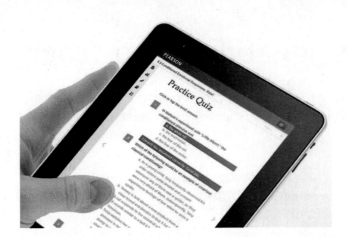

Located throughout REVEL, **quizzing** affords students opportunities to check their understanding at regular intervals before moving on.

REVEL enables students to read and interact with course material on the devices they use, **anywhere** and **anytime**. Responsive design allows students to access REVEL on their tablet devices, with content displayed clearly in both portrait and landscape view.

Highlighting, **note taking**, and a **glossary** personalize the learning experience. Educators can add **notes** for students, too, including reminders or study tips

REVEL's variety of **writing** activities and assignments develop and assess concept **mastery** and **critical thinking**.

Superior assignability and tracking

REVEL's assignability and tracking tools help educators make sure students are completing their reading and understanding core concepts.

REVEL allows educators to indicate precisely which readings must be completed on which dates. This clear, detailed schedule helps students stay on task and keeps them motivated throughout the course.

REVEL lets educators monitor class assignment completion and individual student achievement. It offers actionable information that helps educators intersect with their students in meaningful ways, such as points earned on quizzes and time on task.

Race and Ethnicity in the United States

EIGHTH EDITION

Richard T. Schaefer
DePaul University

Boston Columbus Indianapolis New York San Francisco Amsterdam
Cape Town Dubai London Madrid Milan Munich Paris Montreal Toronto Delhi
Mexico City Sao Paulo Sydney Hong Kong Seoul Singapore Taipei Tokyo

Publisher: Charlyce Jones Owen
Editorial Assistant: Maureen Diana
Product Marketing Manager: Tricia Murphy
Field Marketing Manager: Brittany Pogue-Mohammed
Program Manager: Seanna Breen
Production Team Lead: Denise Forlow
Project Manager: Manuel Echevarria
Senior Operations Supervisor: Mary Fischer
Procurement Specialist: Diane Peirano

Art Director: Maria Lange
Cover Designer: Kristina Mose-Libon
Project Manager, Digital Studio: Claudine Bellanton
Full-Service Project Management: George Jacob, Integra
Printer/Binder: RRD-Crawfordsville
Cover Printer: Phoenix Color
Text Font: Palatino LT Pro 9.5/13

Acknowledgements of third party content appear on page 232, which constitutes an extension of this copyright page.

ISBN-10:   0-13-401196-1
ISBN-13: 978-0-13-401196-7

*To my grandson, may he grow to flourish in
our multicultural society*

Contents

Preface

The first fifteen years of the twenty-first century have witnessed significant changes. The Latino population has overtaken the African American population with the Asian American population growing faster than either. Meanwhile, the population of White non-Hispanic youth has actually become a numerical minority when compared collectively to the other racial and ethnic groups. Yet alongside these demographic changes has been a series of events that serve to underscore the diversity of the American people.

People cheered on May 1, 2011, upon hearing that Osama bin Laden had been found and killed. However, the always patriotic American Indian people were very troubled to learn that the military had assigned the code name "Geronimo" to the infamous terrorist. The Chiricahua Apache of New Mexico were particularly disturbed to learn that the name of their freedom fighter was used in this manner.

Barack Obama may be the son of an immigrant and the first African American president, but that is not the end of his ethnicity. On an official state visit to Ireland, the president made a side trip to the village of Moneygall in County Offaly from where his great-great-grandfather Falmouth Kearney, a shoemaker's son, came to the United States in 1850.

Race and ethnicity are an important part of the national agenda. Thirty years ago, when the first edition of this book was being written, it was noted that race is not a static phenomenon and that, although it is always a part of the social reality, specific aspects change. At that time, the presence of a new immigrant group, the Vietnamese, was duly noted, and the efforts to define affirmative action were described. Today, we seek to describe the growing presence of Salvadorans, Haitians, Tongans, Somalis, Hmong, and Arab Americans.

Specific issues may change over time, but they continue to play out against a backdrop of discrimination that is rooted in the social structure and changing population composition as influenced by immigration and reproduction patterns. One unanticipated change is that the breakup of the Soviet Union and erosion of power of totalitarian leaders in the Middle East have made ethnic, language, and religious divisions even more significant sources of antagonism between and within nations. The old ideological debates about communism and capitalism have been replaced by emotional divisions over religious dogma and cultural traditions.

Changes in the Eighth Edition

As with all previous editions, every line, every source, and every number in this edition have been rechecked for their accuracy. We pride ourselves on providing the most current information possible to document the patterns in intergroup relations in the United States.

Relevant scholarly findings in a variety of disciplines, including economics, anthropology, law, and communication sciences, have been incorporated. Previous users of this book will notice the Spectrum of Intergroup Relations has been given new representation, and appears in five of the book's six chapters.

What's New in the Eighth Edition

The eighth edition includes the following additions and changes:

CHAPTER 1

New opening examples

- New Jeff Parker cartoon on changing racial and ethnic landscape
- Latest American Community Survey 2010 data with updated statistics
- New census data now allows listing of Arab Americans among major racial groups.
- Table of metropolitan segregation data for African Americans, Hispanics, and Asian Americans
- 2012 map of minority population by counties
- Proposed census changes for racial/ethnic categories for 2020
- Racial and ethnic population projections for 2060 including data for Arab and Biracial Americans

CHAPTER 2

- New opening example on impact of racial names on allocating public assistance
- **Research Focus:** Virtual Prejudice and Anti-Prejudice
- **Speaking Out:** Gangsters, Gooks, Geishas, and Geeks, by Helen Zia
- 2012 data on police profiling in New York City
- New section on avoidance of racial and ethnic groups via the Internet
- New cartoon on workplace diversity
- 2012 data on foreign-born workers

CHAPTER 3

New opening examples

- Figure on hate crimes (updated to 2012 release)
- Map of voter identification laws illustrates institutional discrimination
- 2013 HUD study of housing discrimination
- Tables and figure on income by race and sex, holding education constant, updated through 2013 Census reports

- Wealth inequity data updated through the recent economic slowdown
- **Research Focus:** The Unequal Wealth Distribution
- Implications of *Fisher v. University of Texas* 2013 decision outlined
- **Speaking Out:** Arab Problem, by Moustafa Bayoumi
- Recent changes in Craigslist policy on discriminatory advertisements

CHAPTER 4

- Opener on the success of Dr. Alfredo Quiñones-Hinojosa
- Two figures and map on immigration updated through 2012
- **Speaking Out:** Chinese Exclusion Act of 1882, by Judy Chu
- Table on immigrant adaptation to the USA
- **Research Focus:** The Hispanic Dairyland
- Updated figure on languages most frequently spoken at home from 2013 census report
- Cartoons on bilingual language and "borderline schizophrenia"
- Table on refugees updated to 2012

CHAPTER 5

- Opening on Little Italy and Chinese Americans in Manhattan's Little Italy
- **Speaking Out:** The Next Americans, by Tomás Jiménez   153
- Head "Studying Whiteness" rephrased
- More states enact "moment of silence" as a stand-in for prayer in schools
- Romanian language newspaper persists

CHAPTER 6

- **Research Focus:** Tiger Mothers   194
- **Speaking Out:** Holocaust Museum of the Indigenous People Should Be Built at Wounded Knee, by Tim Giago   200
- Updated comparison of schooling, health, and income measures
- Figure: Changes in Minority Population under Age 18, 2000–2010

REVEL™

Educational technology designed for the way today's students read, think, and learn

When students are engaged deeply, they learn more effectively and perform better in their courses. This simple fact inspired the creation of REVEL: an immersive learning experience designed for the way today's students read, think, and learn. Built in collaboration with educators and students nationwide, REVEL is the newest, fully digital way to deliver respected Pearson content.

REVEL enlivens course content with media interactives and assessments— integrated directly within the authors' narrative—that provide opportunities for students to read about and practice course material in tandem. This immersive educational technology boosts student engagement, which leads to better understanding of concepts and improved performance throughout the course.

Learn more about REVEL

http://www.pearsonhighered.com/revel/

Features to Aid Students

Several features are included in the text to facilitate student learning. To help students review, each chapter ends with a conclusion and summary. The key terms are highlighted in bold when they are first introduced in the text and are listed with corresponding page numbers at the end of each chapter. The Spectrum of Intergroup Relations first presented in Chapter 1 also appears in Chapters 3, 4, 5, and 6 to reinforce major concepts while addressing the unique social circumstances of individual racial and ethnic groups.

In addition, there is an end-of-book glossary with full definitions referenced by page numbers. This edition includes both "Review Questions" and "Critical Thinking Questions." The Review Questions are intended to remind the reader of major points, whereas the Critical Thinking Questions encourage students to think more deeply about some of the major issues raised in the chapter. An extensive illustration program, which includes maps and political cartoons, expands the text discussion and provokes thought.

Ancillary Materials

The ancillary materials that accompany this textbook have been carefully created to enhance the topics being discussed.

FOR THE INSTRUCTOR

Instructor's Manual and Test Bank (ISBN 020521634X). This carefully prepared manual includes chapter overviews, key term identification exercises, discussion questions, topics for class discussion, audiovisual resources, and test questions in both multiple-choice and essay format. The Instructor's Manual and Test Bank is available to adopters at www.pearsonhighered.com.

MyTest (ISBN 0205216366). This computerized software allows instructors to create their own personalized exams, to edit any or all of the existing test questions, and to add new questions. Other special features of this program include random generation of test questions, creation of alternate versions of the same test, scrambling question sequence, and test preview before printing. The MyTest is available to adopters at www. pearsonhighered.com.

PPTs (ISBN 0205216374). The Lecture PowerPoint slides follow the chapter outline and feature images from the textbook integrated with the text. The slides are uniquely designed to present concepts in a clear and succinct manner. They are available to adopters at www.pearsonhighered.com.

Acknowledgments

The eighth edition was improved by the suggestions of:

Tanetta Andersson, Central Connecticut State
University
Michelle Bentz, Central Community College-
Columbus Campus
Mary Donaghy, Arkansas State University
Elena Ermolaeva, Marshall University
Mominka Filey, Davenport University
Dr. Lloyd Ganey, College of Southern Nevada
Malcolm Gold, Malone University
Lisa Munoz, Hawkeye Community College
Jose Soto, Southeast Community College
Gerald Titchener, Des Moines Area
Community College

I would also like to thank my Publisher at Pearson, Charlyce Jones-Owen, for developing this eighth edition. Her long experience, love of history, and appreciation of books combine to enrich this and every academic book with which she is associated. My appreciation also extends to Editor in Chief Dickson Musslewhite for his encouragement and support for my textbooks on race and ethnicity.

The truly exciting challenge of writing and researching has always been for me an enriching experience, mostly because of the supportive home I share with my wife, Sandy. She knows so well my appreciation and gratitude, now as in the past and in the future.

Richard T. Schaefer
schaeferrt@aol.com
www.schaefersociology.net

About the Author

Richard T. Schaefer grew up in Chicago at a time when neighborhoods were going through transitions in ethnic and racial composition. He found himself increasingly intrigued by what was happening, how people were reacting, and how these changes were affecting neighborhoods and people's jobs. In high school, he took a course in sociology. His interest in social issues caused him to gravitate to more sociology courses at Northwestern University, where he eventually received a B.A. in sociology.

"Originally as an undergraduate I thought I would go on to law school and become a lawyer. But after taking a few sociology courses, I found myself wanting to learn more about what sociologists studied and was fascinated by the kinds of questions they raised," Dr. Schaefer says. "Perhaps most fascinating and, to me, relevant to the 1960s was the intersection of race, gender, and social class." This interest led him to obtain his M.A. and Ph.D. in sociology from the University of Chicago. Dr. Schaefer's continuing interest in race relations led him to write his master's thesis on the membership of the Ku Klux Klan and his doctoral thesis on racial prejudice and race relations in Great Britain.

Dr. Schaefer went on to become a professor of sociology. He has taught sociology and courses on multiculturalism for 30 years. He has been invited to give special presentations to students and faculty on racial and ethnic diversity in Illinois, Indiana, Missouri, North Carolina, Ohio, and Texas.

Dr. Schaefer is the author of *Racial and Ethnic Diversity in the USA* (Pearson 2014) and *Racial and Ethnic Groups*, fourteenth edition (Pearson, 2014). Dr. Schaefer is the general editor of the three-volume *Encyclopedia of Race, Ethnicity, and Society* (2008). He is also the author of the thirteenth edition of *Sociology* (2012), the eleventh edition of *Sociology: A Brief Introduction* (2015), the third edition of *Sociology: A Modular Approach* (2015), and the sixth edition of *Sociology Matters* (2013). Schaefer coauthored with William Zellner the ninth edition of *Extraordinary Groups* (2011), which, in 2014, was translated into Japanese. His articles and book reviews have appeared in many journals, including *American Journal of Sociology, Phylon: A Review of Race and Culture, Contemporary Sociology, Sociology and Social Research, Sociological Quarterly*, and *Teaching Sociology*. He served as president of the Midwest Sociological Society from 1994 to 1995. In recognition of his achievements in undergraduate teaching, he was named Vincent de Paul Professor of Sociology in 2004.

Chapter 1
Exploring Race and Ethnicity

Learning Objectives

RANKING GROUPS
  1-1 Explain how groups are ranked.

TYPES OF GROUPS
  1-2 Describe the different types of groups.

DOES RACE MATTER?
  1-3 Explain what is meant by race being socially constructed.

BIRACIAL AND MULTIRACIAL IDENTITY: WHO AM I?
  1-4 Define biracial and multiracial identity.

1

SOCIOLOGY AND THE STUDY OF RACE AND ETHNICITY
  1-5 Describe how sociology helps us understand race and ethnicity.
THE CREATION OF SUBORDINATE-GROUP STATUS
  1-6 Restate the creation of subordinate groups.
SPECTRUM OF INTERGROUP STATUS
  1-7 Use the Spectrum of Intergroup Relations.
THE CONSEQUENCES OF SUBORDINATE-GROUP STATUS
  1-8 Restate the consequences of subordinate groups.
RESISTANCE AND CHANGE
  1-9 Articulate how change occurs in racial and ethnic relations.

Lewiston, Maine, was dying. Now Lewiston is thriving, even in the midst of a national recession. This city changed its future. In 2000, the community of about 36,000, of which 96 percent were White, mostly of French and Irish descent, was going nowhere. The textile mills were shuttered and massive social welfare programs were created locally to meet the needs of the people. It was little wonder that a nearby resident, Stephen King, often chose its abandoned mills and other buildings as inspiration for his suspense novels.

In February 2001, Black Africans, originally from Somalia and of the Muslim faith, began to settle in Lewiston from other areas throughout the United States. With few job opportunities and well-known long, cold winters, it seemed an unlikely destination for people whose homeland was hot and mostly arid. Better schools, little crime, cheap housing, and good social welfare programs attracted the initial arrivals. Once a small group was established, more and more Somalis arrived as the first group shared their positive experiences with friends and relatives. Not everyone stayed because of the winters or unrelated explanations, yet they continued to come.

The numbers of arrivals ebbed and flowed—the increased immigration regulations after 9/11 made entry difficult for Arab Muslims such as the Somali immigrants. One mayor in 2002 issued a public letter encouraging Somalis not to come; his actions were widely denounced. Another man threw a pig's head into a local mosque during evening prayers. Muslims by tradition cannot touch, much less eat, pork. Politicians continue to make unwelcoming comments, but they are quickly drowned out by those who are supportive of the 6,000-plus Somali community. For their part, the Somalis have settled in and are raising their children, but they are concerned that their sons and daughters identify more with being American than with being Somali. Despite their limited resources, as a community they send about $300,000 a month to friends and relatives in Somalia who continue to face incredible hardship.

For over ten years, they have come to Lewiston—10 to 30 *every week*. Lewiston is thriving in a state that continues to face many challenges. A decade is not a long time to reach conclusions about race, religion, and immigration. Somalis, who now account for about 15 percent of the population, have graduated from the local community college, run for office, and opened up dozens of previously shuttered businesses. Others commute the 20 miles to L. L. Bean warehouses to work (Canfield 2012; Cullen 2011; Hammond 2010; Huisman et al. 2011; Tice 2007).

The struggles of racial, ethnic, linguistic, and religious minorities have often required their organized efforts to overcome inequities. Not only significant White support but also organized resistance typically mark these struggles. The various groups that make the United States diverse do not speak with one voice. For example, the Somalis of Maine are made up of different ethnic or tribal groups. Most are Bantu, who were targeted during the 1991 civil war, fled to refugee camps in Kenya, came to the United States, and resettled in Maine. They still see themselves as different from other ethnic groups from Somalia.

One aspect of the struggle to overcome inequality is the continuing effort to identify strategies and services to assist minorities in their struggle to overcome prejudice and discrimination. Among the beneficiaries of programs aimed at racial and ethnic minorities are White Americans, who, far from all being affluent themselves, have also experienced challenges in their lives.

The election and reelection of the nation's first African American president (who incidentally carried three states of the former Confederacy) presents the temptation to declare that issues of racial inequality are past or racism is limited to a few troublemakers. Progress has been made and expressions of explicit racism are rarely tolerated, yet challenges remain for immigrants of any color and racial, ethnic, and religious minorities (Massey 2011).

The United States is a diverse nation and is becoming even more so, as shown in Table 1.1. In 2010, approximately 40 percent of the population were members of racial minorities or were Hispanic. This represents one out of three people in the United States, without counting White ethnic groups or foreign-born Whites.

Lewiston, Maine, a town undergoing difficult economic times over the last 20 years, received a boost from the arrival of Somalis from Africa who have now established a viable community.

Table 1.1 Racial and Ethnic Groups in the United States

Classification	Number in Thousands	Percentage of Total Population
RACIAL GROUPS		
Whites (non-Hispanic)	195,371	60.3
Blacks/African Americans	37,686	12.2
Native Americans, Alaskan Natives	2,247	0.7
Asian Americans	15,553	5.0
Chinese	3,347	1.1
Asian Indians	2,843	0.9
Filipinos	2,556	0.8
Vietnamese	1,548	0.5
Koreans	1,424	0.5
Japanese	763	0.2
Pacific Islanders, Native Hawaiians	1,847	0.6
Other Asian Americans	1,225	0.5
Arab Americans	1,517	0.5
Two or more races	9,009	2.9
ETHNIC GROUPS		
White ancestry		
Germans	49,341	16.0
Irish	35,664	11.6
English	26,873	8.7
Italians	17,486	5.7
Poles	9,757	3.2
French	9,159	3.0
Scottish and Scotch-Irish	9,122	3.0
Jews	5,425	1.8
Hispanics (or Latinos)	50,478	16.4
Mexican Americans	31,798	10.3
Puerto Ricans	4,624	1.5
Cubans	1,785	0.6
Salvadorans	1,648	0.5
Dominicans	1,415	0.5
Guatemalans	1,044	0.3
Other Hispanics	8,164	2.7
TOTAL (ALL GROUPS)	308,746	

Note: Arab American population excluded from White total. All data are for 2010. Percentages do not total 100 percent, and when subcategories are added, they do not match totals in major categories because of overlap between groups (e.g., Polish American Jews or people of mixed ancestry such as Irish and Italian).

SOURCE: American Community Survey 2011b: Table C04006; Asi and Beaulieu 2013; DellaPergola 2012; Ennis, Rose-Vargas and Albert 2011; Hixson, Hepler, and Kim 2012; Hoeffel et al. 2012; Humes, Jones, and Ramirez 2011; Norris, Vines, and Hoeffel 2012.

Figure 1.1 Population of the United States by Race and Ethnicity, 2010 and 2060 (Projected)

According to projections by the Census Bureau, the proportion of residents of the United States who are White and non-Hispanic will decrease significantly by the year 2060. By contrast, the proportion of both Hispanic Americans and Asian Americans will rise significantly.

SOURCE: Bureau of the Census 2013b: Table 4, sources listed in Table 1.1, and author estimates.

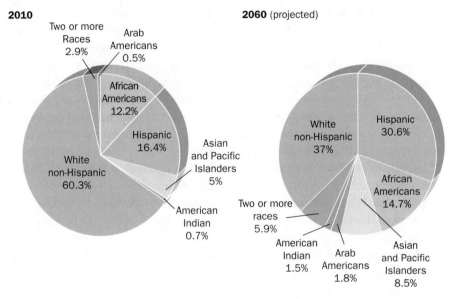

As shown in Figure 1.1, between 2010 and 2060, the Black, Hispanic, Asian, Arab, and Native American population along with those identifying as biracial or multiracial in the United States is expected to increase to about 63 percent. Although the composition of the population is changing, problems of prejudice, discrimination, and mistrust remain.

This trend toward "majority-minority" got underway noticeably in 2011 when Latino and non-White babies outnumbered White newborns for the first time in the United States (Bureau of the Census 2012d).

Ranking Groups

1.1 Explain how groups are ranked.

In every society, not all groups are treated or viewed equally. Identifying a subordinate group or a minority in a society seems to be a simple task. In the United States, the groups readily identified as minorities—Blacks and Native Americans, for example—are outnumbered by non-Blacks and non–Native Americans. However, having minority status is not necessarily a result of being outnumbered. A social minority need not be a mathematical one. A **minority group** is a subordinate group whose members have significantly less control or power over their own lives than do the members of a dominant or majority group. In sociology, *minority* means the same as *subordinate*, and *dominant* is used interchangeably with *majority*.

Confronted with evidence that a particular minority in the United States is subordinate to the majority, some people respond, "Why not? After all, this is a democracy, so the majority rules." However, the subordination of a minority involves more than its inability to rule over society. A member of a subordinate or minority group experiences a narrowing of life's opportunities—for success, education, wealth, the pursuit of happiness—that goes beyond any personal shortcoming he or she may have. A minority group does not share in proportion to its numbers what a given society, such as the United States, defines as valuable.

Being superior in numbers does not guarantee a group has control over its destiny or ensure majority status. In 1920, the majority of people in Mississippi and South Carolina were African Americans. Yet African Americans did not have as much control over their lives as did Whites, let alone control of the states in which they lived. Throughout the United States today are counties or neighborhoods in which the majority of people are African American, Native American, or Hispanic, but White Americans are the dominant force. Nationally, 50.7 percent of the population is female, but males still dominate positions of authority and wealth well beyond their numbers.

A minority or subordinate group has five characteristics: unequal treatment, distinguishing physical or cultural traits, involuntary membership, awareness of subordination, and in-group marriage (Wagley and Harris 1958):

1. Members of a minority experience unequal treatment and have less power over their lives than members of a dominant group have over theirs. Prejudice, discrimination, segregation, and even extermination create this social inequality.

2. Members of a minority group share physical or cultural characteristics such as skin color or language that distinguish them from the dominant group. Each society has its own arbitrary standard for determining which characteristics are most important in defining dominant and minority groups.

3. Membership in a dominant or minority group is not voluntary: People are born into the group. A person does not choose to be African American or White.

4. Minority-group members have a strong sense of group solidarity. William Graham Sumner, writing in 1906, noted that people make distinctions between members of their own group (the in-group) and everyone else (the out-group). When a group is the object of long-term prejudice and discrimination, the feeling of "us versus them" often becomes intense.

5. Members of a minority generally marry others from the same group. A member of a dominant group often is unwilling to join a supposedly inferior minority by marrying one of its members. In addition, the minority group's sense of solidarity encourages marriage within the group and discourages marriage to outsiders.

Figure 1.2 Minority Population by County

In four states (California, Hawaii, New Mexico, and Texas) and the District of Columbia, as well as in about one out of every nine counties, minorities constitute the numerical majority.

SOURCE: Jones-Puthoff 2013: slide 5.

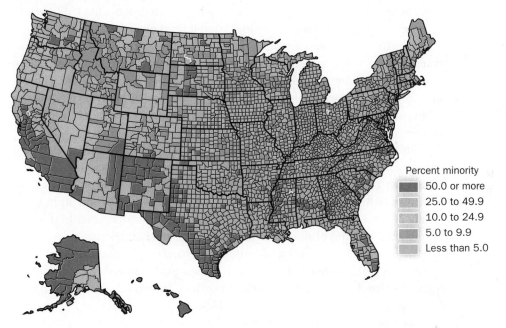

Percent minority
- 50.0 or more
- 25.0 to 49.9
- 10.0 to 24.9
- 5.0 to 9.9
- Less than 5.0

Although "minority" status is not about numbers, there is no denying that the White American majority is diminishing in size relative to the growing diversity of racial and ethnic groups, as illustrated in Figure 1.2.

Using available population projects, which are heavily influenced by estimating future immigration patterns, the White population will be outnumbered by other racial groups and Hispanics somewhere between 2040 and 2045 or before the time people born now turn 30 years of age. The move to a more diverse nation—one in which no group is the numerical minority—will have a social impact on everything, including marriage patterns, housing, political party politics, health care delivery, and education (Bureau of the Census 2013b).

Types of Groups

1-2   Describe the different types of groups.

There are four types of minority or subordinate groups. All four, except where noted, have the five properties previously outlined. The four criteria for classifying minority groups are race, ethnicity, religion, and gender.

Racial Groups

The term **racial group** is reserved for minorities and the corresponding majorities that are socially set apart because of obvious physical differences. Notice the two crucial words in the definition: *obvious* and *physical*. What is obvious? Hair color? Shape of an earlobe? Presence of body hair? To whom are these differences obvious, and why? Each society defines what it finds obvious.

In the United States, skin color is one obvious difference. People in the United States have learned informally that skin color is important. In the United States, people have traditionally classified themselves as either Black or White. There is no in-between state except for people readily identified as Native Americans or Asian Americans. Later in this chapter, we explore this issue more deeply and see how such assumptions about race have complex implications.

Other societies use skin color as a standard but may have a more elaborate system of classification. In Brazil, where hostility between races is less prevalent than in the United States, numerous categories identify people on the basis of skin color or tone. In the United States, a person is Black or White. In Brazil, a variety of terms such as *cafuso, mazombo, preto,* and *escuro* are used to describe various combinations of skin color, facial features, and hair texture.

The designation of a racial group emphasizes physical differences as opposed to cultural distinctions. In the United States, minority races include Blacks, Native Americans (or American Indians), Japanese Americans, Chinese Americans, Arab Americans, Filipinos, Hawaiians, and other Asian peoples. The issue of race and racial differences has been an important one, not only in the United States but also throughout the entire sphere of European influence. Later in this chapter, we examine race and its significance more closely. We should not forget that Whites are a race, too. As we consider in Chapter 4, who is White has been subject to change over history when certain European groups were considered not worthy of being considered White. Partly to compete against a growing Black population, the "Whiting" of some European Americans has occurred. In Chapter 5, we will consider how Italians and Irish for all intents and purposes were once considered not to be White by others.

Some racial groups also may have unique cultural traditions, as we can readily see in the many Chinatowns throughout the United States. For racial groups, however, the physical distinctiveness and not the cultural differences generally prove to be the barrier to acceptance by the host society. For example, Chinese Americans who are faithful Protestants and know the names of all the members of the Baseball Hall of Fame may be bearers of American culture. Yet these Chinese Americans are still part of a minority because they are seen as physically different.

Ethnic Groups

Ethnic minority groups are differentiated from the dominant group on the basis of cultural differences such as language, attitudes toward marriage and parenting, and food habits. **Ethnic groups** are groups set apart from others because of their national origin or distinctive cultural patterns.

Ethnic groups in the United States include a grouping that we call *Hispanics* or *Latinos*, which, in turn, include Mexican Americans, Puerto Ricans, Cubans, and other Latin American residents of the United States. Hispanics can be either Black or White, as in the case of a dark-skinned Puerto Rican who may be taken as Black in central Texas but may be viewed as Puerto Rican in New York City. The ethnic group category also includes White ethnics such as Irish Americans, Polish Americans, and Norwegian Americans.

The cultural traits that make groups distinctive usually originate from their homelands or, for Jews, from a long history of being segregated and prohibited from becoming a part of a host society. Once living in the United States, an immigrant group may maintain distinctive cultural practices through associations, clubs, and worship. Ethnic enclaves such as a Little Haiti or a Greektown in urban areas also perpetuate cultural distinctiveness.

Ethnicity and race has been long recognized as an important source of differentiation. More than a century ago, African American sociologist W. E. B. Du Bois, addressing an audience at a world antislavery convention in London in 1900, called attention to the overwhelming importance of the color line throughout the world. In "Speaking Out," we read the remarks of Du Bois, the first Black person to receive a doctorate from Harvard, who later helped to organize the National Association for the Advancement of Colored People (NAACP). Du Bois's observations give us a historical perspective on the struggle for equality. We can look ahead, knowing how far we have come, and speculate on how much farther we have to go.

We also should appreciate the context of Du Bois's insight. He spoke of his "color-line" prediction in light of then-contemporary U.S. occupation of the Philippines and the relationship of "darker to lighter races" worldwide. So today, he would see race matters not only in the sporadic hate crimes we hear about but also in global conflicts (Roediger 2009).

Religious Groups

Association with a religion other than the dominant faith is the third basis for minority-group status. In the United States, Protestants, as a group, outnumber members of all other religions. Roman Catholics form the largest minority religion. For people who are not a part of the Christian tradition, such as followers of Islam, allegiance to their faith often is misunderstood and stigmatizes people. This stigmatization became especially widespread and legitimated by government action in the aftermath of the attacks of September 11, 2001.

Religious minorities include groups such as the Church of Jesus Christ of Latter-Day Saints (the Mormons), Jehovah's Witnesses, Amish, Muslims, and Buddhists. Cults or sects associated with practices such as animal sacrifice, doomsday prophecy, demon worship, or the use of snakes in a ritualistic fashion

Speaking Out

Problem of the Color Line

W. E. B. Du Bois

In the metropolis of the modern world, in this the closing year of the nineteenth century, there has been assembled a congress of men and women of African blood, to deliberate solemnly upon the present situation and outlook of the darker races of mankind. The problem of the twentieth century is the problem of the color line, the question as to how far differences of race—which show themselves chiefly in the color of the skin and the texture of the hair—will hereafter be made the basis of denying to over half the world the right of sharing to their utmost ability the opportunities and privileges of modern civilization....

To be sure, the darker races are today the least advanced in culture according to European standards. This has not, however, always been the case in the past, and certainly the world's history, both ancient and modern, has given many instances of no despicable ability and capacity among the blackest races of men.

In any case, the modern world must remember that in this age when the ends of the world are being brought so near together, the millions of Black men in Africa, America, and Islands of the Sea, not to speak of the brown and yellow myriads elsewhere, are bound to have a great influence upon the world in the future, by reason of sheer numbers and physical contact. If now the world of culture bends itself toward giving Negroes and other dark men the largest and broadest opportunity for education and self-development, then this contact and influence is bound to have a beneficial effect upon the world and hasten human progress. But if, by reason of carelessness, prejudice, greed, and injustice, the Black world is to be exploited and ravished and degraded, the results must be deplorable, if not fatal—not simply to them, but to the high ideals of justice, freedom and culture which a thousand years of Christian civilization have held before Europe....

Let the world take no backward step in that slow but sure progress which has successively refused to let the spirit of class, of caste, of privilege, or of birth, debar from life, liberty, and the pursuit of happiness a striving human soul.

Let not color or race be a feature of distinction between White and Black men, regardless of worth or ability....

Thus we appeal with boldness and confidence to the Great Powers of the civilized world, trusting in the wide spirit of humanity, and the deep sense of justice of our age, for a generous recognition of the righteousness of our cause.

SOURCE: Du Bois 1900 [1969a], *An ABC of Color*, pp. 20–21, 23.

also constitute religious minorities. Jews are excluded from this category and placed among ethnic groups. Culture is a more important defining trait for Jewish people worldwide than is religious doctrine. Jewish Americans share a cultural tradition that goes beyond theology. In this sense, it is appropriate to view them as an ethnic group rather than as members of a religious faith.

Gender Groups

Gender is another attribute that creates dominant and subordinate groups. Males are the social majority; females, although numerous, are relegated to the position of the social minority. Women are considered a minority even though they do not exhibit all the characteristics outlined earlier (e.g., there is little in-group marriage). Women encounter prejudice and discrimination and are physically distinguishable. Group membership is involuntary, and many women have developed a sense of sisterhood.

Women who are members of racial and ethnic minorities face special challenges to achieving equality. They suffer from greater inequality because they belong to two separate minority groups: a racial or ethnic group plus a subordinate gender group.

Other Subordinate Groups

This book focuses on groups that meet a set of criteria for subordinate status. People encounter prejudice or are excluded from full participation in society for many reasons. Racial, ethnic, religious, and gender barriers are the main ones, but there are others. Age, disability status, physical appearance, and sexual orientation are among the factors that are used to subordinate groups of people.

Does Race Matter?

1-3 Explain what is meant by race being socially constructed.

We see people around us—some of whom may look quite different from us. Do these differences matter? The simple answer is no, but because so many people have for so long acted as if differences in physical characteristics as well as geographic origin and shared culture do matter, distinct groups have been created in people's minds. Race has many meanings for many people. Often these meanings are inaccurate and based on theories scientists discarded generations ago. As we will see, race is a socially constructed concept (Young 2003).

Biological Meaning

The way the term *race* has been used by some people to apply to human beings lacks any scientific basis. Distinctive physical characteristics for groups of human beings cannot be identified the same way that scientists distinguish one animal species from another. The idea of **biological race** is based on the mistaken notion of a genetically isolated human group.

ABSENCE OF PURE RACES Even past proponents of the belief that sharp, scientific divisions exist among humans had endless debates over what the races of the world were. Given people's frequent migration, exploration, and invasions, pure

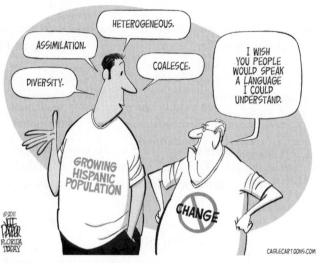

The changing landscape of the United States is hard to miss, but not all people equally embrace it.

genetic types have not existed for some time, if they ever did. There are no mutually exclusive races. Skin tone among African Americans varies tremendously, as it does among White Americans. There is even an overlapping of dark-skinned Whites and light-skinned African Americans. If we grouped people by genetic resistance to malaria and by fingerprint patterns, then Norwegians and many African groups would be the same race. If we grouped people by lactose intolerance some Africans, Asians, and Southern Europeans would be of one group and West Africans and Northern Europeans of another (Leehotz 1995; Shanklin 1994).

Biologically, no pure, distinct races exist. Research as a part of the Human Genome Project mapping human deoxyribonucleic acid (DNA) has served to confirm genetic diversity only, with differences within traditionally regarded racial groups (e.g., Black Africans) much greater than that between groups (e.g., between Black Africans and Europeans). Contemporary studies of DNA on a global basis have determined that about 90 percent of human genetic variation is within "local populations," such as within the French or within the Afghan people. The remaining 10 percent of total human variation is what we think of today as constituting races and accounts for skin tone, hair texture, nose shape, and so forth (Feldman 2010).

Research has also been conducted to determine whether personality characteristics such as temperament and nervous habits are inherited among minority groups. It is no surprise that the question of whether races have different innate levels of intelligence has led to the most explosive controversies (Bamshad and Olson 2003; El-Haj 2007).

INTELLIGENCE TESTS Typically, intelligence is measured as an **intelligence quotient (IQ)**, which is the ratio of a person's mental age to his or her

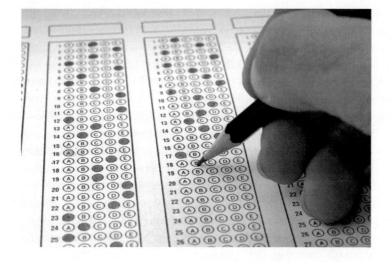

chronological age, multiplied by 100, with 100 representing average intelligence and higher scores representing greater intelligence. It should be noted that there is little consensus over just what intelligence is, other than as defined by such IQ tests. Intelligence tests are adjusted for a person's age so that ten-year-olds take a different test from someone 20 years old. Although research shows that certain learning strategies can improve a person's IQ, generally IQ remains stable as one ages.

A great deal of debate continues over the accuracy of IQ tests. Are they biased toward people who come to the tests with knowledge similar to that of the test writers? Skeptics argue that questions in IQ tests do not truly measure intellectual potential. The question of cultural bias in tests remains a concern. The most recent research shows that differences in intelligence scores between Blacks and Whites are almost eliminated when adjustments are made for social and economic characteristics (Brooks-Gunn, Klebanov, and Duncan 1996; Kagan 1971; Young 2003).

In 1994, an 845-page book unleashed another national debate on the issue of IQ. The research efforts of psychologist Richard J. Herrnstein and social scientist Charles Murray, published in *The Bell Curve* (1994), concluded that 60 percent of IQ is inheritable and that racial groups offer a convenient means to generalize about any differences in intelligence. Unlike most other proponents of the race–IQ link, the authors offered policy suggestions that included ending welfare to discourage births among low-IQ poor women and changing immigration laws so that the IQ pool in the United States is not diminished. Herrnstein and Murray even made generalizations about IQ levels among Asians and Hispanics in the United States, groups subject to even more intermarriage. In spite of *The Bell Curve* "research," it is not possible to generalize about absolute differences between groups, such as Latinos versus Whites, when almost half of Latinos in the United States marry non-Hispanics.

More than a decade later, the mere mention of the "bell curve" still signals to many people a belief in a racial hierarchy, with Whites toward the top and Blacks near the bottom. The research present then and repeated today points to the difficulty in definitions: What is intelligence, and what constitutes a racial group, given generations (if not centuries) of intermarriage? How can we speak of definitive inherited racial differences if there has been intermarriage between people of every color? Furthermore, as people on both sides of the debate have noted, regardless of the findings, we would still want to strive to maximize the talents of each individual. All research shows that the differences within a group are much greater than any alleged differences between group averages.

Why does such IQ research reemerge if the data are subject to different interpretations? The argument that "we" are superior to "them" is appealing to the dominant group. It justifies receiving opportunities that are denied to others. We can anticipate that the debate over IQ and the allegations of significant group differences will continue. Policymakers need to acknowledge the difficulty in treating race as a biologically significant characteristic.

Social Construction of Race

If race does not distinguish humans from one another biologically, then why does it seem to be so important? It is important because of the social meaning people have attached to it. The 1950 (UNESCO) Statement on Race maintains that the scientific use of race is not a biological phenomenon (Montagu 1972: 118).

Race is a social construction, and this process benefits the oppressor, who defines which groups of people are privileged and which groups are not. The acceptance of race in a society as a legitimate category allows racial hierarchies to emerge to the benefit of the dominant "races." For example, inner-city drive-by shootings are now seen as a race-specific problem worthy of local officials cleaning up troubled neighborhoods. Yet school shootings are viewed as a societal concern and placed on the national agenda.

People could speculate that if human groups have obvious physical differences, then they could have corresponding mental or personality differences. No one disagrees that people differ in temperament, potential to learn, and sense of humor, among other characteristics. In its social sense, race implies that groups that differ physically also bear distinctive emotional and mental abilities or disabilities. These beliefs are based on the notion that humankind can be divided into distinct groups. We have already seen the difficulties associated with pigeonholing people into racial categories. Despite these difficulties, belief in the inheritance of behavior patterns and in an association between physical and cultural traits is widespread. It is called **racism** when this belief is coupled with the feeling that certain groups or races are inherently superior to others. Racism is a doctrine of racial supremacy that states one race is superior to another (Bash 2001; Bonilla-Silva 1996).

We questioned the biological significance of race in the previous section. In modern complex industrial societies, we find little adaptive utility in the presence or absence of prominent chins, epicanthic eye fold associated with Eastern and Central Asian peoples, or the comparative amount of melanin in the skin. It is of little importance that people are genetically different; what is important is that they approach one another with dissimilar perspectives. It is in the social setting that race is decisive. Race is significant because people have given it significance.

Race definitions are crystallized through what Michael Omi and Howard Winant (1994) called **racial formation**, a sociohistorical process by which racial categories are created, inhabited, transformed, and destroyed. Those in power define groups of people in a certain way that depends on a racist social structure. As in the United States, these definitions can become systematic and embedded in many aspects of society for a significant length of time. No one escapes the extent and frequency to which we are subjected to racial formation. The creation of a category called Native Americans and of the reservation system for them in the late 1800s is an example of this racial formation. The federal American Indian policy combined previously distinctive tribes into a single group (Feagin, Cobas, and Elias 2012).

With rising immigration from Latin America in the latter part of the twentieth century, the fluid nature of racial formation is evident. As if it happened in one day, people in the United States have spoken about the Latin Americanization of the United States or stated that the biracial order of Black and White has been replaced with a *triracial* order. We examine this social context of the changing nature of diversity to understand how scholars have sought to generalize about intergroup relations in the United States and elsewhere (Bonilla-Silva and Dietrich 2011; Frank, A Kresh, and Lu 2010).

In the southern United States, the social construction of race was known as the "one-drop rule." This tradition stipulated that if a person had even a single drop of "Black blood," that person was defined and viewed as Black. Today, children of biracial or multiracial marriages try to build their own identities in a country that seems intent on placing them in some single, traditional category—a topic we look at next.

Biracial and Multiracial Identity: Who Am I?

1-4 Define biracial and multiracial identity.

People are now more willing to accept and advance identities that do not fit neatly into mutually exclusive categories. Hence, increasing numbers of people are identifying themselves as biracial or multiracial or, at the very least, explicitly viewing themselves as reflecting a diverse racial and ethnic identity. Barack

Obama is the most visible person with a biracial background. President Obama has explicitly stated he sees himself as a Black man, although his mother was White and he was largely raised by his White grandparents. Yet in 2010, he chose only to check the "Black, African American, or Negro) box on his household's census form. Obviously, biracial does not mean biracial identity.

The diversity of the United States today has made it more difficult for many people to place themselves on the racial and ethnic landscape. It reminds us that racial formation continues to take place. Obviously, the racial and ethnic landscape, as we have seen, is constructed not naturally but socially and, therefore, is subject to change and different interpretations. Although our focus is on the United States, almost every nation faces the same problems.

The United States tracks people by race and ethnicity for myriad reasons, ranging from attempting to improve the status of oppressed groups to diversifying classrooms. But how can we measure the growing number of people whose ancestry is mixed by anyone's definition? In "Research Focus," we consider how the U.S. Bureau of the Census dealt with this issue.

Besides the increasing respect for biracial identity and multiracial identity, group names undergo change as well. Within little more than a generation during the twentieth century, labels that were applied to subordinate groups changed from *Negroes* to *Blacks* to *African Americans*, from *American Indians* to *Native Americans* or *Native Peoples*. However, more Native Americans prefer the use of their tribal name, such as *Seminole*, instead of a collective label. The old 1950s statistical term of "people with a Spanish surname" has long been discarded, yet there is disagreement over a new term: *Latino* or *Hispanic*. Like Native Americans, Hispanic Americans avoid such global terms and prefer their native names, such as *Puerto Ricans* or *Cubans*. People of Mexican ancestry indicate preferences for a variety of names, such as *Mexican American*, *Chicano*, or simply *Mexican*.

Research Focus

Multiracial Identity

Approaching Census 2000, a movement was spawned by people who were frustrated by government questionnaires that forced them to indicate only one race. Take the case of Stacey Davis in New Orleans. The young woman's mother is Thai and her father is Creole, a blend of Black, French, and German. People seeing Stacey confuse her for a Latina, Filipina, or Hawaiian. Officially, she has been "White" all her life because she looks White. The census in 2000 for the first time gave people the option to check off one or more racial groups. "Biracial" or "multiracial" was not an option because pretests showed very few people would use it. This meant that in Census 2000 the government recognized different social constructions of racial identity—that is, a person could be Asian American and White.

Most people did select one racial category in Census 2000 and again in 2010. Overall, approximately 9 million people, or 2.9 percent of the total population, selected two or more racial groups in

Figure 1.3 Multiple-Race Choices in Census 2010

This figure shows the percentage distribution of the 9 million people who chose two or more races (out of the total population of 309 million).

SOURCE: Humes, Jones, and Ramirez 2011: 10.

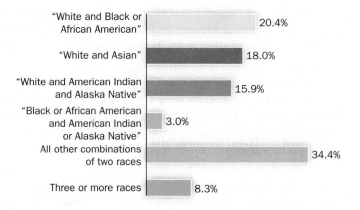

2010. This was a smaller proportion than many observers had anticipated. In fact, not even the majority of mixed-race couples identified their children with more than one racial classification. As shown in Figure 1.3, Whites and African Americans were the most common multiple identity, with 1.8 million people or so selecting that response. As a group, American Indians were most likely to select a second category and Whites least likely. Race is socially defined.

Complicating the situation is that, in the Census, people are asked separately whether they are Hispanic or non-Hispanic. So a Hispanic person can be any race. In the 2010 Census, 94 percent indicated they were one race, but 6 percent indicated two or more races; this proportion was twice as high than among non-Hispanics. Therefore, Latinos are more likely than non-Hispanics to indicate a multiracial ancestry.

Changes in measuring race and ethnicity are not necessarily over. Already Bureau officials are considering for 2020 Census adding categories for people of Middle Eastern, North African, or Asian descent. "Hispanic" may even be added as a "race category"

along with White, African American, Asian, and American Indian/Alaska Native and Pacific Islander.

Regardless of government definitions, we know that people do change their racial identity over time, choosing to self-identify as something different. This fluidity in individual actions could well be increased if the nation as a whole appears to be more accepting of biracial and multiracial categories.

The Census Bureau's decision does not necessarily resolve the frustration of hundreds of thousands of people such as Stacey Davis, who daily face people trying to place them in some racial or ethnic category that is convenient. However, it does underscore the complexity of social construction and trying to apply arbitrary definitions to the diversity of the human population. A symbol of this social construction of race can be seen in President Barack Obama, born of a White woman and a Black immigrant from Kenya. Although he has always identified himself as a Black man, it is worthy to note he was born in Hawaii, a state in which 23.6 percent of people see themselves as more than one race, compared to the national average of 2.9 percent.

SOURCES: DaCosta 2007; Dade 2012a; Grieco and Cassidy 2001; Humes, Jones, and Ramirez 2011: 2–11; Jones and Smith 2001; Saperstein and Penner 2012; Saulny 2011; Welch 2011; Williams 2005.

In the United States and other multiracial, multiethnic societies, **panethnicity**, the development of solidarity between ethnic subgroups, has emerged. The coalition of tribal groups as Native Americans or American Indians to confront outside forces, notably the federal government, is one example of panethnicity. Hispanics or Latinos and Asian Americans are other examples of panethnicity. Although it is rarely recognized by the dominant society, the very term *Black* or *African American* represents the descendants of many different ethnic or tribal groups, such as Akamba, Fulani, Hausa, Malinke, and Yoruba (Lopez and Espiritu 1990).

Is *panethnicity* a convenient label for "outsiders" or a term that reflects a mutual identity? Certainly, many people outside the group are unable or unwilling to recognize ethnic differences and prefer umbrella terms such as *Asian Americans*. For some small groups, combining with others is emerging as a useful way to make them heard, but there is always a fear that their own distinctive culture will become submerged. Although many Hispanics share the Spanish language and many are united by Roman Catholicism, only one in four native-born people of Mexican, Puerto Rican, or Cuban descent prefers a panethnic label to nationality or ethnic identity. Yet the growth of a variety of panethnic associations among many groups, including Hispanics, continues into the twenty-first century (de la Garza et al. 1992; Espiritu 1992; Steinberg 2007).

Another challenge to identity is **marginality**: the status of being between two cultures, as in the case of a person whose mother is a Jew and father a Christian. A century ago, Du Bois (1903) spoke eloquently of the "double consciousness" that Black Americans feel—caught between being a citizen of the United States but viewed as something quite apart from the dominant social forces of society. Incomplete assimilation by immigrants also results in marginality. Although a Filipino woman migrating to the United States may take on the characteristics of her new host society, she may not be fully accepted and may, therefore, feel neither Filipino nor American. Marginalized individuals often encounter social situations in which their identities are sources of tension, especially when the expression of multiple identities is not accepted, and they find themselves being perceived differently in different environments, with varying expectations (Park 1928; Stonequist 1937; Townsend, Markos, and Bergsieker 2009).

Yet another source of marginality comes from children of biracial or multiracial parental backgrounds and children adopted by parents of a different racial or ethnic background. For these children or adolescents, developing their racial or ethnic identity says more about society's desire to fix labels onto their own actions (Fryer et al. 2012).

As we seek to understand diversity in the United States, we must be mindful that ethnic and racial labels are just that: labels that have been socially constructed. Yet these social constructs can have a powerful impact, whether self-applied or applied by others.

Sociology and the Study of Race and Ethnicity

1-5   Describe how sociology helps us understand race and ethnicity.

Before proceeding further with our study of racial and ethnic groups, let us consider several sociological perspectives that provide insight into dominant–subordinate relationships. **Sociology** is the systematic study of social behavior and human groups, so it is aptly suited to enlarge our understanding of intergroup relations. The study of race relations has a long, valuable history in sociology. Admittedly, it has not always been progressive; indeed, at times it has reflected the prejudices of society. In some instances, sociology scholars who are members of racial, ethnic, and religious minorities, as well as women, have not been permitted to make the kind of contributions they are capable of making to the field.

Stratification by Class and Gender

That some members of society have unequal amounts of wealth, prestige, or power is a characteristic of all societies. Sociologists observe that entire groups may be assigned less or more of what a society values. The hierarchy that emerges is called **stratification**. Stratification is the structured ranking of entire groups of people that perpetuates unequal rewards and power in a society.

Much discussion of stratification identifies the **class**, or social ranking, of people who share similar wealth, according to sociologist Max Weber's classic definition. Mobility from one class to another is not easy to achieve. Movement into classes of greater wealth may be particularly difficult for subordinate-group members faced with lifelong prejudice and discrimination (Banton 2008; Gerth and Mills 1958).

Recall that the first property of subordinate-group standing is unequal treatment by the dominant group in the form of prejudice, discrimination, and segregation. Stratification is intertwined with the subordination of racial, ethnic, religious, and gender groups. Race has implications for the way people are treated; so does class. One also must add the effects of race and class together. For example, being poor and Black is not the same as being either one by itself. A wealthy Mexican American is not the same as an affluent Anglo American or Mexican Americans as a group.

Public discussion of issues such as housing or public assistance often is disguised as a discussion of class issues, when, in fact, the issues are based primarily on race. Similarly, some topics such as the poorest of the poor or the working poor are addressed in terms of race when the class component should be explicit. Nonetheless, the link between race and class in society is abundantly clear (Winant 2004).

Another stratification factor that we need to consider is gender. How different is the situation for women as contrasted with men? Returning again to the first property of minority groups—unequal treatment and less control—women do not receive treatment that equals that received by men. Whether the issue is jobs or poverty, education or crime, women typically have more difficult experiences. In addition, the situations women face in areas such as health care and welfare raise different concerns than they do for men. Just as we need to consider the role of social class to understand race and ethnicity better, we also need to consider the role of gender.

Theoretical Perspectives

Sociologists view society in different ways. Some see the world basically as a stable and ongoing entity. The endurance of a Chinatown, the general sameness of male–female roles over time, and other aspects of intergroup relations impress them. Some sociologists see society as composed of many groups in conflict, competing for scarce resources. Within this conflict, some people or even entire groups may be labeled or stigmatized in a way that blocks their access to what a society values. We examine three theoretical perspectives that are widely used by sociologists today: the functionalist, conflict, and labeling perspectives.

FUNCTIONALIST PERSPECTIVE In the view of a functionalist, a society is like a living organism in which each part contributes to the survival of the whole. The **functionalist perspective** emphasizes how the parts of society are structured to maintain its stability. According to this approach, if an aspect of social life does not contribute to a society's stability or survival, then it will not be passed on from one generation to the next.

It seems reasonable to assume that bigotry between races offers no such positive function, and so we ask, Why does it persist? Although agreeing that racial hostility is hardly to be admired, the functionalist would point out that it serves some positive functions from the perspective of the racists. We can identify five functions that racial beliefs have for the dominant group:

1. Racist ideologies provide a moral justification for maintaining a society that routinely deprives a group of its rights and privileges.
2. Racist beliefs discourage subordinate people from attempting to question their lowly status and why they must perform "the dirty work"; to do so is to question the very foundation of the society.
3. Racial ideologies not only justify existing practices but also serve as a rallying point for social movements, as seen in the rise of the Nazi Party or present-day Aryan movements.
4. Racist myths encourage support for the existing order. Some argue that if there were any major societal change, the subordinate group would suffer even greater poverty, and the dominant group would suffer lower living standards.
5. Racist beliefs relieve the dominant group of the responsibility to address the economic and educational problems faced by subordinate groups.

As a result, racial ideology grows when a value system (e.g., that underlying a colonial empire or slavery) is being threatened (Levin and Nolan 2011: 115–145; Nash 1962).

Prejudice and discrimination also cause definite dysfunctions. **Dysfunctions** are elements of society that may disrupt a social system or decrease its stability. Racism is dysfunctional to a society, including to its dominant group, in six ways:

1. A society that practices discrimination fails to use the resources of all individuals. Discrimination limits the search for talent and leadership to the dominant group.
2. Discrimination aggravates social problems such as poverty, delinquency, and crime and places the financial burden of alleviating these problems on the dominant group.
3. Society must invest a good deal of time and money to defend the barriers that prevent the full participation of all members.
4. Racial prejudice and discrimination undercut goodwill and friendly diplomatic relations between nations. They also negatively affect efforts to increase global trade.
5. Social change is inhibited because change may assist a subordinate group.
6. Discrimination promotes disrespect for law enforcement and for the peaceful settlement of disputes.

That racism has costs for the dominant group as well as for the subordinate group reminds us that intergroup conflict is exceedingly complex (Bowser and Hunt 1996; Feagin, Vera, and Batur 2000; Rose 1951).

CONFLICT PERSPECTIVE   In contrast to the functionalists' emphasis on stability, conflict sociologists see the social world as being in continual struggle. The **conflict perspective** assumes that the social structure is best understood in terms of conflict or tension between competing groups. The result of this conflict is significant economic disparity and structural inequality in education, the labor market, housing, and health care delivery. Specifically, society is in a struggle between the privileged (the dominant group) and the exploited (the subordinate group). Such conflicts need not be physically violent and may take the form of immigration restrictions, real estate practices, or disputes over cuts in the federal budget.

The conflict model often is selected today when one is examining race and ethnicity because it readily accounts for the presence of tension between competing groups. According to the conflict perspective, competition takes place between groups with unequal amounts of economic and political power. The minorities are exploited or, at best, ignored by the dominant group. The conflict perspective is viewed as more radical and activist than functionalism because conflict theorists emphasize social change and the redistribution of resources.

Those who follow the conflict approach to race and ethnicity have remarked repeatedly that the subordinate group is criticized for its low status. That the dominant group is responsible for subordination is often ignored. William Ryan (1976) calls this an instance of **blaming the victim**: portraying the problems of racial and ethnic minorities as their fault rather than recognizing society's responsibility.

Conflict theorists consider the costs that come with residential segregation. Besides the more obvious cost of reducing housing options, racial and social class isolation reduces for people (including Whites) all available options in schools, retail shopping, and medical care. People, however, can travel to access services and businesses, and it is more likely that racial and ethnic minorities will have to make that sometimes costly and time-consuming trip (Carr and Kutty 2008).

LABELING THEORY Related to the conflict perspective and its concern over blaming the victim is **labeling theory**, a concept introduced by sociologist Howard Becker to explain why certain people are viewed as deviant and others engaging in the same behavior are not. Students of crime and deviance have relied heavily on labeling theory. According to labeling theory, a youth who misbehaves may be considered and treated as a delinquent if he or she comes from the "wrong kind of family." Another youth from a middle-class family who commits the same sort of misbehavior might be given another chance before being punished.

From the conflict perspective, the emphasis should not be primarily on the attributes of the individual (i.e., "blaming the victim") but on structural factors such as the labor market, affordable housing, and availability of programs to assist people with addiction or mental health issues.

The labeling perspective directs our attention to the role that negative stereotypes play in race and ethnicity. The image that prejudiced people maintain of a group toward which they hold ill feelings is called a **stereotype**. Stereotypes are unreliable generalizations about all members of a group that do not take individual differences into account. The warrior image of Native American (American Indian) people is perpetuated by the frequent use of tribal names or even names such as "Indians" and "Redskins" for sports teams. In Chapter 2, we review some of the research on the stereotyping of minorities. This labeling is not limited to racial and ethnic groups, however. For instance, age can be used to exclude a person from an activity in which he or she is qualified to engage. Groups are subjected to stereotypes and discrimination in such a way that their treatment resembles that of social minorities. Social prejudice as a result of stereotyping exists toward ex-convicts, gamblers, alcoholics, lesbians, gays, prostitutes, people with AIDS, and people with disabilities, to name a few.

The labeling approach points out that stereotypes, when applied by people in power, can have negative consequences for people or groups identified falsely. A crucial aspect of the relationship between dominant and subordinate groups is the prerogative of the dominant group to define society's values. U.S. sociologist William I. Thomas (1923), an early critic of racial and gender discrimination, saw that the "definition of the situation" could mold the personality of the individual. In other words, Thomas observed that people respond not only to the objective features of a situation (or person) but also to the meaning these features have for them. So, for example, a lone walker seeing a young Black man walking toward him may perceive the situation differently than if the oncoming person is an older woman. Sociologist Elijah Anderson (2011) has long seen passers-by scrutinize him and other African American males more closely and suspiciously than they would women or White males. In this manner, we can create false images or stereotypes that become real in their social consequences.

In certain situations, we may respond to negative stereotypes and act on them, with the result that false definitions become accurate. This is known as a **self-fulfilling prophecy**. A person or group described as having particular characteristics begins to display the very traits attributed to him or her. Thus, a child who is praised for being a natural comic may focus on learning to become funny to gain approval and attention.

Self-fulfilling prophecies can be devastating for minority groups (Figure 1.4). Such groups often find that they are allowed to hold only low-paying jobs with little prestige or opportunity for advancement. The rationale of the dominant society is that these minority people lack the ability to perform in more important and lucrative positions. Training to become scientists, executives, or physicians is denied to many subordinate-group individuals (SGIs), who are then locked into society's inferior jobs. As a result, the false definition of the self-fulfilling prophecy becomes real. The subordinate group becomes inferior because it was defined at the start as inferior and was, therefore, prevented from achieving the levels attained by the majority.

Because of this vicious circle, a talented subordinate-group person may come to see the fields of entertainment and professional sports as his or her only hope for achieving wealth and fame. Thus, it is no accident that successive waves of Irish, Jewish, Italian, African American, and Hispanic performers and athletes have made their mark on culture in the United States. Unfortunately, these very successes may convince the dominant group that its original stereotypes were valid—that these are the only areas of society in which subordinate-group members can excel. Furthermore, athletics and the arts are highly competitive areas. For every LeBron James and Jennifer Lopez who makes it, many, many more SGIs will end up disappointed.

Figure 1.4 Self-Fulfilling Prophecy

The self-validating effects of dominant-group definitions are shown here. The subordinate-group individual attends a poorly financed school and is left unequipped to perform jobs that offer high status and pay. He or she then gets a low-paying job and must settle for a much lower level of society's standard of living. Because the person shares these societal standards, he or she may begin to feel self-doubt and self-hatred.

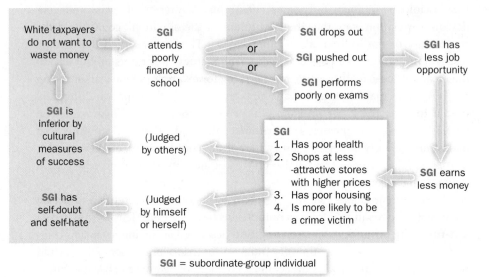

SGI = subordinate-group individual

The Creation of Subordinate-Group Status

1-6 Restate the creation of subordinate groups.

Three situations are likely to lead to the formation of a relationship between a subordinate group and the dominant group. A subordinate group emerges through migration, annexation, and colonialism.

Migration

People who emigrate to a new country often find themselves a minority there. Cultural or physical traits or religious affiliation may set the immigrant apart from the dominant group. Immigration from Europe, Asia, and Latin America has been a powerful force in shaping the fabric of life in the United States. **Migration** is the general term used to describe any transfer of population. **Emigration** (by emigrants) describes leaving a country to settle in another. **Immigration** (by immigrants) denotes coming into the new country. As an example, from Vietnam's perspective, the "boat people" were emigrants from

Vietnam to the United States, but in the United States they were counted among this nation's immigrants.

Although some people migrate because they want to, leaving one's home country is not always voluntary. Millions have been transported as slaves against their will. Conflict and war have displaced people throughout human history. In the twentieth century, we saw huge population movements caused by two world wars; revolutions in Spain, Hungary, and Cuba; the partition of British India; conflicts in Southeast Asia, Korea, and Central America; and the confrontations between Arabs and Israelis.

In all types of movement, even when a U.S. family moves from Ohio to Florida, but especially regarding emigration, two sets of forces operate: push factors and pull factors. Push factors discourage a person from remaining where he or she lives. Religious persecution and economic factors such as dissatisfaction with employment opportunities are possible push factors. Pull factors, such as a better standard of living, friends and relatives who have already emigrated, and a promised job, attract an immigrant to a particular country.

Although generally we think of migration as a voluntary process, much of the population transfer that has occurred in the world has been involuntary. Such forced movement of people into another society guarantees a subordinate role. Involuntary migration is no longer common; although enslavement has a long history, all industrialized societies today prohibit such practices. Of course, many contemporary societies, including the United States, bear the legacy of slavery.

Migration has taken on new significance in the twenty-first century partly because of **globalization**, or the worldwide integration of government policies, cultures, social movements, and financial markets through trade and the exchange of ideas. The increased movement of people and money across borders has made the distinction between temporary and permanent migration less meaningful. Although migration has always been fluid, people in today's global economy are connected across societies culturally and economically as never before. Even after they have relocated, people maintain global linkages to their former country and with a global economy (Richmond 2002).

Annexation

Nations, particularly during wars or as a result of war, incorporate or attach land. This new land is contiguous to the nation, such as in the German annexation of Austria and Czechoslovakia in 1938 and 1939 and in the U.S. Louisiana Purchase of 1803. The Treaty of Guadalupe Hidalgo that ended the Mexican–American War in 1848 gave the United States California, Utah, Nevada, most of New Mexico, and parts of Arizona, Wyoming, and Colorado. The indigenous peoples in some of this huge territory were dominant in their society one day, only to become minority-group members the next.

When annexation occurs, the dominant power generally suppresses the language and culture of the minority. Such was the practice of Russia with the Ukrainians and Poles and of Prussia with the Poles. Minorities try to maintain their cultural integrity despite annexation. Poles inhabited an area divided into territories ruled by three countries but maintained their own culture across political boundaries.

Colonialism

Colonialism has been the most common way for one group of people to dominate another. **Colonialism** is the maintenance of political, social, economic, and cultural dominance over people by a foreign power for an extended period (Bell 1991). Colonialism is rule by outsiders but, unlike annexation, does not involve actual incorporation into the dominant people's nation. The long-standing control that was exercised by the British Empire over much of North America, parts of Africa, and India is an example of colonial domination (see Figure 1.5).

Societies gain power over a foreign land through military strength, sophisticated political organization, and investment capital. The extent of power may

---

Figure 1.5 World Colonial Empires (1900)

Events of the nineteenth century increased European dominance over the world. By 1900, most independent African nations had disappeared, and the major European powers and Japan took advantage of China's internal weakness to gain both trading ports and economic concessions.

SOURCE: Divine, Breen, Williams, Gross & Brands, *America: Past and Present,* Volume 2, 10/e ©2013 | Pearson.

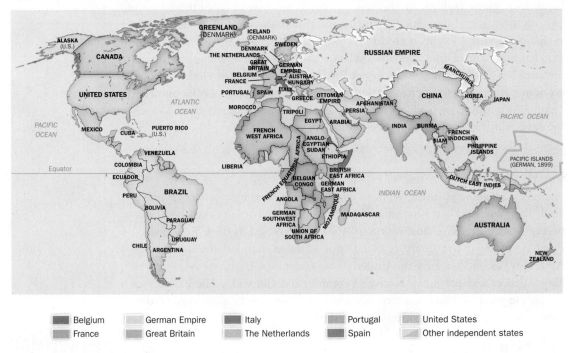

also vary according to the dominant group's scope of settlement in the colonial land. Relations between the colonizing nation and the colonized people are similar to those between a dominant group and exploited subordinate groups. Colonial subjects generally are limited to menial jobs and the wages from their labor. The natural resources of their land benefit the members of the ruling class.

By the 1980s, colonialism, in the sense of political rule, had become largely a phenomenon of the past, yet industrial countries of North America and Europe still dominated the world economically and politically. Drawing on the conflict perspective, sociologist Immanuel Wallerstein (1974) views the global economic system of today as much like the height of colonial days. Wallerstein has advanced the **world systems theory**, which views the global economic system as divided between nations that control wealth and those that provide natural resources and labor. The limited economic resources available in developing nations exacerbate many of the ethnic, racial, and religious conflicts noted at the beginning of this chapter. In addition, the presence of massive inequality between nations only serves to encourage immigration generally and, more specifically, the movement of many of the most skilled from developing nations to the industrial nations.

Spectrum of Intergroup Status

1-7 Use the Spectrum of Intergroup Relations.

Relationships between and among racial, ethnic, and religious groups as well as other dominate–subordinate relationships are not static. These relations change over time, sometimes in one's own lifetime. To better illustrate this, we can use the Spectrum of Intergroup Relations illustrated here.

These relationships can be viewed among a continuum from those largely unacceptable to the subordinate group such as extermination and expulsion to those that are more tolerant such as assimilation and pluralism. In the next section we will explore these consequences of group inequality in more detail.

Spectrum of Intergroup Relations

EXPULSION	SEGREGATION	ASSIMILATION
INCREASINGLY UNACCEPTABLE		MORE TOLERABLE

EXTERMINATION	SECESSION	FUSION	PLURALISM
or genocide	or partitioning	or amalgamation or melting pot	or multiculturalism

The Consequences of Subordinate-Group Status

1-8 **Restate the consequences of subordinate groups.**

A group with subordinate status is faced with several consequences. These differ in their degree of harshness, ranging from physical annihilation to absorption into the dominant group. In this section, we examine six consequences of subordinate-group status: extermination, expulsion, secession, segregation, fusion, and assimilation.

Extermination

The most extreme way to deal with a subordinate group is to eliminate it. Today, the term **genocide** is used to describe the deliberate, systematic killing of an entire people or nation. This term is often used in reference to the Holocaust, Nazi Germany's extermination of 12 million European Jews and other ethnic minorities during World War II. The **Holocaust** was the state-sponsored systematic persecution and annihilation of European Jewry by Nazi Germany and its collaborators. The move to eliminate Jews from the European continent started slowly, with Germany gradually restricting the rights of Jews: preventing them from voting, living outside the Jewish ghetto, and owning businesses. Much anti-Semitic cruelty was evident before the beginning of the war. Dramatically, *Kristallnacht*, or the "Night of Broken Glass," in Berlin on November 9, 1938, was a turning point toward genocide. Ninety Berlin Jews were murdered, hundreds of homes and synagogues were set on fire or ransacked, and thousands of Jewish store windows were broken.

Despite the obvious intolerance they faced, Jews desiring to immigrate were often turned back by government officials in Europe and the Americas (DellaPergola 2007; Institute for Jewish and Community Research 2008).

The term **ethnic cleansing** refers to the forced deportation of people, accompanied by systematic violence including death. The term was introduced in 1992 to the world's vocabulary as ethnic Serbs instituted a policy intended to "cleanse"—eliminate—Muslims from parts of Bosnia. Again in 1994, a genocidal war between the Hutu and Tutsi people in Rwanda left 300,000 school-age children orphaned (Chirot and Edwards 2003; Naimark 2004).

Genocide also appropriately describes White policies toward Native Americans in the nineteenth century. In 1800, the American Indian population in the United States was approximately 600,000; by 1850, it had been reduced to 250,000 through warfare with the U.S. Army, disease, and forced relocation to inhospitable environments.

In 2008, the Australian government officially apologized for past treatment of its native people, the Aboriginal population. Not only did this involve brutality and neglect, but also a quarter of their children, the so-called lost generation, were taken from their families and places in orphanages, foster homes, or put up for adoption by White Australians until the policy was finally abandoned in 1969 (Johnston 2008).

Expulsion

Dominant groups may choose to force a specific subordinate group to leave certain areas or even vacate a country. Expulsion, therefore, is another extreme consequence of minority-group status. European colonial powers in North America and eventually the U.S. government itself drove almost all Native Americans out of their tribal lands and into unfamiliar territory.

More recently, beginning in 2009, France expelled over 10,000 ethnic Roma (or Gypsies), forcing their return to their home countries of Bulgaria and Romania. This appeared to violate the European Union's (EU) ban against targeting ethnic groups as well as Europe's policy of "freedom of movement." In 2011, the EU withdrew its threat of legal action against France when the government said it would no longer expel Roma in particular but only those living in "illegal camps," which many observers felt was only a technical way for the country to get around long-standing human rights policies.

Secession

A group ceases to be a subordinate group when it secedes to form a new nation or moves to an already-established nation, where it becomes dominant. After Great Britain withdrew from Palestine, Jewish people achieved a dominant position in 1948, attracting Jews from throughout the world to the new state of Israel. Similarly, Pakistan was created in 1947 when India was partitioned. The predominantly Muslim areas in the north became Pakistan, making India predominantly Hindu. Throughout this century, minorities have repudiated dominant customs. In this spirit, the Estonian, Latvian, Lithuanian, and Armenian peoples, not content to be merely tolerated by the majority, all seceded to form independent states after the demise of the Soviet Union in 1991. In 1999, ethnic Albanians fought bitterly for their cultural and political recognition in the Kosovo region of Yugoslavia.

Some African Americans have called for secession. Suggestions dating back to the early 1700s supported the return of Blacks to Africa as a solution to racial problems. The settlement target of the American Colonization Society was Liberia, but proposals were also advanced to establish settlements in other areas. Territorial separatism and the emigrationist ideology were recurrent and interrelated themes among African Americans from the late nineteenth century well into the 1980s. The Black Muslims, or Nation of Islam, once expressed the desire for complete separation in their own state or territory within the modern borders of the United States. Although a secession of Blacks from the United States has not taken place, it has been proposed.

Stigmatizing and expelling minority groups is not an action of the distance past. Here, police in Paris round up Roma (Gypsies) for subsequent expulsion from the country.

Segregation

Segregation is the physical separation of two groups in residence, workplace, and social functions. Generally, the dominant group imposes segregation on a subordinate group. Segregation is rarely complete; however, intergroup contact inevitably occurs even in the most segregated societies.

Sociologists Douglas Massey and Nancy Denton wrote *American Apartheid* (1993), which described segregation in U.S. cities on the basis of 1990 data. The title of their book was meant to indicate that neighborhoods in the United States resembled the segregation of the rigid government-imposed racial segregation that prevailed for so long in the Republic of South Africa.

Analysis of census data shows continuing segregation despite racial and ethnic diversity in the United States. Scholars use a segregation index to measure separation. This index ranges from 0 (complete integration) to 100 (complete segregation), where the value indicates the percentage of the minority group that needs to move to be distributed exactly like Whites. So a segregation index of 60 for Blacks–Whites would mean that 60 percent of all African Americans would have to move to be residing just like Whites.

In Table 1.2, we look at the most segregated metropolitan areas with large African American, Latino, and Asian American populations. Blacks and Whites are most separated from each other in Detroit; the Los Angeles/long beach metropolitan area finds Whites and Latinos most living apart; and the New Brunswick, New Jersey, area is where Asians and Whites are most segregated from each other. Typically half to three-quarters of the people would have to move to achieve even distribution throughout the city and surrounding suburbs.

Table 1.2 Segregated Metro America

BLACK–WHITE	
1. Detroit	79.6
2. Milwaukee	79.6
3. New York/White Plains	79.1
4. Newark	78.0
5. Chicago/Naperville	75.9
6. Philadelphia	73.7
7. Miami/Miami Beach	73.0
8. Cleveland	72.6
HISPANIC–WHITE	
1. Los Angeles/Long Beach	63.4
2. New York/White Plains	63.1
3. Newark	62.6
5. Boston	62.0
6. Salinas, CA	60.0
7. Philadelphia	58.8
8. Chicago/Naperville	57.0
9. Oxford/Venture, CA	54.5
ASIAN–WHITE	
1. Edison/New Brunswick, NJ	53.7
2. New York/White Plains	49.5
3. Houston	48.7
4. Los Angeles/Long Beach	47.6
5. Boston	47.4
6. Sacramento, CA	46.8
7. San Francisco	46.7
8. Warren/Farmington Hills MI	46.3

Note: The higher the value, the more segregated the metropolitan area.
SOURCE: Logan and Stults 2011.

Over the last 40 years, Black–White segregation has declined modestly. Hispanic–White segregation, while lower, has not changed significantly in the last 30 years. Asian–White segregation is even a bit lower but also has been mostly unchanged over the three decades. Even when we consider social class, the patterns of minority segregation persist. Despite the occasional multiracial neighborhood, segregation prevails (Bureau of the Census 2010b; Frey 2011; Iceland, Sharp, and Timberlake 2013; Krysan, Farley, and Couper 2008).

This focus on metropolitan areas should not cause us to ignore the continuing legally sanctioned segregation of Native Americans on reservations.

Although the majority of our nation's first inhabitants live outside these tribal areas, the reservations play a prominent role in the identity of Native Americans. Although it is easier to maintain tribal identity on the reservation, economic and educational opportunities are more limited in these areas, which are segregated from the rest of society.

A particularly troubling pattern has been the emergence of **resegregation**, or the physical separation of racial and ethnic groups reappearing after a period of relative integration. Resegregation has occurred in neighborhoods and schools after a transitional period of desegregation. For example, in 1954, only 1 in 100,000 Black students attended a majority White school in the South. Thanks to the civil rights movement and a series of civil rights measures, by 1968, the percentage of Black students in White majority schools rose to 23 percent and then to 47 percent by 1988.

The latest analysis, however, shows continuing racial isolation. A 2012 report documents that nationwide, 43 percent of Latinos and 38 percent of Blacks attend schools in which fewer than 10 percent of their classmates are White (Orfield 2007;Orfield, Kucsera and Siegel-Hawley 2012; Orfield and Lee 2005; Rich 2008).

Given segregation patterns, many Whites in the United States have limited contact with people of other racial and ethnic backgrounds. In one study of 100 affluent powerful White men that looked at their experiences past and present, it was clear they had lived in a "White bubble"—their neighborhoods, schools, elite colleges, and workplaces were overwhelmingly White. The continuing pattern of segregation in the United States means our diverse population grows up in very different nations. For many urban Blacks and Latinos, segregation in neighborhoods with limited job opportunities is a social fact (Bonilla-Silva and Embrick 2007; Feagin and O'Brien 2003; Massey 2012).

Segregation by race, ethnicity, religion, tribal or clan affiliation, and sometimes even language grouping occurs throughout the world. The most dramatic government-engineered segregation in recent memory was in South Africa. In 1948, the Great Britain granted South Africa its independence, and the National Party, dominated by a White minority, assumed control of the government. The rule of White supremacy, well under way as the custom in the colonial period, became more and more formalized into law. To deal with the multiracial population, the Whites devised a policy called apartheid to ensure their dominance. **Apartheid** (in Afrikaans, the language of the White Afrikaners, it means *separation* or *apartness*) came to mean a policy of separate development, euphemistically called *multinational development* by the government. Black South Africans were relegated to impoverished urban townships or rural areas and their mobility within the country strictly regulated. Events took a significant turn in 1990, when the South African prime minister legalized once-banned Black organizations and freed Nelson Mandela, leader of the African National Congress (ANC), after 27 years of imprisonment. Mandela's triumphant return was soon followed by him becoming head of the government, and a half-century of apartheid came to an end.

Fusion

Fusion occurs when a minority and a majority group combine to form a new group. This combining can be expressed as $A + B + C \longrightarrow D$, where A, B, and C represent the groups present in a society and D signifies the result, an ethnocultural–racial group that shares some of the characteristics of each initial group. Mexican people are an example of fusion, originating as they do from the mixing of Spanish and indigenous Indian cultures. Theoretically, fusion does not entail intermarriage, but it is very similar to **amalgamation**, or the process by which a dominant group and a subordinate group combine through intermarriage into a new people. In everyday speech, the words *fusion* and *amalgamation* are rarely used, but the concept is expressed in the notion of a human **melting pot** in which diverse racial or ethnic groups form a new creation, a new cultural entity (Newman 1973).

The analogy of the cauldron, the "melting pot," was first used to describe the United States by the French observer Crèvecoeur in 1782. The phrase dates back to the Middle Ages, when alchemists attempted to change less-valuable metals into gold and silver. Similarly, the idea of the human melting pot implied that the new group would represent only the best qualities and attributes of the different cultures contributing to it. The belief in the United States as a melting pot became widespread in the early twentieth century. This belief suggested that the United States had an almost divine mission to destroy artificial divisions and create a single kind of human. However, the dominant group had indicated its unwillingness to welcome such groups as Native Americans, Blacks, Hispanics, Jews, Asians, and Irish Roman Catholics into the melting pot. It is a mistake to think of the United States as an ethnic mixing bowl. Although superficial signs of fusion are present, as in a cuisine that includes sauerkraut and spaghetti, most contributions of subordinate groups are ignored (Gleason 1980).

Marriage patterns indicate the resistance to fusion. People are unwilling, in varying degrees, to marry outside their own ethnic, religious, and racial groups. Until relatively recently, interracial marriage was outlawed in much of the United States. At the time that President Barack Obama's White mother and Black father were married in Hawaii, their union would have been illegal and unable to occur in 22 other states. Surveys show that 20 to 50 percent of various White ethnic groups report single ancestry. When White ethnics do cross boundaries, they tend to marry within their religion and social class. For example, Italians are more likely to marry Irish, who are also Catholic, than they are to marry Protestant Swedes.

Although it may seem that interracial matches are everywhere, there is only modest evidence of a fusion of races in the United States. Racial intermarriage has been increasing. In 1980, there were 651,000 interracial marriages, but by 2010, there were 5.4 million. That is still less than 7 percent of married couples but it is increasing significantly. Among unmarried couples it rises to 14 percent and among same-sex couples to 15 percent.

While still not typical, more couples are crossing racial and ethnic boundaries in the United States today than any generation before. Clearly this will increase the potential for their children to identify as biracial or multiracial rather than in a single category.

Among couples in which at least one member is Hispanic, marriages with a non-Hispanic partner account for 28 percent. Taken together, all interracial and Hispanic–non-Hispanic marriages account for 10 percent of married opposite-sex couples today. But this includes decades of marriages. Among new couples, about 15 percent of marriages are between people of different races or between Hispanics and non-Hispanics (Bureau of the Census 2010a: Table 60; Lofquist et al. 2012; Passel, Wang, and Taylor 2010).

Assimilation

Assimilation is the process by which a subordinate individual or group takes on the characteristics of the dominant group and is eventually accepted as part of that group. Assimilation is a majority ideology in which $A + B + C \longrightarrow A$. The majority (A) dominates in such a way that the minorities (B and C) become indistinguishable from the dominant group. Assimilation dictates conformity to the dominant group, regardless of how many racial, ethnic, or religious groups are involved (Newman 1973: 53).

To be complete, assimilation must entail an active effort by the minority-group individual to shed all distinguishing actions and beliefs and the unqualified acceptance of that individual by the dominant society. In the United States, dominant White society encourages assimilation. The assimilation perspective tends to devalue alien culture and to treasure the dominant. For example, assimilation assumes that whatever is admirable among Blacks was adapted from Whites and that whatever is bad is inherently Black. The assimilation solution to Black–White conflict has been typically defined as the development of a consensus around White American values.

Assimilation is very difficult. The person being assimilated must forsake his or her cultural tradition to become part of a different, often antagonistic culture. However, assimilation should not be viewed as if immigrants are extraterrestrials. Cross-border movement is often preceded by adjustments and awareness of the culture that awaits the immigrant (Skrentny 2008).

Assimilation does not occur at the same pace for all groups or for all individuals in the same group. Typically, the assimilation process is not completed by the first generation—the new arrivals. Assimilation tends to take longer under the following conditions:

- The differences between the minority and the majority are large.
- The majority is not receptive, or the minority retains its own culture.

One aspect of assimilation is when immigrants seek to learn the language of the host society, as shown in this adult English as a Second Language class in Minneapolis, Minnesota.

- The minority group arrives over a short period of time.
- The minority-group residents are concentrated rather than dispersed.
- The arrival is recent, and the homeland is accessible.

Assimilation is not a smooth process (Warner and Srole 1945).

Segmented assimilation describes the outcome of immigrants and their descendants moving in to different classes of the host society. It emphasizes that there is not a single, uniform lifestyle in the United States and that much of the assimilation is into the working or even lower classes. For a very small portion, such as high-level and elite engineers and other professionals, the movement might be into the higher reaches of class divisions. However, for many, assimilation may be into a lower class than that enjoyed in their home country and may represent downward mobility even while assimilation progresses (Haller, Portes, and Lynch 2011).

Many people view assimilation as unfair or even dictatorial. However, members of the dominant group see it as reasonable that subordinate people shed their distinctive cultural traditions. In public discussions today, assimilation is the ideology of the dominant group in forcing people how to act. Consequently, the social institutions in the United States—the educational system, economy, government, religion, and medicine—all push toward assimilation, with occasional references to the pluralist approach.

The Pluralist Perspective

Thus far, we have concentrated on how subordinate groups cease to exist (removal) or take on the characteristics of the dominant group (assimilation). The alternative to these relationships between the majority and the minority is pluralism. **Pluralism** implies that various groups in a society have mutual respect for one another's culture, a respect that allows minorities to express their own culture without suffering prejudice or discrimination. Whereas the assimilationist or integrationist seeks the elimination of ethnic boundaries, the pluralist believes in maintaining many of them.

There are limits to cultural freedom. A Romanian immigrant to the United States cannot expect to avoid learning English and still move up the occupational ladder. To survive, a society must have a consensus among its members on basic ideals, values, and beliefs. Nevertheless, there is still plenty of room for variety. Earlier, fusion was described as $A + B + C \longrightarrow D$ and assimilation as $A + B + C \longrightarrow A$. Using this same scheme, we can think of pluralism as $A + B + C \longrightarrow A + B + C$, with groups coexisting in one society (Manning 1995; Newman 1973; Simpson 1995).

In the United States, cultural pluralism is more an ideal than a reality. Although there are vestiges of cultural pluralism—in the various ethnic neighborhoods in major cities, for instance—the rule has been for subordinate groups to assimilate. Yet as the minority becomes the numerical majority, the ability to live out one's identity becomes a bit easier. African Americans, Hispanics, American Indians, and Asian Americans already outnumber Whites in most of the largest cities. The trend is toward even greater diversity. Nonetheless, the cost of cultural integrity throughout the nation's history has been high. The various Native American tribes have succeeded to a large extent in maintaining their heritage, but the price has been bare subsistence on federal reservations.

The United States is experiencing a reemergence of ethnic identification by groups that had previously expressed little interest in their heritage. Groups that make up the dominant majority also are reasserting their ethnic heritages. Various nationality groups are rekindling interest in almost forgotten languages, customs, festivals, and traditions. In some instances, this expression of the past has taken the form of a protest against exclusion from the dominant society. For example, Chinese youths chastise their elders for forgetting the old ways and accepting White American influence and control.

The most visible expression of pluralism is language use. As of 2008, nearly one in every five people (19.1 percent) over age five spoke a language other than English at home. Later, in Chapter 4, we consider how language use figures into issues relating to immigration and education (American Community Survey 2009: Table S1601).

Facilitating a diverse and changing society affects just about every aspect of that society. Yet another nod to pluralism, although not nearly so obvious as language to the general population, has been the changes within the funeral industry. Where Christian and Jewish funeral practices once dominated, funeral home professionals are now being trained to accommodate a variety of practices. Latinos often expect 24-hour viewing of their deceased, whereas Muslims may wish to participate in washing the deceased before burial in a grave pointing toward Mecca. Hindu and Buddhist requests to participate in cremation are now being respected (Brulliard 2006).

Resistance and Change

1-9   Articulate how change occurs in racial and ethnic relations.

By virtue of wielding power and influence, the dominant group may define the terms by which all members of society operate. This is particularly evident in a slave society, but even in contemporary industrialized nations, the dominant group has a disproportionate role in shaping immigration policy, the curriculum of the schools, and the content of the media.

Subordinate groups do not merely accept the definitions and ideology proposed by the dominant group. A continuing theme in dominant–subordinate relations is the minority group's challenge to its subordination. Resistance by subordinate groups is well documented as they seek to promote change that will bring them more rights and privileges, if not true equality. Often, traditional notions of racial formation are overcome not only through panethnicity but also because Black people, along with Latinos and sympathetic Whites, join in the resistance to subordination (Moulder 1996; Winant 2004).

Resistance can be seen in efforts by racial and ethnic groups to maintain their identity through newspapers and organizations and in today's technological age through cable television stations, blogs, and Internet sites. Resistance manifests itself in social movements such as the civil rights movement, the feminist movement, and gay rights efforts. The passage of such legislation as the Age Discrimination Act or the Americans with Disabilities Act marks the success of oppressed groups in lobbying on their own behalf.

Resistance efforts may begin through small actions. For example, residents of a reservation question why a toxic waste dump is to be located on their land.

Through recent efforts of collective action, African American farmers successfully received Congressional approval in 2010 for compensation denied them in the latter 1900s by the Department of Agriculture.

Although it may bring in money, they question the wisdom of such a move. Their concerns lead to further investigations of the extent to which American Indian lands are used disproportionately as containment areas for dangerous materials. This action in turn leads to a broader investigation of the ways in which minority-group people often find themselves "hosting" dumps and incinerators. As we discuss later, these local efforts eventually led the Environmental Protection Agency to monitor the disproportionate placement of toxic facilities in or near racial and ethnic minority communities. There is little reason to expect that such reforms would have occurred if the reservation residents had relied on traditional decision-making processes alone.

Change has occurred. At the beginning of the twentieth century, lynching was practiced in many parts of the country. At the beginning of the twenty-first century, laws punishing hate crimes were increasingly common and embraced a variety of stigmatized groups. Although this social progress should not be ignored, the nation still must focus concern on the significant social inequalities that remain. It is too easy to look at the accomplishments of Barack Obama and Hillary Clinton and conclude "mission accomplished" in terms of racial and gender injustices (Best 2001).

An even more basic form of resistance is to question societal values. In this book, we avoid using the term *American* to describe people of the United States because geographically, Brazilians, Canadians, and El Salvadorans are Americans as well. It is easy to overlook how our understanding of today has been shaped by the way institutions and even the very telling of history have been presented by members of the dominant group. African American studies scholar Molefi Kete Asante (2007, 2008) has called for an **Afrocentric perspective** that emphasizes the customs of African cultures and how they have pervaded the history, culture, and behavior of Blacks in the United States and around the world. Afrocentrism seeks to balance Eurocentrism and works toward a multiculturalist or pluralist orientation in which no viewpoint is suppressed. The Afrocentric approach could become part of our school curriculum, which has not adequately acknowledged the importance of this heritage.

The Afrocentric perspective has attracted much attention in education. Opponents view it as a separatist view of history and culture that distorts both past and present. Its supporters counter that African peoples everywhere can come to full self-determination only when they are able to overthrow the dominance of White or Eurocentric intellectual interpretations (Conyers 2004).

The remarkable efforts by members of racial and ethnic minorities working with supportive White Americans beginning in the 1950s through the early 1970s successfully targeted overt racist symbols or racist and sexist actions. Today's targets are more intractable and tend to emerge from institutional discrimination. Sociologist Douglas Massey (2011) argued that a central goal must be to reform the criminal justice system by demanding repeal of the following: the three-strikes law, mandatory minimum sentencing, and harsher penalties for crack than for powdered cocaine. Such targets are quite different from laws that prevented Blacks and women from serving on juries.

In considering the inequalities present today, as we do in the chapters that follow, it is easy to forget how much change has taken place. Much of the resistance to prejudice and discrimination in the past, either to slavery or to women's prohibition from voting, took the active support of members of the dominant group. The indignities still experienced by subordinate groups continue to be resisted as subordinate groups and their allies among the dominant group seek further change.

Conclusion

One hundred years ago, sociologist and activist W. E. B. Du Bois took another famed Black activist, Booker T. Washington, to task for saying that the races could best work together apart, like fingers on a hand. Du Bois felt that Black people had to be a part of all social institutions and not create their own. With an African American elected and now reelected to the presidency, Whites, African Americans, and other groups continue to debate what form society should take. Should we seek to bring everyone together into an integrated whole? Or do we strive to maintain as much of our group identities as possible while working as cooperatively as necessary?

In this chapter, we have attempted to organize our approach to subordinate–dominant relations in the United States. We observed that subordinate groups do not necessarily contain fewer members than the dominant group. Subordinate groups are classified into racial, ethnic, religious, and gender groups. Racial classification has been of interest, but scientific findings do not explain contemporary race relations. Biological differences of race are not supported by scientific data. Yet as the continuing debate over standardized tests demonstrates, attempts to establish a biological meaning of race have not been swept entirely into the dustbin of history. However, the social meaning given to physical differences is very significant. People have defined racial differences in such a way as to encourage or discourage the progress of certain groups.

Subordinate-group members' reactions include the seeking of an alternative avenue to acceptance and success: "Why should we give up what we are, to be accepted by them?" In response to this question, there continues to be strong ethnicity identification. Pluralism describes a society in which several different groups coexist, with no dominant or subordinate groups. People individually choose what cultural patterns to keep and which to let go.

Subordinate groups have not and do not always accept their second-class status passively. They may protest, organize, revolt, and resist society as defined by the dominant group. Patterns of race and ethnic relations are changing, not stagnant. Indicative of the changing landscape, biracial and multiracial children present us with new definitions of identity emerging through a process of racial formation, reminding us that race is socially constructed.

In the twenty-first century, we are facing new challenges to cooperation. There has been a marked increase in the population of minority racial and ethnic groups to the point that collectively they will be in the majority well before today's college students reach 40 years of age. Society is not static, but dynamic and evolving. Little wonder that scholars are now talking about "super-diversity" and considering whether past notions of race and ethnicity are passé (Bobo 2013).

Continuing immigration and the explosive growth of the Hispanic population—more than double since 1990—fuel this population growth. Latinos are now settling in to the point that the Spanish-language Telemundo network is now introducing English-language subtitles to ensure their Latino viewers can fully comprehend their programming.

Barack Obama's historic campaign and becoming the 44th president of the United States in January 2009 marks a significant time in U.S. history. The fact that he is the first African American (and also the first non-White person) to serve as president demonstrates how much progress has been achieved in race relations in this country. It also underscores both how long it has taken and how much more needs to be accomplished for the United States to truly be "a more perfect union" as stated in the Constitution.

The two significant forces that are absent in a truly pluralistic society are prejudice and discrimination. In an assimilation society, prejudice disparages out-group differences, and discrimination financially rewards those who shed their past. In the next two chapters, we explore the nature of prejudice and discrimination in the United States.

Summary

1. When sociologists define a minority group, they are concerned primarily with the economic and political power, or powerlessness, of the group.

2. A racial group is set apart from others primarily by physical characteristics; an ethnic group is set apart primarily by national origin or cultural patterns.

3. People cannot be sorted into distinct racial groups, so race is best viewed as a social construct that is subject to different interpretations over time.

4. A small but still significant number of people in the United States—more than 7 million—readily see themselves as having a biracial or multiracial identity.

5. The study of race and ethnicity in the United States often considers the role played by class and gender.

6. Subordinate-group status has emerged through migration, annexation, and colonialism.

7. The Spectrum of Intergroup Relations illustrates the patterns between racial and ethnic groups ranging from those extremely harsh to more tolerant.

8. The social consequences of subordinate-group status include extermination, expulsion, secession, segregation, fusion, assimilation, and pluralism.

9. Racial, ethnic, and other minorities maintain a long history of resisting efforts to restrict their rights.

Key Terms

Afrocentric perspective, p. 38
amalgamation, p. 33
apartheid, p. 32
assimilation, p. 34
biological race, p. 11
blaming the victim, p. 22
class, p. 19
colonialism, p. 26
conflict perspective, p. 21
dysfunction, p. 21
emigration, p. 24
ethnic cleansing, p. 28
ethnic group, p. 9

functionalist perspective, p. 20
fusion, p. 33
genocide, p. 28
globalization, p. 25
Holocaust, p. 28
immigration, p. 24
intelligence quotient (IQ), p. 12
labeling theory, p. 22
marginality, p. 18
melting pot, p. 33
migration, p. 24
minority group, p. 5
panethnicity, p. 18

pluralism, p. 36
racial formation, p. 15
racial group, p. 8
racism, p. 14
resegregation, p. 32
segmented assimilation, p. 35
segregation, p. 30
self-fulfilling prophecy, p. 23
sociology, p. 19
stereotype, p. 22
stratification, p. 19
world systems theory, p. 27

Review Questions

1. What are the characteristics of subordinate and minority groups?
2. Distinguish between racial and ethnic groups.
3. In what different ways is race viewed?
4. How do biracial and multiracial categories call into question traditional groupings in the United States?
5. How do the conflict, functionalist, and labeling approaches apply to the social construction of race?
6. How do subordinate groups emerge?
7. Describe the Spectrum of Intergroup Relations.
8. Characterize the range of intergroup relations from those which are most tolerant to those that are most unacceptable to minority groups.
9. What role do subordinate groups play in their own destiny?

Critical Thinking

1. How do the concepts of "biracial" and "multiracial" relate to W. E. B. Du Bois's notion of a "color line"?
2. How diverse is your city? Can you see evidence that some group is being subordinated? What social construction of categories do you see that may be different in your community as compared to elsewhere?
3. Select a racial or ethnic group and apply the Spectrum of Intergroup Relations. Can you provide an example today or in the past where each relationship occurs?
4. Identify some protest and resistance efforts by subordinated groups in your area. Have they been successful? Even though some people say they favor equality, why are they uncomfortable with such efforts? How can people unconnected with such efforts either help or hinder such protests?

Chapter 2
Prejudice

Learning Objectives

PREJUDICE AND DISCRIMINATION
2-1 Differentiate between prejudice and discrimination.

WHITE PRIVILEGE
2-2 Apply White privilege.

THEORIES OF PREJUDICE
2-3 Paraphrase the theories of prejudice.

STEREOTYPES
2-4 Describe stereotyping.

COLOR-BLIND RACISM
2-5 Put into your own words color-blind racism.

THE MOOD OF THE OPPRESSED
2-6 Discuss how members of subordinate groups respond to prejudice.

INTERGROUP HOSTILITY
2-7 Explain how hostility is present among racial and ethnic groups.

REDUCING PREJUDICE
2-8 Illustrate research on reducing prejudice.

CONCLUSION
2-9 Identify ways to reduce hate.

These are tough economic times—hard to find jobs and when one does find a job they often are part-time and do not pay a good wage. Government funds to help the jobless make it while they look for work or training opportunities are limited. So imagine you are in the difficult position to allocate government assistance and you want the money to be effective.

A study published in 2013 gave people the choice to extend $1,500 of assistance to applicants based on a completed questionnaire—some with an excellent work ethic, others with a poor work ethic. You also had the alternative not to spend the money and help reduce the state's budget deficit—another very real challenge. Oh, there was more piece of information you were given besides the assessment of the person's work ethic: their name—either Laurie and Emily or Keisha and Latoya.

Looking at how the nationwide sample of 1,000 adults responded to this task, the results were clear. Not surprisingly hard workers were given more assistance than those judged to be poor. Faced with a "lazy" recipient, the hypothetical decision-makers were more likely to use the money to offset the budget deficit. However, what seemed to make the real difference was the name. Hardworking Emily was given ten times as much money as hardworking Keisha. Similarly idle Emily received much more than lazy Latoya. In fact, money allocated to the lazy White-sounding name applicant started to approach what the hardworking Black could expect to be awarded.

In summary, Keisha and Latoya were not given the same credit as Emily and Latoya and were more likely to be punished where it hurt with assistance withheld (DeSante 2012).

Prejudice is so prevalent that it is tempting to consider it inevitable or, even more broadly, part of human nature. Such a view ignores its variability from individual to individual and from society to society. Not everyone punished "Keisha" and rewarded "Emily." People learn prejudice as children before they exhibit it as adults. Therefore, prejudice is a social phenomenon, an acquired characteristic. A truly pluralistic society would lack unfavorable distinctions made through prejudicial attitudes among racial and ethnic groups.

Figure 2.1 Change in Minority Population by County, 2000–2010

Growth in the minority population has occurred in the last decade across the country, including in many areas that previously had few members of racial and ethnic minorities.

SOURCE: Humes, Jones, and Ramirez 2011: 21.

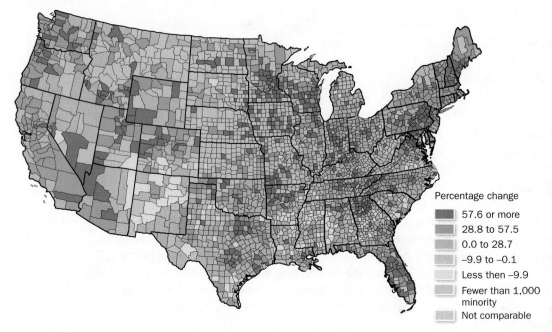

Percentage change

- 57.6 or more
- 28.8 to 57.5
- 0.0 to 28.7
- −9.9 to −0.1
- Less then −9.9
- Fewer than 1,000 minority
- Not comparable

Holding ill feelings based on a person's race or ethnicity is more of an issue because our nation is so increasingly diverse. In Figure 2.1, we look at the increase in minority presence in the first decade of the twenty-first century. Many counties far removed from urban centers or historic areas with Black and Latino populations saw population increases in the years from 2000 to 2010. The likelihood that prejudices will be expressed, dealt with, or hidden is beginning to become a truly nationwide phenomenon as majority–minority interaction pervades more and more communities.

Ill feeling among groups of different races, ethnicities, or cultures may result from **ethnocentrism**, or the tendency to believe that one's culture and way of life are superior to all others'. The ethnocentric person judges other groups and other cultures by the standards of his or her own group. This attitude makes it quite easily for people to view other cultures as inferior. We see a woman wearing a veil and may regard it as strange and backward, yet we are baffled when other societies think U.S. women in short skirts are dressed inappropriately. Ethnocentrism and other expressions of prejudice are often voiced; but unfortunately, such expressions sometimes become the motivation for criminal acts.

Prejudice and Discrimination

2-1 Differentiate between prejudice and discrimination.

Prejudice and discrimination are related concepts but are not the same. **Prejudice** is a negative attitude toward an entire category of people. The important components in this definition are *attitude* and *entire category*. Prejudice involves attitudes, thoughts, and beliefs—not actions. Prejudice often is expressed using **ethnophaulisms**, or ethnic slurs, which include derisive nicknames such as *honky*, *gook*, and *wetback*. Ethnophaulisms also include speaking to or about members of a particular group in a condescending way, such as saying, "José does well in school for a Mexican American" or referring to a middle-aged woman as "one of the girls."

Research Focus

Virtual Prejudice and Anti-Prejudice

More and more of our daily lives are spent not directly talking or seeing other people but in time online. Sometimes this may include indirectly communicating with friends through social media, but it includes a large amount of time spent in some virtual world separated from our reality. What impact can this have on reinforcing or undercutting prejudice?

Researchers have looked at video games and found minorities are vastly underrepresented, and when they do appear it is usually as thugs or athletes. Even when given the opportunity to interact with games, White players are more likely to recall Black characters as violent and aggressive.

Yet like real society, virtual society can seek to have a positive impact. User-generated video sites like YouTube abound with videos reflecting all sorts of representations of racial and ethnic groups. However, one study found that generally images of American Indians provoke positive responses in online comments. However, there were some important qualifications. Viewers seemed most positive when videos were historical rather than dealing with present-day situations. And if ill-treatment toward today's Native Americans was central to the video, negative comments began to escalate.

The complexity of online representations and prejudice is highlighted in the May 2013 Cheerios advertisement. In the 30-second spot a White mom is shown telling her biracial daughter that is it true that Cheerios is heart-healthy. The six-year-old then scampers into the next room spilling Cheerios on her Black father's chest while he is napping on the living room couch. People weighed in to General Mills with comments 10-1 favorable toward the biracial household but the company was forced to disable the comment section because of all the racist remarks that were left.

Not to be outdone, a parody was mounted within days on YouTube by comedian Kenji America showing a girl dumping the breakfast cereal on her Black mother in a household of biracial lesbian parents with their cute biracial daughter. Humor was used to deflect prejudice aimed at earlier video.

Researchers of online prejudice admit the depth of hostility is difficult to assess since many commercial venues and news outlets monitor, at some expense, comments and selectively delete them, giving to the casual online user an inaccurate view of how the general public is responding to racially charged topics. It also appears that those who wish to express racist views are retreating to online sites where such rhetoric will not be challenged. As in everyday life, one cannot assume the absence of overt prejudice means tolerance.

SOURCES: Burgess et al. 2011; Hughley and Daniels 2013; Kenji America 2013; Kopacz and Lawton 2013; Nudd 2013)

A prejudiced belief also leads to categorical rejection. Prejudice means you dislike someone not because you find his or her behavior objectionable; it means you dislike an entire racial or ethnic group, even if you have had little or no contact with that group. A college student is not prejudiced because he requests a room change after three weeks of enduring his roommate's sleeping all day, playing loud music all night, and piling garbage on his desk. However, he is displaying prejudice if he requests a change after arriving at school and learning his new roommate is of a different nationality.

Prejudice is a belief or attitude; discrimination is action. **Discrimination** is the denial of opportunities and equal rights to individuals and groups because of prejudice or for other arbitrary reasons. Unlike prejudice, discrimination involves *behavior* that excludes members of a group from certain rights, opportunities, or privileges. Like prejudice, it is categorical, except for a few rare exceptions. If an employer refuses to hire an illiterate Italian American as a computer analyst, that is not discrimination. If an employer refuses to hire all Italian Americans because he or she thinks they are incompetent and makes no effort to determine if an applicant is qualified, that is discrimination.

Prejudice is a complicated aspect of our behavior and has been extensively researched as you will see in this chapter. To give you just a sample, consider the "Research Focus" dealing with online expressions of prejudice.

Merton's Typology

Prejudice does not necessarily coincide with discriminatory behavior. In exploring the relationship between negative attitudes and negative behavior, sociologist Robert Merton (1949, 1976) identified four major categories (Figure 2.2). The label added to each of Merton's categories may more readily identify the type of person described:

1. The unprejudiced nondiscriminator—or all-weather liberal
2. The unprejudiced discriminator—or reluctant liberal
3. The prejudiced nondiscriminator—or timid bigot
4. The prejudiced discriminator—or all-weather bigot

As the term is used in types 1 and 2, liberals are committed to equality among people. The all-weather liberal believes in equality and practices it. Merton was quick to observe that all-weather liberals may be far removed from any real contact with subordinate groups such as African Americans or women. Furthermore, such people may be content with their own behavior and do little to change it. The reluctant liberal is not completely committed to equality between groups. Social pressure may cause such a person to discriminate. Fear of losing employees may lead a manager to avoid promoting women to supervisory capacities. Equal-opportunity legislation may be the best way to influence a reluctant liberal.

Types 3 and 4 do not believe in equal treatment for racial and ethnic groups, but they vary in their willingness to act. The timid bigot, type 3, will not

Figure 2.2 Prejudice and Discrimination

As sociologist Robert Merton's formulation shows, prejudice and discrimination are related but are not the same.

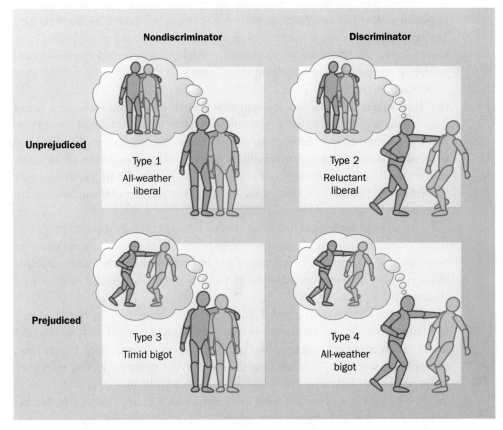

discriminate if discrimination costs money or reduces profits or if peers or the government apply pressure against doing so. The all-weather bigot acts without hesitation on the prejudiced beliefs he or she holds.

LaPiere's Study

Merton's typology points out that attitudes should not be confused with behavior. People do not always act as they believe. More than a half-century ago, Richard LaPiere (1934, 1969) exposed the relationship between racial attitudes and social conduct. From 1930 to 1932, LaPiere traveled throughout the United States with a Chinese couple. Despite an alleged climate of intolerance of Asians, LaPiere observed that the couple was treated courteously at hotels, motels, and restaurants. He was puzzled by the good reception they received; all the conventional attitude surveys showed extreme prejudice by Whites toward the Chinese.

Was it possible that LaPiere was fortunate during his travels and consistently stopped at places operated by tolerant members of the dominant group? To test this possibility, he sent questionnaires asking the places at which they had been served whether the owner would "accept members of the Chinese race as guests in your establishment." More than 90 percent responded no, even though LaPiere's Chinese couple were treated politely at all of these establishments. How can this inconsistency be explained? People who returned questionnaires reflecting prejudice were unwilling to act based on those asserted beliefs; they were timid bigots.

The LaPiere study is not without flaws. First, he had no way of knowing whether the respondent to the questionnaire was the person who had served him and the Chinese couple. Second, he accompanied the couple, but the questionnaire suggested that the guests would be unescorted (and, in the minds of some, uncontrolled) and might consist of many Chinese people. Third, personnel may have changed between the time of the visit and the mailing of the questionnaire (Deutscher, Pestello, and Pestello 1993).

The LaPiere technique has been replicated with similar results. This technique questions whether attitudes are important if they are not reflected in behavior. But if attitudes are not important in small matters, they are important in other ways: Lawmakers legislate and courts may reach decisions based on what the public thinks.

This is not just hypothetical. Legislators in the United States often are persuaded to vote a certain way by what they perceive are changed attitudes toward immigration, affirmative action, and prayer in public schools. Sociologists have enumerated some of prejudice's functions. For the majority group, prejudice maintains privileged occupations and more power for its members.

The following sections examine theories of why prejudice exists and discuss the content and extent of prejudice today.

White Privilege

2-2 Apply White privilege.

White travelers, unlike LaPiere's Chinese couple, rarely, if ever, would be concerned about second-class treatment because of race. Being White in the United States may not assure success and wealth, but it does limit encounters with intolerance.

White privilege refers to the rights or immunities granted as a particular benefit or favor for being White. This advantage exists unconsciously and is often invisible to the White people who enjoy it (Ferber 2008).

Scholar Peggy McIntosh of the Wellesley College Center for Research on Women looked at the privilege that comes from being White and the added privilege of being male. The other side of racial oppression is the privilege enjoyed by dominant groups. Being White or being successful in establishing a White

Being White means having distinct advantages, which has been called *White privilege*. For example, one can seek assistance and assume your race will not work against you.

identity carries with it distinct advantages. Among those that McIntosh (1988) identified were the following:

- Being considered financially reliable when using checks, credit cards, or cash
- Taking a job without having coworkers suspect it came about because of race
- Never having to speak for all the people of your race
- Watching television or reading a newspaper and seeing people of your own race widely represented
- Speaking effectively in a large group without being called a credit to your race
- Assuming that if legal or medical help is needed, your race will not work against you

Whiteness does carry privileges, but most White people do not consciously think of them except on the rare occasions when they are questioned. Returning to the research described at the beginning of the chapter, we saw how easily "Emily" and "Laurie" were privileged over "Latoya" and "Keisha" in being awarded government assistance.

Typically, White people do not see themselves as privileged in the way many African Americans and Latinos see themselves as disadvantaged. When asked to comment on their "Whiteness," White people most likely see themselves devoid of ethnicity ("no longer Irish," for example), stigmatized as racist, and victims of reverse discrimination. Privilege for many White people may be easy to exercise in one's life, but it is difficult to acknowledge (McKinney 2008).

Theories of Prejudice

2-3 Paraphrase the theories of prejudice.

Prejudice is learned. Friends, relatives, newspapers, books, movies, television, and the Internet all teach it. Awareness of the differences among people that society judges to be important begins at an early age. Several theories have been advanced to explain the rejection of certain groups in a society. We examine four theoretical explanations. The first two, scapegoating and authoritarian personality, are psychological and emphasize why a particular person harbors ill feelings. The second two, exploitation and normative, are sociological and view prejudice in the context of our interaction in a larger society.

Scapegoating Theory

People use some expressions of prejudice so they can blame others and refuse to accept responsibility. **Scapegoating theory** says that prejudiced people believe they are society's victims.

The term *scapegoat* comes from a biblical injunction telling the Hebrews to send a goat into the wilderness to symbolically carry away the people's sins. Similarly, the theory of scapegoating suggests that, rather than accepting guilt for some failure, a person transfers the responsibility for failure to a vulnerable group.

In the major tragic twentieth-century example, Adolf Hitler used the Jews as the scapegoat for all German social and economic ills in the 1930s. This premise led to the passage of laws restricting Jewish life in pre–World War II Germany and eventually escalated into the mass extermination of Europe's Jews. Scapegoating of Jews persists. A national survey in 2009 showed that one out of four people in the United States blame "the Jews" for the recent financial crisis. **Anti-Semitism**—anti-Jewish prejudice and discrimination—remains a very real phenomenon (Malhotra and Margalit 2009).

Today in the United States, both legal and illegal immigrants often are blamed by "real Americans" for their failure to secure jobs or desirable housing. The immigrant becomes the scapegoat for one's own lack of skills, planning, or motivation. It is so much easier to blame someone else.

Authoritarian Personality Theory

Prejudice may be influenced by one's upbringing and the lessons taught—and learned—early in life. Several efforts have been made to detail the prejudiced personality, but the most comprehensive effort culminated in a volume titled *The Authoritarian Personality* (Adorno et al. 1950). Using a variety of tests and relying on more than 2,000 respondents, ranging from middle-class Whites to inmates of San Quentin State Prison (California), the authors claimed they had isolated the characteristics of the authoritarian personality.

In Adorno and colleagues' (1950) view, the **authoritarian personality** has basic characteristics that mean it is a personality type that is likely to be prejudiced. It encompasses adherence to conventional values, uncritical acceptance of authority, and concern with power and toughness. With obvious relevance to the development of intolerance, the authoritarian personality also was characterized by aggressiveness toward people who did not conform to conventional norms or obey authority. According to the researchers, this personality type developed from the experience of harsh discipline in early childhood. A child with an authoritarian upbringing was obedient to authority figures and then later treated others as he or she had been raised.

This study has been widely criticized, but the very existence of such wide criticism indicates the influence of the study. Critics have attacked the study's equation of authoritarianism with right-wing politics (although liberals also can be rigid); its failure to see that prejudice is more closely related to other individual traits, such as social class, than to authoritarianism as it was defined; the research methods used; and the emphasis on extreme racial prejudice rather than on more common expressions of hostility.

Despite these concerns about specifics in the study, which was completed 60 years ago, annual conferences continue to draw attention to how authoritarian attitudes contribute to racism, sexism, and even torture (Kinloch 1974; O'Neill 2008).

Exploitation Theory

Racial prejudice is often used to justify keeping a group in a subordinate economic position. Conflict theorists, in particular, stress the role of racial and ethnic hostility as a way for the dominant group to keep its position of status and power intact. Indeed, this approach maintains that even the less-affluent White working class uses prejudice to minimize competition from upwardly mobile minorities.

This **exploitation theory** is clearly part of the Marxist tradition in sociological thought. Karl Marx emphasized exploitation of the lower class as an integral part of capitalism. Similarly, the exploitation or conflict approach explains how racism can stigmatize a group as inferior to justify the exploitation of that group. As developed by Oliver Cox (1942), exploitation theory saw prejudice against Blacks as an extension of the inequality faced by the entire lower class.

The exploitation theory of prejudice is persuasive. Japanese Americans were the object of little prejudice until they began to enter occupations that brought them into competition with Whites. The movement to keep Chinese out of the country became strongest during the late nineteenth century, when Chinese immigrants and Whites fought over dwindling numbers of jobs. Both the enslavement of African Americans and the removal westward of Native Americans were to a significant degree economically motivated.

Table 2.1 Theories of Prejudice

No single explanation of why prejudice exists is satisfactory, but several approaches taken together offer insight.

Theory	Explanation	Example
Scapegoating	People blame others for their own failures.	An unsuccessful applicant assumes that a minority member or a woman got "his" job.
Authoritarian	Childrearing leads one to develop intolerance as an adult.	The rigid personality type dislikes people who are different.
Exploitation	People use others unfairly for economic advantage.	A minority member is hired at a lower wage level.
Normative	Peer and social influences encourage tolerance or intolerance.	A person from an intolerant household is more likely to be openly prejudiced.

Normative Approach

Although personality factors are important contributors to prejudice, normative or situational factors also must be given serious consideration. The **normative approach** takes the view that prejudice is influenced by societal norms and situations that encourage or discourage the tolerance of minorities.

Analysis reveals how societal influences shape a climate for tolerance or intolerance. Societies develop social norms that dictate not only what foods are desirable (or forbidden) but also what racial and ethnic groups are to be favored (or despised). Social forces operate in a society to encourage or discourage tolerance. The force may be widespread, such as the pressure on White Southerners to oppose racial equality even though there was slavery or segregation, which would seem to make concerns about equality irrelevant. The influence of social norms may be limited, as when one man finds himself becoming more sexist as he competes with three women for a position in a prestigious law firm.

The four approaches to prejudice summarized in Table 2.1 are not mutually exclusive. Social circumstances provide cues for a person's attitudes; personality determines the extent to which people follow social cues and the likelihood that they will encourage others to do the same. Societal norms may promote or deter tolerance; personality traits suggest the degree to which a person will conform to norms of intolerance. To understand prejudice, we must use all four approaches together.

Stereotypes

2-4 Describe stereotyping.

On Christmas Day 2001, Arab American Walied Shater boarded an American Airlines flight from Baltimore to Dallas carrying a gun. The cockpit crew refused to let him fly, fearing that Shater would take over the plane and use it as a weapon of mass destruction. However, Walied Shater carried documentation identifying him as a Secret Service agent, and calls to Washington, D.C., confirmed that he was flying to join a presidential protection force at President George W. Bush's ranch in Texas. Nevertheless, the crew could not get past the stereotype of Arab American men posing a lethal threat (Leavitt 2002).

What Are Stereotypes?

In Chapter 1, we saw that stereotypes play a powerful role in how people come to view dominant and subordinate groups. **Stereotypes** are unreliable generalizations about all members of a group and do not take individual differences into account. Numerous scientific studies have been made of these exaggerated images. This research has shown the willingness of people to assign positive and negative traits to entire groups of people, which are then applied to particular individuals. Stereotyping causes people to view Blacks as superstitious, Whites as uncaring, and Jews as shrewd. Over the last 80 years of such research, social scientists have found that people have become less willing to express such views openly, but prejudice persists, as we will see later in this chapter (Quillian 2006).

If stereotypes are exaggerated generalizations, then why are they so widely held, and why are some traits assigned more often than others? Evidence for traits may arise out of real conditions. For example, more Puerto Ricans live in poverty than Whites, so the prejudiced mind associates Puerto Ricans with laziness. According to the New Testament, some Jews were responsible for the crucifixion of Jesus, so, to the prejudiced mind, all Jews are Christ killers. Some activists in the women's movement are lesbians, so all feminists are seen as lesbians. From a kernel of fact, faulty generalization creates a stereotype.

In "Speaking Out," journalist Helen Zia, born in New Jersey of parents who emigrated from Shanghai, comments about how immigrant parents grapple with the prejudice their children feel. Should they teach their children their language and perhaps heighten stereotypes and ill feelings from others or push them to become American as fast as possible?

Labeling individuals through negative stereotypes has strong implications for the self-fulfilling prophecy. Studies show that people are all too aware of the negative images others have of them. When asked to estimate the prevalence of hard-core racism among Whites, one in four Blacks agrees that more than half "personally share the attitudes of groups like the Ku Klux Klan toward Blacks"; only one Black in ten says "only a few" share such views. Stereotypes not only influence how people feel about themselves but also, and perhaps equally important, affect how people interact with others. If people feel that others hold incorrect, disparaging attitudes toward them, then it undoubtedly makes it difficult to have harmonious relations (Sigelman and Tuch 1997).

Although explicit expressions of stereotypes are becoming less common, it is much too soon to write the obituary of racial and ethnic stereotypes. In addition, stereotyping is not limited to racial and ethnic groups. Other groups are

Speaking Out

Gangsters, Gooks, Geishas, and Geeks

Helen Zia

Ah so. No tickee, no washee. So sorry, so sollee. Chinkee, Chink. Jap, Nip, zero, kamikaze. Dothead, flat face, flat nose, slant eye, slope. Slit, mamasan, dragon lady. Gook, VC, Flip, Hindoo.

By the time I was ten, I'd heard such words so many times I could feel them coming before they parted lips. I knew they were meant in the unkindest way. Still, we didn't talk about these incidents at home; we just accepted them as part of being in America, something to learn to rise above.

The most common taunting didn't even utilize words but a string of unintelligible gobbledygook that kids—and adults—would spew as they pretended to speak Chinese or some other Asian language. It was a mockery of how they imagined my parents talked to me.

Truth was that Mom and Dad rarely spoke to us in Chinese, except to scold or call us to dinner. Worried that we might develop an accent,

my father insisted that we speak English at home. This, he explained, would lessen the hardships we might encounter and make us more acceptable as Americans.

I'll never know if my father's language decision was right. On the one hand, I, like most Asian Americans, have been complimented countless times on my spoken English by people who assumed I was a foreigner. "My, you speak such good English," they'd cluck. "No kidding, I ought to," I would think to myself, then wonder: should I thank them for assuming that English isn't my native language? Or should I correct them on the proper usage of "well" and "good"?

More often than feeling grateful for my American accent, I've wished that I could jump into a heated exchange of rapid-fire Chinese, volume high and spit flying. But with a vocabulary limited to "Ni hao?" (How are you?) and "Ting bu dong" (I hear but don't understand), meaningful exchanges are woefully impossible. I find myself smiling and nodding like a dashboard ornament. I'm envious of the many people I know who grew up speaking an Asian language yet converse in English beautifully.

Armed with standard English and my flat New Jersey "a," I still couldn't escape the name-calling. I became all too familiar with other names and faces that supposedly matched mine—Fu Manchu, Suzie Wong, Hop Sing, Madame Butterfly, Charlie Chan, Ming the Merciless—the "Asians" produced for mass consumption. Their faces filled me with shame whenever I saw them on TV or in the movies. They defined my face to the rest of the world: a sinister Fu, Suzie the whore, subservient Hop Sing, pathetic Butterfly, cunning Chan, and warlike Ming. Inscrutable Orientals all, real Americans none.

SOURCE: Zia 2000: 109–110.

subjected to stereotyping. Probably easiest to see in daily life and the mass media is sexism. **Sexism** is the ideology that one sex is superior to the other. Images and descriptions of women and even girls often reinforce sexism. **Homophobia**, the fear of and prejudice toward homosexuality, is present in every facet of life: the family, organized religion, the workplace, official policies, and the mass media. Like the myths and stereotypes of race and gender, those about homosexuality keep gay men and lesbian women oppressed as a group and may also prevent sympathetic members of the dominant group, the heterosexual community, from supporting them. We next consider the use of stereotypes in the contemporary practice of racial profiling.

Stereotyping in Action: Racial Profiling

A Black dentist, Elmo Randolph, testified before a state commission that he was stopped dozens of times in the 1980s and 1990s while traveling the New Jersey Turnpike to work. Invariably state troopers asked, "Do you have guns or drugs?" "My parents always told me, be careful when you're driving on the turnpike," said Dr. Randolph, age 44. "White people don't have that conversation" (Purdy 2001: 37; see also Fernandez and Fahim 2006).

Little wonder that Dr. Randolph was pulled over. Although African Americans accounted for only 17 percent of the motorists on that turnpike, they were 80 percent of the motorists pulled over. Such occurrences gave rise to the charge that a new traffic offense was added to the books: DWB, or "driving while Black" (Bowles 2000).

In recent years, the government has given its attention to a social phenomenon with a long history: racial profiling. According to the Department of Justice, **racial profiling** is any police-initiated action based on race, ethnicity, or national origin rather than the person's behavior. Generally, profiling occurs when law enforcement officers, including customs officials, airport security, and police,

The majority of people in the United States think that ethnic and religious profiling should be taken into account to maintain security.

assume that people fitting certain descriptions are likely to be engaged in something illegal. In 2012, national attention was drawn to the incident of a man on a neighborhood watch patrol shooting dead 17-year-old Trayvon Martin, a Black youth visiting his father's fiancée in a gated Florida community. While the legal system slowly investigated, many felt the boy would still be alive had he been White and the shooter immediately arrested if Black. So unsettling was the event that it prompted President Obama in the midst of his public nomination of the head of the World Bank to express sympathy for Martin's parents and say, "If I had a son, he'd look like Trayvon" (White House 2012).

Racial profiling persists despite overwhelming evidence that it not a predictive approach toward identifying potential troublemakers. Whites are more likely to be found with drugs in the areas in which minority group members are disproportionately targeted. A federal study made public in 2005 found little difference nationwide in the likelihood of being stopped by law enforcement officers, but African Americans were twice as likely to have their vehicles searched, and Latinos were five times more likely. A similar pattern emerged in the likelihood of force being used against drivers: It was three times more likely for Latinos and Blacks than White drivers. A study of New York City police officers describing some 4.43 million stops between 2004 and mid-2012 found that Blacks and Latinos accounted for 83 percent of people who were stopped and frisked, and a related study found that Whites were 50 percent more likely to be carrying weapons (Center for Constitutional Rights 2011; Goldstein 2013; Herbert 2010; Tomaskovic-Devey and Warren 2009).

Back in the 1990s, increased attention to racial profiling led not only to special reports and commissions but also to talk of legislating against it. This proved difficult. The U.S. Supreme Court in *Whren v. United States* (1996) upheld the constitutionality of using a minor traffic infraction as an excuse to stop and search a vehicle and its passengers. Nonetheless, states and other government units are discussing policies and training that would discourage racial profiling. At the same time, most law enforcement agencies reject the idea of compiling racial data on traffic stops, arguing that it would be a waste of money and staff time.

Efforts to stop racial profiling came to an abrupt end after the September 11, 2001, terrorist attacks on the United States. Suspicions about Muslims and Arabs in the United States became widespread. Foreign students from Arab countries were summoned for special questioning. Legal immigrants identified as Arab or Muslim were scrutinized for any illegal activity and were prosecuted for routine immigration violations that were ignored for people of other ethnic backgrounds and religious faiths (Withrow 2006).

National surveys have found little change since 2001 in support for profiling Arab Americans at airports. In 2010, 53 percent of Americans favored "ethnic and religious profiling," even for U.S. citizens, and wanted requirements that Arab Americans undergo special and more-intensive security checks before boarding planes in the United States (Zogby 2010).

Color-Blind Racism

2-5 **Put into your own words color-blind racism.**

Over the last three generations, nationwide surveys have consistently shown growing support by Whites for integration, interracial dating, and having members of minority groups attain political office, including becoming president of the United States. Yet how can this be true when the hatred described at the beginning of the chapter persists and thousands of hate crimes occur annually?

Color-blind racism refers to the use of race-neutral principles to defend the racially unequal status quo. Yes, "no discrimination for college admission" should exist, yet the disparity in educational experiences means that formal admissions criteria will privilege White high school graduates. "Healthcare is for all," but if you do not have workplace insurance, you likely cannot afford it.

Color-blind racism has also been referred to as laissez-faire, postracialism, or aversive racism, but the common theme is that notions of racial inferiority are rarely expressed and that proceeding color-blind into the future will perpetuate inequality. In the post–civil rights era and with the election of President Barack Obama, people are more likely to assume discrimination is long past and express views that are more proper—that is, lacking the overt expressions of racism of the past.

An important aspect of color-blind racism is the recognition that race is rarely invoked in public debates on social issues. Instead, people emphasize lower social class, the lack of citizenship, or illegal aliens; these descriptions serve as proxies for race. Furthermore, the emphasis is on individuals failing rather than on recognizing patterns of groups being disadvantaged. This leads many White people to declare they are not racist and that they do not know anyone who is racist. It also leads to the mistaken conclusion that more progress has been made toward racial and ethnic equality and even tolerance than has really taken place.

When we survey White attitudes toward African Americans, three conclusions are inescapable. First, attitudes are subject to change; during periods of dramatic social upheaval, dramatic shifts can occur within one generation. Second, less progress was made in the late twentieth and beginning of the twentieth-first centuries than was made in the relatively brief period of the 1950s and 1960s. Third, the pursuit of a color-blind agenda has created lower levels of support for politics that could reduce racial inequality if implemented.

Economically less-successful groups such as African Americans and Latinos have been associated with negative traits to the point that issues such as urban decay, homelessness, welfare, and crime are viewed as race issues even though race is rarely mentioned explicitly. Besides making it harder to resolve difficult social issues, this is another instance of blaming the victim.

These perceptions come at a time when the willingness of the government to address domestic ills is limited by increasing opposition to new taxes and continuing commitments to fight terrorism here and abroad. The color line remains, even if more people are unwilling to accept its divisive impact on everyone's lives (Ansell 2008; Bonilla-Silva 2006; Bonilla-Silva and Embrick with Seamster 2011; Kang and Lane 2010; Mazzocco et al. 2006; Quillian 2006; Winant 2004: 106–108).

The Mood of the Oppressed

2-6   Discuss how members of subordinate groups respond to prejudice.

Sociologist W. E. B. Du Bois relates an experience from his youth in a largely White community in Massachusetts. He tells how, on one occasion, the boys and girls were exchanging cards, and everyone was having a lot of fun. One girl, a newcomer, refused his card as soon as she saw that Du Bois was Black. He wrote:

> Then it dawned upon me with a certain suddenness that I was different from others...shut out from their world by a vast veil. I had therefore no desire to tear down that veil, to creep through; I held all beyond it in common contempt and lived above it in a region of blue sky and great wandering shadows. (1903: 2)

In using the image of a veil, Du Bois describes how members of subordinate groups learn they are being treated differently. In his case and that of many others, this leads to feelings of contempt toward all Whites that continue for a lifetime.

Opinion pollsters have been interested in White attitudes on racial issues longer than they have measured the views of subordinate groups. This neglect of minority attitudes reflects, in part, the bias of the White researchers. It also stems from the contention that the dominant group is more important to study because it is in a better position to act on its beliefs. The results of a nationwide survey conducted in the United States offer insight into sharply different views on the state of race relations today (Figure 2.3). Latinos, African Americans, and Asian Americans all have strong reservations about the state of race relations in the United States. They are skeptical about the level of equal opportunity and perceive a lot of discrimination. It is interesting to note that Hispanics and Asian Americans, overwhelmingly immigrants, are more likely to feel they will succeed if they work hard. Yet the majority of all three groups have a positive outlook for the next ten years (New America Media 2007; Preston 2007).

National surveys showed that the 2008 successful presidential bid of Senator Barack Obama led to a sense of optimism and national pride among African Americans, even though political observers noted that Obama ran a race-neutral campaign and rarely addressed issues specifically of concern to African Americans. Unlike Whites or Hispanics, Black voters still saw President

Figure 2.3 What Is the State of Race Relations? Three Views

Note: Answers mean respondent believes "very important problem" or "strongly agree" regarding the statements listed. Based on 1,105 interviews in August–September 2007, with bilingual questioners used as necessary.

SOURCE: New America Media 2007: 6, 12, 14, 24, 26.

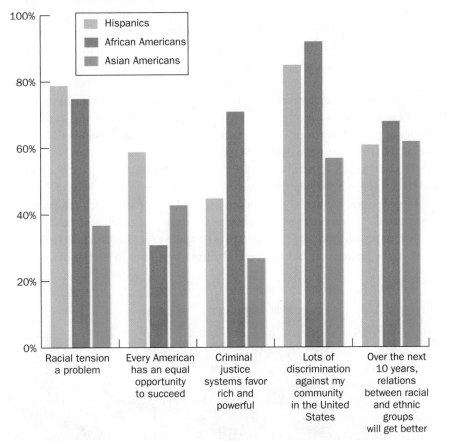

Obama's campaign as addressing issues important to the Black community. Survey researchers closely followed these perceptions after the 2008 election.

Optimism about the present and future increased significantly among African Americans during the Obama campaign and first year of his presidency. Ironically, White optimism about positive racial change was even more optimistic during the early period of the Obama administration. Yet other data show little evidence of a new nationwide perspective on race following the election. For example, only 35.3 percent of first-year college students in September 2012 indicated a goal of "helping to promote racial understanding" compared to 46 percent in 1992 (Pew Research Center 2010; Pryor et al. 2012: 43).

We have focused so far on what comes to mind when we think about prejudice: one group hating another group. But there is another form of prejudice that has been proposed in the past: A group may come to hate itself. Members of groups held in low esteem by society may, as a result, either hate themselves or have low self-esteem, as many social scientists once believed. Research literature of the 1940s through the 1960s emphasized the low self-esteem of minorities. Usually, the subject was African American, but the argument also has been generalized to include any subordinate racial, ethnic, or nationality group.

This view is no longer accepted. We should not assume that minority status influences personality traits in either a good or a bad way. First, such assumptions may create a stereotype. We cannot describe a Black personality any more accurately than we can a White personality. Second, characteristics of minority-group members are not entirely the result of subordinate racial status; they also are influenced by low incomes, poor neighborhoods, and so forth. Third, many studies of personality imply that certain values are normal or preferable, but the values chosen are those of dominant groups.

If assessments of a subordinate group's personality are so prone to misjudgments, then why has the belief in low self-esteem been so widely held? Much of the research rests on studies with preschool-age Black children who were asked to express their preferences for dolls with different facial colors. Indeed, one such study by psychologists Kenneth and Mamie Clark (1947) was cited in the arguments before the U.S. Supreme Court in the landmark 1954

Another sign that Muslim Americans are being recognized in the mainstream: in 2013 Marvel Comics introduced a new superhero, Kamala Khan, who lives in New Jersey and whose family came from Pakistan. The young Muslim American comes to realize she has superhuman strength and is a polymorph—that is, she can change her shape. All this as she experiences the usual angst of being in high school and dealing with her conservative parents and brother.

case *Brown v. Board of Education.* The Clarks' study showed that Black children preferred White dolls, a finding that suggested the children had developed a negative self-image. Although subsequent doll studies have sometimes shown Black children's preference for white-faced dolls, other social scientists contend that this shows a realization of what most commercially sold dolls look like rather than documenting low self-esteem (Bloom 1971; Powell-Hopson and Hopson 1988).

Because African American children, as well as other subordinate groups' children, realistically see that Whites have more power and resources and, therefore, rate them higher does not mean that they personally feel inferior. Children who experience overt discrimination are more likely to continue to display feelings of distress and anxiety later in life. However, studies, even those with children, show that when the self-images of middle-class or affluent African Americans are measured, their feelings of self-esteem are more positive than those of comparable Whites (Coker et al. 2009; Gray-Little and Hafdahl 2000).

Intergroup Hostility

2-7   Explain how hostility is present among racial and ethnic groups.

Prejudice is as diverse as the nation's population. It exists not only between dominant and subordinate peoples but also among specific subordinate groups. Unfortunately, until recently little research existed on this subject except for a few social distance scales administered to racial and ethnic minorities.

Do we get along? Although this question often is framed in terms of the relationships between White Americans and other racial and ethnic groups, we should recognize the prejudice between groups. In a national survey, people were asked whether they felt they could generally get along with members of other groups. In Figure 2.4, we can see that Whites felt they had the most difficulty getting along with Blacks. We also see the different views that Blacks, Latinos, Asian Americans, and American Indians hold toward other groups.

It is curious to find that some groups feel they get along better with Whites than with other minority groups. Why would that be? Often, low-income people compete daily with other low-income people and do not readily see the larger societal forces that contribute to their low status. The survey results reveal that many Hispanics are more likely to believe Asian Americans are getting in their way than the White Americans who are the real decision makers in their community.

Most troubling is when intergroup hostility becomes violent. Ethnic and racial tensions among African Americans, Latinos, and immigrants may become manifest in hate crimes. Violence can surface in neighborhoods where people compete for scarce resources such as jobs and housing. Gangs become organized along racial lines, much like private clubs "downtown." In recent years, Los

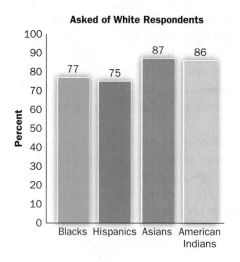

Asked of White Respondents

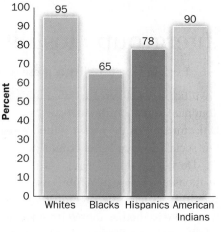

Asked of Black Respondents

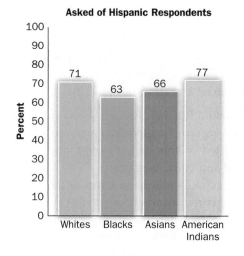

Asked of Hispanic Respondents

Asked of Asian Respondents

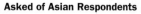

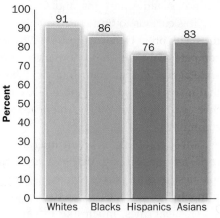

Asked of American Indian Respondents[1]

Figure 2.4 Do We Get Along?

Percentage saying groups get along with each other
("Don't Knows" excluded).

[1]Sample size for American Indians is very small and subject to large sample
variance.

Note: The wording of the question was, "We hear a lot these days about how
various groups in society get along with each other. I'm going to mention
several groups and ask whether you think they generally get along with each
other or generally do not get along with each other." So, in the "Asked of
White Respondents" graph, Whites are asked how Whites get along with
each ethnic group; in the "Asked of Black Respondents" graph, Blacks are
asked how Blacks get along with each ethnic group, and so on.

SOURCE: Smith 2006: 65. Reprinted by permission of the author.

Angeles has been particularly concerned about rival Black and Hispanic gangs. Conflict theorists see this violence as resulting from larger structural forces, but for the average person in such areas, life itself becomes more of a challenge (Archibold 2007).

Reducing Prejudice

2-8 Illustrate research on reducing prejudice.

Focusing on how to eliminate prejudice involves an explicit value judgment: Prejudice is wrong and causes problems for those who are prejudiced and for their victims. As individuals, we can act to stop prejudice, as indicated in Table 2.2. The important thing to remember is not to ignore prejudice when you witness it.

The obvious way to eliminate prejudice is to eliminate its causes: the desire to exploit, the fear of being threatened, and the need to blame others for one's own failure. These might be eliminated by personal therapy, but therapy, even if it works for every individual, is no solution for an entire society in which prejudice is a part of everyday life.

Table 2.2 Ways to Fight Prejudice

1. *Act.* Do something. In the face of hatred, apathy will be taken as acceptance, even by the victims of prejudice themselves.

2. *Unite.* Call a friend or coworker. Organize a group of like-thinking friends from school or your place of worship or club. Create a coalition that is diverse and includes the young, the old, law enforcement representatives, and the media.

3. *Support the victims.* Victims of hate crimes are especially vulnerable. Let them know you care by words, in person, or by e-mail. If you or your friend is a victim, report it.

4. *Do your homework.* If you suspect a hate crime has been committed, do your research to document it.

5. *Create an alternative.* Never attend a rally where hate is a part of the agenda. Find another outlet for your frustration, whatever the cause.

6. *Speak up.* You, too, have First Amendment rights. Denounce the hatred, the cruel jokes. If you see a news organization misrepresenting a group, speak up.

7. *Lobby leaders.* Persuade policymakers, business heads, community leaders, and executives of media outlets to take a stand against hate.

8. *Look long term.* Participate or organize events such as annual parades or cultural fairs to celebrate diversity and harmony. Supplement it with a website that can be a 24/7 resource.

9. *Teach acceptance.* Prejudice is learned, and parents and teachers can influence the content of curriculum. In a first-grade class in Seattle, children paint self-portraits, mixing colors to match their skin tone.

10. *Dig deeper.* Look into the issues that divide us—social inequality, immigration, and sexual orientation. Work against prejudice. Dig deep inside yourself for prejudices and stereotypes you may embrace. Find out what is happening and act!

SOURCE: Author, based on Southern Poverty Law Center 2010; Willoughby 2004.

The answer appears to rest with programs directed at society as a whole. Prejudice is attacked indirectly when discrimination is attacked. Despite prevailing beliefs to the contrary, we *can* legislate against prejudice: Statutes and decisions do affect attitudes. In the past, people firmly believed that laws could not overcome norms, especially racist ones. Recent history, especially after the civil rights movement began in 1954, has challenged that once-common belief. Laws and court rulings that have equalized the treatment of Blacks, and Whites have led people to reevaluate their beliefs about what is right and wrong. The increasing tolerance by Whites during the civil rights era from 1954 to 1965 supports this conclusion.

Much research has been done to determine how to change negative attitudes toward groups of people. The most encouraging findings point to education, mass media, intergroup contact, and workplace training programs.

Education

Research on education and prejudice considers special programs aimed at promoting mutual respect as well as what effect more formal schooling generally has on expressions of bigotry.

Most research studies show that well-constructed programs have a positive effect on reducing prejudice, at least temporarily. The reduction is rarely as much as one might want, however. The difficulty is that a single program is insufficient to change lifelong habits, especially if little is done to reinforce the program's message once it ends. Persuasion to respect other groups does not operate in a clear field because, in their ordinary environments, people are still subjected to situations that promote prejudicial feelings. Children and adults are encouraged to laugh at Polish jokes and cheer for a team named the *Redskins*. Black adolescents may be discouraged by peers from befriending a White youth. All this undermines the effectiveness of prejudice-reduction programs (Allport 1979).

Studies document that increased formal education, regardless of content, is associated with racial tolerance. Research data show that highly educated people are more likely to indicate respect and liking for groups different from themselves. Why should more education have this effect? It might promote a broader outlook and make a person less likely to endorse myths that sustain racial prejudice. Formal education teaches the importance of qualifying statements such as "even though they have lower test scores, you need to remember the neighborhoods from which they come." Education introduces one to the almost indefinite diversity of social groups and the need to question rigid categorizations, if not reject them altogether. Colleges increasingly include a graduation requirement that students complete a course that explores diversity or multiculturalism. Another explanation is that education does not reduce intolerance but instead makes people more careful about revealing it. Formal education may simply instruct people in the appropriate responses. Despite the lack of a clear-cut explanation, either theory suggests that the continued trend toward a better-educated population will contribute to a reduction in overt prejudice.

However, college education may not reduce prejudice uniformly. For example, some White students might believe that minority students did not earn their admission into college. Students may feel threatened to see large groups of people of different racial and cultural backgrounds congregating and forming their own groups. Racist confrontations do occur outside the classroom and, even if they involve only a few individuals, the events will be followed by hundreds more. Therefore, some aspects of the college experience may only foster "we" and "they" attitudes (Schaefer 1986, 1996).

Mass Media

Mass media, like schools, may reduce prejudice without requiring specially designed programs. Television, radio, motion pictures, newspapers, magazines, and the Internet present only a portion of real life, but what effect do they have on prejudice if the content is racist or antiracist, sexist or antisexist? As with measuring the influence of programs designed to reduce prejudice, coming to strong conclusions on mass media's effect is hazardous, but the evidence points to a measurable effect.

Today, over 56 percent of all youth less than 14 years of age in the United States are children of color, yet few faces they see on television reflect their race or cultural heritage. What is more, the programs shown earlier in the evening, when young people are most likely to watch television, are the least diverse of all. It is not surprising that young people quickly develop expectations of the roles that various racial and ethnic group members play in mass media such as television and motion pictures. A national survey of teens (ages 12–18) asked what characters members of racial and ethnic groups would be likely to play. The respondents' perception of media, as shown in Table 2.3, shows a significant amount of stereotyping occurring in their minds, in the media, or both.

Table 2.3 Stereotyping in the Twenty-First Century

When asked to identify the role a person of a particular ethnic or racial background would be most likely to play in a movie or on television, teenagers cited familiar stereotypes.

Group	Media Roles Identified
African American	Athlete, gang member, police officer
Arab American	Terrorist, convenience store clerk
Asian American	Physician, lawyer, CEO, factory worker
Hispanic	Gang member, factory worker
Irish American	Drunkard, police officer, factory worker
Italian American	Crime boss, gang member, restaurant worker
Jewish American	Physician, lawyer, CEO, teacher
Polish American	Factory worker

Note: Based on national survey of 1,264 people between ages 13 and 18.
SOURCE: Zogby 2001.

Why the underrepresentation? Incredibly, network executives seemed surprised by the research demonstrating an all-White season. Producers, writers, executives, and advertisers blamed each other for the alleged oversight. In recent years, the rise of cable television and the Internet has fragmented the broadcast entertainment market, siphoning viewers away from the general-audience sitcoms and dramas of the past. With the proliferation of cable channels such as Black Entertainment Television (BET) and the Spanish-language Univision and websites that cater to every imaginable taste, there no longer seems to be a need for broadly popular series such as *The Cosby Show*, whose tone and content appealed to Whites as well as Blacks in a way that newer series do not. The result of these sweeping technological changes has been a sharp divergence in viewer preferences. Black comedian and director Tyler Perry is an immensely popular and successful actor, director, and producer but his popularity is largely limited to the African American community.

The absence of racial and ethnic minorities in television is well documented. They are less likely to play recurring roles and are far underrepresented in key decision-making positions such as directors, producers, and casting agents. Television series are only part of the picture. News broadcasting is done predominantly by Whites, and local news emphasizes crime, often featuring Black or Hispanic perpetrators; print journalism is nearly the same (Media Matters for America 2013; Writers Guild of America West 2013).

This is especially troubling given another finding in a research study creating simulations where the participants can choose to act in a possible crime situation. Research showed that people were quicker to "shoot" an armed Black person than a White man in a video simulation. In another variation of that same study, the researchers showed subjects fake newspaper articles describing a string of armed robberies that showed either Black or White suspects. The subjects were quicker to "shoot" the armed suspect if he was Black but reading the articles had no impact on their willingness to "shoot" the armed White criminal. This is a troubling aspect of the potential impact of media content (Correll et al. 2007a, 2007b).

Reality or unscripted television programs have dominated prime time television for the last few years. Popular with consumers and relatively inexpensive to produce, broadcast and cable networks alike rushed into production shows that featured everyday people or, at least, C-list celebrities thrust into challenges. While unscripted shows have been routinely criticized on many artistic grounds, it is hard not to see the diverse nature of the participants. Reality programs have been analyzed as representing the diversity of the population. They represent a new and significant exception to television dominated by White actors and actresses.

In one area of unscripted television, the color line remains in place. Reality shows that promote creation of romantic partnerships such as *The Bachelor* and *The Bachelorette* do so in an all-White dating gallery—at least that has been the case for the first 24 seasons through late 2012. Meanwhile, back on scripted television, in a recent year, only four of the nearly 70 pilot projects under development by the four major networks had a minority person cast in a starring role (Belton 2009; Braxton 2009; NAACP 2008; Ratledge 2012; Wyatt 2009).

Avoidance versus Friendship

Is prejudice reduced or intensified when people cross racial and ethnic boundaries? Two parallel paths have been taken to look at this social distance and equal-status contact.

THE SOCIAL DISTANCE SCALE   Robert Park and Ernest Burgess (1921: 440) first defined **social distance** as the tendency to approach or withdraw from a racial group. Emory Bogardus (1968) conceptualized a scale that could measure social distance empirically. His social distance scale is so widely used that it is often called the **Bogardus scale**.

The scale asks people how willing they would be to interact with various racial and ethnic groups in specified social situations. The situations describe different degrees of social contact or social distance. The items used, with their corresponding distance scores, follow. People are asked whether they would be willing to work alongside someone or be a neighbor to someone of a different group, and, showing the least amount of social distance, be related through marriage. Over the 70-year period in which the tests were administered, certain patterns emerged. In the top third of the hierarchy are White Americans and Northern Europeans. Held at greater social distance are Eastern and Southern Europeans, and generally near the bottom are racial minorities (Bogardus 1968; Song 1991; Wark and Galliher 2007).

Generally, the researchers also found that among the respondents who had friends of different racial and ethnic origins, they were more likely to show greater social distance—that is, they were less likely to have been in each other's homes, shared in fewer activities, and were less likely to talk about their problems with each other. This is unlikely to promote mutual understanding.

Who does the guy pick on *The Bachelor*? Who does the gal pick on *The Bachelorette*? If the first 24 seasons of the two shows are any indication, the person choosing will definitely be White and the choices will most likely be White.

EQUAL STATUS CONTACT   An impressive number of research studies have confirmed the **contact hypothesis**, which states that intergroup contact between people of equal status in harmonious circumstances causes them to become less prejudiced and to abandon previously held stereotypes. The importance of equal status in interaction cannot be stressed enough. If a Puerto Rican is abused by his employer, little interracial harmony is promoted. Similarly, the situation in which contact occurs must be pleasant, making a positive evaluation likely for both individuals. Contact between two nurses, one Black and the other White, who are competing for one vacancy as a supervisor may lead to greater racial hostility. On the other hand, being employed together in a harmonious workplace or living in the same neighborhood would work against harboring stereotypes or prejudices (Krysan, Farley, and Couper 2008; Schaefer 1976).

The key factor in reducing hostility, in addition to equal-status contact, is the presence of a common goal. If people are in competition, as already noted, contact may heighten tension. However, bringing people together to share a common task has been shown to reduce ill feelings when these people belong to different racial, ethnic, or religious groups. A study released in 2004 traced the transformations that occurred over the generations in the composition of the Social Service Employees Union in New York City. Always a mixed membership, the union was founded by Jews and Italian Americans, only to experience an influx of Black Americans. More recently in other parts of the United States, it comprises Latin Americans, Africans, West Indians, and South Asians. At each transformation, the common goals of representing the workers effectively overcame the very real cultural differences among the rank and file of Mexican and El Salvadoran immigrants in Houston. The researchers found that when the new arrivals had contact with African Americans, intergroup relations generally improved, and the absence of contact tended to foster ambivalent, even negative, attitudes (Fine 2008; Foerstrer 2004; Paluck and Green 2009).

The limited amount of intergroup contact is of concern given the power of the contact hypothesis. If there is no positive contact, then how can we expect a decrease in prejudice? National surveys show prejudice directed toward Muslim Americans, but social contact bridges that hatred. In a 2006 survey, 50 percent of people who were not acquainted with a Muslim favored special identification for Muslim Americans, but only 24 percent of those who knew a Muslim embraced that same view. Similarly, people personally familiar with Muslims are more than one-third less likely to endorse special security checks just for Muslims and are less nervous to see Muslim men on the same flight with themselves. Although negative views are common toward Muslim Americans today, they are much less likely to be endorsed by people who have had intergroup contact (Saad 2006).

As African Americans and other subordinate groups slowly gain access to better-paying and more-responsible jobs, the contact hypothesis takes on greater significance. Usually, the availability of equal-status interaction is taken for granted; yet in everyday life, intergroup contact does not conform to the equal-status idea of the contact hypothesis. Furthermore, as we have seen, in a highly segregated society such as the United States, contact tends to be brief and superficial, especially between Whites and minorities. The apartheid-like friendship patterns prevent us from learning firsthand not just how to get along but also how to revel in interracial experiences (Bonilla-Silva and Embrick 2007; Miller 2002).

AVOIDANCE VIA THE INTERNET   The emergence of the Internet, smartphones, and social media are often heralded as transforming social behavior, allowing us to network globally. While this may be the case in some instances, avoiding people online who are racially, ethnically, and religiously different is just another means of doing what one's parents and grandparents did face-to-face.

Take dating, for example. While in the past, one avoided people who looked different at social occasions, Internet daters have a new tool for such avoidance. Studies document that people who use Internet dating services typically use filters or respond to background questions to exclude contact with people different from themselves. While many daters use such means, Whites are least open to dating racial and ethnic groups different from themselves, African Americans are most open, and Latinos and Asian Americans are somewhere between the two extremes (Robnett and Feliciano 2011).

Sometimes the avoidance is not necessarily initiated by people but by the helpful technology. There is growing concern that because of an increasingly wired world, in a more subtle fashion we are less likely to benefit from intergroup contacts, not to mention friendships, in the future. Through Facebook, Classmate, and LinkedIn, the Internet allows us to reach out to those who are different from ourselves—or does it? The search engines we use to navigate the Internet are personalized. Google, for example, uses as many as 57 sources of information, including a person's location and past searches, to make calculated guesses about the sites a person might like to visit. Its searches have been personalized in this way since 2009. Keep in mind that Google accounts for 82 percent of the global Internet searches and captures 98 percent of the mobile phone searches. In 2012, Google carried the process one step further by collecting information from the websites that people "friend" or "like" through social media, and then use that information to direct their web searches.

Although Google's approach may at first sound convenient, critics charge that it can trap users in their own worlds by routing them ever more narrowly in the same direction. In his book *The Filter Bubble,* online political activist Eli Pariser (2011a, 2011b) contends that when a search engine filters our searches, it encloses us in a kind of "invisible bubble" or "walled garden" that limits what we see to what we are already familiar with. Thus, we are not likely to discover people, places, and ideas that are outside our comfort zone. Secure in our online bubble, which we may not even realize is there, we have little interaction with people different from ourselves (Katz 2012; Zittrain 2008).

What is wrong with that? Given a choice, most of us go only to restaurants whose food we enjoy and read and listen to only those books and radio programs we know we like. Yet, wasn't the Internet supposed to open new vistas to us? If we are investigating a major news event, shouldn't we all see the same information when we search for it? Pariser describes what happened when two friends searched for the term "BP" in the spring of 2010, during the Deepwater Horizon oil rig's accidental discharge of crude oil into the Gulf of Mexico. Using the same browser, the two friends got very different results. One saw links to information about the oil spill; the other saw links to information about BP's CEO, intended for investors.

Corporate Response: Diversity Training

Prejudice carries a cost. This cost is not only to the victim but also to any organization that allows prejudice to interfere with its functioning. Workplace hostility can lead to lost productivity and even staff attrition. Furthermore, if left unchecked, an organization—whether a corporation, government agency, or nonprofit enterprise—can develop a reputation for having a "chilly climate."

If a business has a reputation that it is unfriendly to people of color or to women, qualified people are discouraged from applying for jobs there and potential clients might seeking products or services elsewhere.

In an effort to improve workplace relations, most organizations have initiated some form of diversity training. These programs are aimed at eliminating circumstances and relationships that cause groups to receive fewer rewards,

We often are unaware of all the social situations that allow us to meet people of different ethnic and racial backgrounds. Such opportunities may increase understanding.

resources, or opportunities. Typically, programs aim to reduce ill-treatment based on race, gender, and ethnicity. In addition, diversity training may deal with (in descending order of frequency) age, disability, religion, and language as well as other aspects, including citizenship status, marital status, and parental status (Society for Human Resource Management 2010, 2011).

It is difficult to make broad generalization about the effectiveness of diversity-training programs because they vary so much in structure between organizations. At one extreme are short presentations that seem to have little support from management. People file into the room feeling it is something they need to get through quickly. Such training is unlikely to be effective and may be counterproductive by heightening social tensions. At the other end of the continuum is a diversity training program that is integrated into initial job training, reinforced periodically, and presented as part of the overall mission of the organization, with full support from all levels of management. In such businesses, diversity is a core value, and management demands a high degree of commitment from all employees

Remarkably, the prevalence of any diversity programs in organizations remains slow (10 to 30 percent), even in the 30 plus years after the diversity-management paradigm was first widely viewed as good for business. Even inexpensive steps are not widely adopted. Unfortunately, corporations with lower representation of women and minorities are less likely to embrace diversity programs.

Research into different corporate policies has found two that are particularly effective. Diversity task forces that bring together people from different departments to brainstorm about opening up hiring opportunities appear to eventually increase the diversity in upper management. A second successful policy is the diversity mentoring programs designed for aspiring women and minorities, as well as White men, to achieve their career goals. Unfortunately, research suggests that if White men perceive African Americans are the primary organizers of such efforts, networking progress can actually have a negative impact.

As shown in Figure 2.5, the workforce is becoming more diverse, and management is taking notice. An increasing proportion of the workforce is foreign-born, and the numbers of U.S.-born African Americans, Latinos, and Asian Americans also are growing. Growing research in business and the social sciences documents that diversity is an asset in bringing about creative changes. The benefits of workplace diversity are especially true at management levels where leadership teams can develop innovative solutions and creative ideas. However, it is troubling to note that organizations that have the least diverse leadership are less likely to adopt any kind of diversity program, whatever its effectiveness (DiTomaso, Post, and Parks-Yancy 2007; Dobbin and Kalev 2013; Dobbin, Kalev, and Kelly 2007; Dobbin, Kim, and Kalev 2011; Gose 2013; Kalev, Dobbin, and Kelly 2006; Leung et al. 2008; Page 2007).

It is not in an organization's best interests if employees start to create barriers based on, for example, racial lines. Earlier, we learned that equal-status

Figure 2.5 Foreign-Born Workers in the United States, by Country

About 16 percent of the civilian labor force is foreign-born, with Mexico the largest source.

SOURCE: Data for 2012 from Mosisa 2013: 2.

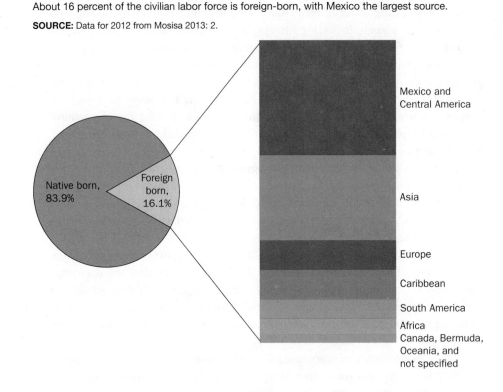

contact can reduce hostility. However, in the workplace, people compete for promotions, desirable work assignments, and better office space, to name a few sources of friction. When done well, an organization undertakes diversity training to remove ill feelings among workers, which often reflect the prejudices present in larger society.

To have a lasting impact, diversity training also should not be separated from other aspects of the organization. For example, even the most inspired program will have little effect on prejudice if the organization promotes a sexist or ethnically offensive image in its advertising. The University of North Dakota launched an initiative in 2001 to become one of the top institutions for Native Americans in the nation. Yet at almost the same time, the administration reaffirmed its commitment, despite tribal objections, to have the "Fighting Sioux" as its mascot for athletic teams. In 2005, the National Collegiate Athletic Association began to review logos and mascots that could be considered insulting to Native Americans. Some colleges have resisted suggestions to change or alter their publicity images, although others have abandoned the practice. Finally, 68 percent of the voters of the state voted to abandon the logo. It does little to present diversity training if overt actions by an organization propel it in the opposite direction (Kolpack 2012).

Despite the problems inherent in confronting prejudice, an organization with a comprehensive, management-supported program of diversity training can go a long way toward reducing prejudice in the workplace. The one major qualifier is that the rest of the organization must also support mutual respect.

Conclusion

2-9   Identify ways to reduce hate.

This chapter has examined theories of prejudice and measurements of its extent. Prejudice has a long history in the United States. Whispering campaigns suggested that Presidents Martin Van Buren and William McKinley were secretly working with the Pope. This whispering emerged into the national debate when John F. Kennedy became the first Roman Catholic to become president. Much more recently, in 2010, 18 percent of Americans believed President Obama to be a Muslim and only 34 percent a Christian (Kristof 2010; Pew Forum on Religion and Public Life 2010).

Are some minority groups now finally being respected? People cheered on May 1, 2011, on hearing that Osama bin Laden had been found and killed. However, the always-patriotic American Indian people were troubled to learn that the military had assigned the code name "Geronimo" to the operation to capture the terrorist. The Chiricahua Apache of New Mexico were particularly disturbed to learn that the name of their freedom fighter was associated with a global terrorist. In response, the U.S. Defense Department said no disrespect was meant to Native Americans. Of course, one can imagine that the operation never would have been named "Operation Lafayette" or "Operation Jefferson" (Dally 2011).

Several theories try to explain why prejudice exists. Theories for prejudice include two that tend to be psychological scapegoating and authoritarian personality—and emphasize why a particular person harbors ill feelings. Others are more sociological-exploitation and normative—and view prejudice in the context of our interaction in a larger society.

Surveys conducted in the United States over the past 60 years point to a reduction of prejudice as measured by the willingness to express stereotypes or maintain social distance. Survey data also show that African Americans, Latinos, Asian Americans, and American Indians do not necessarily feel comfortable with each other. They have adopted attitudes toward other oppressed groups similar to those held by many White Americans.

The absence of widespread public expression of prejudice does not mean prejudice itself is absent. Recent prejudice aimed at Hispanics, Asian Americans, and large recent immigrant groups such as Arab Americans and Muslim Americans is well documented. Issues such as immigration and affirmative action reemerge and cause bitter resentment. Furthermore, ill feelings exist between subordinate groups in schools, on the streets, and in the workplace. Color-blind racism allows one to appear to be tolerant while allowing racial and ethnic inequality to persist.

Equal-status contact may reduce hostility between groups. However, in a highly segregated society defined by inequality, such opportunities are not typical. The mass media can help reduce discrimination, but they have not done enough and may even intensify ill feelings by promoting stereotypical images.

Even though we can be encouraged by the techniques available to reduce intergroup hostility, sizable segments of the population still do not want to live in integrated neighborhoods, do not want to work for or be led by someone of a different race, and certainly object to the idea of their relatives marrying outside their own group. People still harbor stereotypes toward one another, and this tendency includes racial and ethnic minorities having stereotypes about one another.

Reducing prejudice is important because it can lead to support for policy change. There are steps we can take as individuals to confront prejudice and overcome hatred. Another real challenge and the ultimate objective are to improve the social condition of oppressed groups in the United States. To consider this challenge, we turn to discrimination in Chapter 3. Discrimination's costs are high to both dominant and subordinate groups. With this fact in mind, we examine some techniques for reducing discrimination.

Summary

1. Prejudice consists of negative attitudes, and discrimination consists of negative behavior toward a group.

2. Typically unconsciously, White people accept privilege automatically extended to them in everyday life.

3. Among explanations for prejudice are the theories of scapegoating, authoritarian personality, and exploitation as well as the normative approach.

4. Stereotypes present the content or images that prejudiced people hold but also become accepted as reality.

5. Although evidence indicates that the public expression of prejudice has declined, ample evidence exists that people are expressing race-neutral principles or color-blind racism that still serves to perpetuate inequality in society.

6. Typically, members of minority groups have a significantly more negative view of social inequality and are more pessimistic about the future compared to Whites.

7. Not only do people in dominant positions direct prejudice at racial and ethnic minorities but intergroup hostility among the minorities themselves also persists and may become violent.

8. Various techniques are utilized by the corporate sector to reduce prejudice, including educational programs, mass media, friendly intergroup contact, and diversity-training programs.

9. Ten steps have been identified that individuals can take to reduce or end prejudice.

Key Terms

anti-Semitism, p. 50
authoritarian personality, p. 51
Bogardus scale, p. 67
color-blind racism, p. 57
contact hypothesis, p. 68
discrimination, p. 46

ethnocentrism, p. 44
ethnophaulisms, p. 45
exploitation theory, p. 51
homophobia, p. 54
normative approach, p. 52
prejudice, p. 45

racial profiling, p. 55
scapegoating theory, p. 50
sexism, p. 54
social distance, p. 67
stereotypes, p. 53
White privilege, p. 48

Review Questions

1. How are prejudice and discrimination both related and unrelated to each other?

2. If White people are privileged, how do we explain the presence of poverty among Whites?

3. How do theories of prejudice relate to different expressions of prejudice?

4. What is the impact of stereotypes on how we interact with others?

5. How is color-blind racism expressed?

6. What toll can prejudice take on the people subjected to bigotry?

7. How would you describe the presence or absence of prejudice expressed between racial and ethnic subordinate groups?

8. Describe the efforts to reduce prejudice through education and the mass media.

9. Describe the ways that a community or individual can combat prejudice and hatred.

Critical Thinking

1. What might a contemporary version of the LaPiere study look like? Instead of using a Chinese couple, one might look at the treatment of a Muslim man accompanied by his veiled wife.

2. What privileges do you have that you do not give much thought to? Are they in any way related to race, ethnicity, religion, or social class?

3. Identify stereotypes associated with a group of people such as older adults or people with physical disabilities.

4. Consider the television programs you watch the most. In terms of race and ethnicity, how well do the programs you watch reflect the diversity of the population in the United States?

5. Can you identify any steps that have been taken against prejudice in your community?

Chapter 3
Discrimination

WEALTH INEQUALITY: DISCRIMINATION'S LEGACY
3-5 Illustrate how wealth inequality is discrimination's legacy.

ENVIRONMENTAL JUSTICE
3-6 Discuss environmental justice.

AFFIRMATIVE ACTION
3-7 Explain affirmative action.

REVERSE DISCRIMINATION
3-8 Analyze reverse discrimination.

THE GLASS CEILING
3-9 Put into your own words the glass ceiling.

"I didn't get the job" is a frequent complaint that soon leads to reasons "I" did not get the job for which I applied. Sometimes people think it's because of their race. Is discrimination still the case?

A dramatic confirmation of discrimination came with research begun by sociologist Devah Pager in 2003. She sent White, Black, and Latino men out as trained "testers" to look for entry-level jobs in Milwaukee and New York City that required no experience or special training. Each tester was in his twenties and was college educated, but each one presented himself as having only a high school diploma and similar job history.

The job-seeking experiences with different employers were vastly different among the men. Why? Besides having different racial and ethnic background, some testers indicated in the job application that they had served 18 months in jail for a felony conviction (possession of cocaine with intent to distribute). As you can see in Figure 3.1, applicants with a prison record received significantly fewer callbacks. Although a criminal record made a dramatic difference, race was clearly more important. In another study, Pager documented that Latino job applicants were at a disadvantage similar to that of the African American testers (Pager, Western, and Bonikowski 2009; Pager and Western 2012).

The differences were so pointed that a White job applicant with a jail record received more callbacks for further consideration than a Black man with no

---

Figure 3.1 Discrimination in Job Seeking

SOURCE: Pager 2003: 958. Reprinted by permission of the University of Chicago.

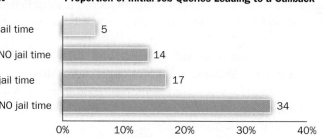

criminal record. Whiteness has a privilege even when it comes to jail time; race, it seems, was more of a concern to potential employers than a criminal background. It is no surprise that an analysis of labor patterns after release from prison finds that wages grow at a 21 percent slower rate for Black compared to White ex-inmates.

"I expected there to be an effect of race, but I did not expect it to swamp the results as it did," Pager told an interviewer. Her finding was especially significant because one in three African American men and one in six Hispanic men are expected to serve time in prison during their lifetime compared to one in 17 White men (Greenhouse 2012; Kroeger 2004).

Pager's research, which was widely publicized, eventually contributed to a change in public policy. In his 2004 State of the Union address, and specifically referring to Pager's work, President George W. Bush announced a $300 million monitoring program for ex-convicts who are attempting to reintegrate into society.

Discrimination has a long history, right up to the present, of taking its toll on people. **Discrimination** is the denial of opportunities and equal rights to individuals and groups because of prejudice or other arbitrary reasons. We examine the many faces of discrimination, its many victims, and the many ways scholars have documented its presence today in the United States. We not only return to more examples of discrimination in housing but also look at differential treatment in employment opportunities, wages, voting, vulnerability to environmental hazards, and even access to membership in private clubs.

Understanding Discrimination

3-1   Distinguish between relative and absolute deprivation.

People in the United States find it difficult to see discrimination as a widespread phenomenon. "After all," it is often said, "these minorities drive cars, hold jobs, own their homes, and go to college, and may even become president of the United States."

Relative vs. Absolute Deprivation

An understanding of discrimination in modern industrialized societies such as the United States must begin by distinguishing between relative and absolute deprivation.

Conflict theorists have said correctly that it is not absolute, unchanging standards that determine deprivation and oppression. Although minority groups may be viewed as having adequate or even good incomes, housing, healthcare, and educational opportunities, it is their position relative to some other group that offers evidence of discrimination.

Relative deprivation is defined as the conscious experience of a negative discrepancy between legitimate expectations and present actualities. After settling in the United States, immigrants often enjoy better material comforts and more political freedom than was possible in their old countries. If they compare themselves with most other people in the United States, however, they will feel deprived because, although their standards have improved, the immigrants still perceive relative deprivation.

Absolute deprivation, on the other hand, implies a fixed standard based on a minimum level of subsistence below which families should not be expected to exist. Discrimination does not necessarily mean absolute deprivation. A Japanese American who is promoted to a management position may still be a victim of discrimination if he or she had been passed over for years because of corporate reluctance to place an Asian American in a highly visible position.

Dissatisfaction also is likely to arise from feelings of relative deprivation. The members of a society who feel most frustrated and disgruntled by the social and economic conditions of their lives are not necessarily worse off in an objective sense. Social scientists have long recognized that what is most significant is how people perceive their situations. Karl Marx pointed out that although the misery of the workers was important in reflecting their oppressed state, so was their position relative to the ruling class. In 1847, Marx wrote, "Although the enjoyment of the workers has risen, the social satisfaction that they have has fallen in comparison with the increased enjoyment of the capitalist" (Marx and Engels 1955: 94).

This statement explains why the groups or individuals who are most vocal and best organized against discrimination are not necessarily in the worst economic and social situation. However, they are likely to be those who most strongly perceive that, relative to others, they are not receiving their fair share. Resistance to perceived discrimination, rather than the actual amount of absolute discrimination, is the key.

Hate Crimes

3-2   Define hate crimes.

Although prejudice certainly is not new in the United States, it is receiving increased attention as it manifests itself in hate crimes in neighborhoods, at meetings, and on college campuses. The Hate Crime Statistics Act, which became law in 1990, directs the Department of Justice to gather data on hate or bias crimes.

What Are Hate Crimes?

The government defines an ordinary crime as a **hate crime** when offenders are motivated to choose a victim because of some characteristic—for example, race, ethnicity, religion, sexual orientation, or disability—and provide evidence that hatred prompted them to commit the crime. Hate crimes also are sometimes referred to as *bias crimes*.

The Hate Crime Statistics Act created a national mandate to identify such crimes, whereas previously only 12 states had monitored hate crimes. The act has since been amended to include disabilities, physical and mental, as well as sexual orientation as factors that could be considered a basis for hate crimes.

In 2013, law enforcement agencies released hate crime data submitted by police agencies. Even though many hate crimes are not reported (less than one in seven participating agencies reported an incident), a staggering number of offenses that come to law agencies' attention were motivated by hate. While most incidents receive relatively little attention, some become the attention of headlines and online sites for days. Such was the case in 2009 when a Maryland man with a long history of ties to neo-Nazi groups walked into the U.S. Holocaust Memorial Museum in Washington, D.C., and opened fire, killing a security guard.

Official reports noted more than 5,700 hate crimes and bias-motivated incidents in 2012. As indicated in Figure 3.2, race was the apparent motivation for the bias in approximately 48 percent of the reports, and religion, sexual orientation, and ethnicity accounted for 11 to 20 percent each. Vandalism against property and intimidation were the most common crimes, but among the more than 3,200 incidents directed against people, 61 percent involved assault, rape, or murder.

In "Speaking Out," Moustafa Bayoumi (2009, 2010), a Brooklyn College, City University of New York, literature professor draws on Du Bois's work to describe how Arab Americans are viewed which in some instances could escalate into a hate crime.

Arab Americans and Muslim Americans, like other subordinate groups, interact with others that, at times, lead to violent encounters. The vast majority of hate crimes are directed by members of the dominant group toward those who

Figure 3.2 Distribution of Reported Hate Crimes

SOURCE: Incidents reported for 2012 by Federal Bureau of Investigation 2013.

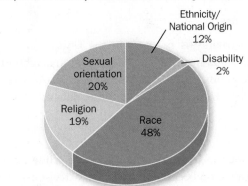

Speaking Out

Arab Problem

Moustafa Bayoumi

Sade and four of his 20-something friends are at a hookah café almost underneath the Verrazano-Narrows Bridge in Brooklyn. It's late, but the summer heat is strong and hangs in the air. They sit on the sidewalk in a circle, water pipes bubbling between their white plastic chairs.

Sade is upset. He recently found out that his close friend of almost four years was an undercover police detective sent to spy on him, his friends, and his community. Even the guy's name, Kamil Pasha, was fake, which particularly irked the 24-year-old Palestinian American. After appearing as a surprise witness at a recent terrorism trial in Brooklyn, Pasha vanished. That's when Sade discovered the truth.

"I was very hurt," he says. "Was it friendship, or was he doing his job?" He takes a puff from his water pipe. "I felt betrayed." The smoke comes out thick and smells like apples. "How could I not have seen this? The guy had four bank accounts! He was always asking for a receipt wherever we went. He had an empty apartment: a treadmill, a TV, and a mattress. No food, no wardrobe." He shakes his head. "We were stupid not to figure it out."

"You have to know the family," Sade says. He points to those around the circle. "His mother is my aunt. I've known him since I was in second grade. I know where his family lives, and he's also my cousin," he says, ticking off each person in turn. He gets to me. "You I'm not so sure about!" he says, and all the young men laugh loudly.

Informants and spies are regular conversation topics in the age of terror, a time when friendships are tested, trust disappears, and tragedy becomes comedy. If questioning friendship isn't enough, Sade has also had other problems to deal with. Sacked from his Wall Street job, he is convinced that the termination stemmed from his Jerusalem birthplace. Anti-Arab and anti-Muslim invectives were routinely slung at him there, and he's happier now in a technology firm owned and staffed by other hyphenated Americans. But the last several years have taken their toll. I ask him about life after September 11 for Arab Americans. "We're the new blacks," he says. "You know that, right?"

How does it feel to be a problem? Just over a century ago, W. E. B. Du Bois asked that very question in his American classic *The Souls of Black Folk,* and he offered an answer. "Being a problem is a strange experience," he wrote, "peculiar even," no doubt evoking the "peculiar institution" of slavery. Du Bois composed his text during Jim Crow, a time of official racial segregation that deliberately obscured to the wider world the human details of African American life. Determined to pull back "the veil" separating populations, he showed his readers a fuller picture of the Black experience, including "the meaning of its religion, the passion of its human sorrow, and the struggle of its greater souls."

It seems barely an exaggeration to say that Arab and Muslim Americans are constantly talked about but almost never heard from. The problem is not that they lack representations but that they have too many. And these are all abstractions. Arabs and Muslims have become a foreign-policy issue, an argument on the domestic agenda, a law-enforcement priority, and a point of well-meaning concern. They appear as shadowy characters on terror television shows, have become objects of sociological inquiry, and get paraded around as puppets from public diplomacy. Pop culture is awash with their images. Hookah cafés entice East Village socialites, fashionistas appropriate the checkered kaffiyah scarf, and Prince sings an ode to a young Arab American girl. They are floating everywhere in the virtual landscape of the national imagination, as either villains of Islam or victims of Arab culture. Yet as in the postmodern world in which we live, sometimes when you are everywhere, you are really nowhere.

Frankly, it's beleaguering; like living on a treadmill, an exhausting condition. University of Michigan anthropologists Sally Howell and Andrew Shryock succinctly describe the situation when they write that "in the aftermath of 9/11, Arab and Muslim Americans have been compelled, time and again, to apologize for acts they did not commit, to condemn acts they never condoned and to openly profess loyalties that, for most U.S. citizens, are merely assumed." Yet despite the apologies, condemnations, and professions, their voices still aren't heard. And while so many terrible things have happened in the past years, plenty of good things have also occurred, from Japanese American groups speaking out against today's wartime policies, to prominent civil-rights activists fighting for due process for Muslim and Arab clients, to ordinary people

reaching out to one another in everyday encounters. Much of this happens quietly in church basements, in mosques holding open houses, in Jewish centers, or in university or community halls, but such events too are often obscured, drowned out by the ideology of our age. Yet what most remains in the shadows today are the human dimensions to how Arabs and Muslims live their lives, the rhythms of their work and days, the varieties of their religious experiences, the obstacles they face, and the efforts they shoulder to overcome them. In other words, what is absent is how they understand the meanings of their religion, the passions of their sorrow, and the struggle of their souls. But in today's landscape, none of that seems to matter. One could say that in the dawning years of the twenty-first century, when Arabs are the new chic and Islam is all the rage, Muslims and Arabs have become essentially a nagging problem to solve, one way or another.

And being a problem is a strange experience—frustrating, even.

SOURCE: Bayoumi 2009: 1–2, 5–6.

---

are, relatively speaking, powerless. Only one in five bias incidents based on race are anti-White. Hate crimes, except for those that are most horrific, receive little media attention, and anti-White incidents probably receive even less. Hostility based on race knows no boundaries (Department of Justice 2011; Witt 2007).

The official reports of hate or bias crimes appear to be only the tip of the iceberg. Government-commissioned surveys conducted over a national cross section indicate that 192,000 people annually report they have been victims of hate crimes, but only half of these are reported to police. Of these, only one out of ten, according to the victims, are confirmed as hate crimes. Although definitions vary, a considerable amount of racial hostility in this country becomes violent (Harlow 2005; Perry 2003).

National legislation and publicity have made *hate crime* a meaningful term, and we are beginning to recognize the victimization associated with such incidents. A current proposal would make a violent crime a federal crime if it were motivated by racial or religious bias. Although passage is uncertain, the serious consideration of the proposal indicates a willingness to consider a major expansion of federal jurisdiction. Currently, federal law prohibits crimes motivated by race, color, religion, or national origin only if they violate a federally guaranteed right such as voting.

Victimized groups do more than experience and observe hate crimes and other acts of prejudice. Watchdog organizations play an important role in documenting bias-motivated violence; among such groups are the Anti-Defamation League, the National Institute Against Prejudice and Violence, the Southern Poverty Law Center, and the National Gay and Lesbian Task Force.

To further their agenda, established hate groups have even set up propaganda sites on the World Wide Web. This also creates opportunities for previously unknown haters and hate groups to promote themselves. However, hate crime legislation does not affect such outlets because of legal questions involving freedom of speech. An even more recent technique of hate groups has been to use instant messaging software, which enables Internet users to create a private chat room with another individual. Enterprising bigots use directories to target their attacks through instant messaging, much as harassing telephone calls were placed in the past. Even more creative and subtle are people who have constructed websites to attract people who are surfing for information on Martin Luther King, Jr., only to find a site that looks educational but savagely discredits the civil rights activist. A close inspection reveals that a White-supremacist organization hosts the site (Davis 2008; Simon Wiesenthal Center 2008; Working 2007).

Why Do Hate Crimes Carry Harsher Penalties?

Frequently, one hears the identification of a crime as a hate crime being questioned. After all, is not hate involved in every assault or act of vandalism? While many non-hate crimes may include a motivation of hatred toward an individual or organization, a hate or bias crime toward a minority is intended to carry a message well beyond the individual victim. When a person is assaulted because they are gay or lesbian, the act is meant to terrorize all gay and lesbians. Vandalizing a mosque or synagogue is meant to warn all Muslims or Jews that they are not wanted and their religious faith is considered inferior.

In many respects, today's hate crimes are like the terrorist efforts of the Ku Klux Klan of generations ago. Targets may be randomly selected, but the group being terrorized is carefully chosen. In many jurisdictions, having a crime being classified as a hate crime can increase the punishment. For example, a misdemeanor like vandalism can be increased to a felony. A felony that is a hate crime can carry a greater prison sentence. These sanctions were upheld by the Supreme Court in the 1993 decision *Mitchell v. Wisconsin*, which recognized that greater harm may be done by hate-motivated crimes (Blazak 2011).

Institutional Discrimination

3-3 **Summarize how institutions discriminate.**

Individuals practice discrimination in one-on-one encounters, and institutions practice discrimination through their daily operations. Indeed, a consensus is growing today that institutional discrimination is more significant than acts committed by prejudiced individuals.

Social scientists are particularly concerned with how patterns of employment, education, criminal justice, housing, healthcare, and government operations maintain the social significance of race and ethnicity. **Institutional discrimination** is the denial of opportunities and equal rights to individuals and groups that results from the normal operations of a society.

Civil rights activist Stokely Carmichael and political scientist Charles Hamilton are credited with introducing the concept of institutional racism. *Individual discrimination* refers to overt acts of individual Whites against individual Blacks; Carmichael and Hamilton reserved the term *institutional racism* for covert acts committed collectively against an entire group. From this perspective, discrimination can take place without an individual intending to deprive others of privileges and even without the individual being aware that others are being deprived (Ture and Hamilton 1992).

How can discrimination be widespread and unconscious at the same time? A few documented examples of institutional discrimination follow:

1. Standards for assessing credit risks work against African Americans and Hispanics who seek to establish businesses because many lack conventional credit references. Businesses in low-income areas where these groups often reside also have much higher insurance costs.
2. IQ testing favors middle-class children, especially the White middle class, because of the types of questions included.
3. The entire criminal justice system, from the patrol officer to the judge and jury, is dominated by Whites who find it difficult to understand life in poverty areas.
4. Hiring practices often require several years' experience at jobs only recently opened to members of subordinate groups.
5. Many jobs automatically eliminate people with felony records or past drug offenses, a practice that disproportionately reduces employment opportunities for people of color.

Institutional discrimination is so systemic that it takes on the pattern of what has been termed "woodwork racism" in that racist outcomes become so widespread that African Americans, Latinos, Asian Americans, and others endure them as a part of everyday life (Feagin and McKinney 2003).

At the beginning of this chapter, we noted how employers routinely pass over job applicants who are felons. To casual observers, this may seem reasonable; however, Black and Latino job applicants are more likely to be passed over than Whites. This is a form of institutional discrimination. Recognizing this, the Equal Opportunity Commission ruled in 2012 that while employers may consider criminal records, a policy that excludes all applicants with a conviction could violate employment discrimination laws because of this differential impact. This does not mean employers must hire ex-felons, only that blanket exclusions are to be avoided (Greenhouse 2012).

Despite the positive step, concern grows over another potential example of institutional discrimination in the area of voting requirements. How do we establish the authenticity of a person's right to vote? States are now considering requiring a government-issued ID *with the person's photograph* to vote. Numerous states (see Figure 3.3) have enacted laws requiring voters to show a photo ID, presumably to prevent voter fraud. However, there is little evidence that people have been impersonating eligible voters at the polls.

Courts have been reluctant to uphold such laws, contending that accessibility is not ensured for all eligible voters to obtain such a credential. Such laws disproportionately disenfranchise members of minority groups, as well as the elderly, simply because they do not have a driver's license. National surveys found 25 percent of African Americans and 16 percent of Latino citizens do not have a valid government-issued photo ID, compared to 8 percent of White citizens. So, court decisions aside, what we have is another case of institutional discrimination in that through the normal operation of voting regulations equal rights are more likely to be denied to people of color (Brennan Center 2006, 2013; Dade 2012b).

Figure 3.3 Voter ID Requirements

SOURCE: National Conference of State Legislatures 2013.

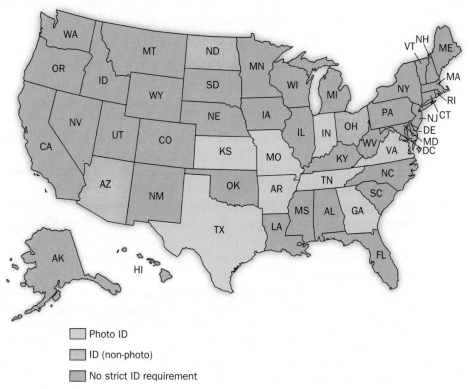

☐ Photo ID

☐ ID (non-photo)

☐ No strict ID requirement

In other situations, even apparently neutral institutional standards can lead a college's policy to have discriminatory effects. African American students at a Midwestern state university protested a policy under which fraternities and sororities that wanted to use campus facilities for a dance were required to post a security deposit to cover possible damage. The Black students complained that this policy had a discriminatory impact on minority student organizations. Campus police countered that the university's policy applied to all student groups interested in using these facilities. However, because almost all White fraternities and sororities at the school had their own houses, which they used for dances, the policy affected only African American and other subordinate groups' organizations.

Institutional discrimination continuously imposes more hindrances on and awards fewer benefits to certain racial and ethnic groups than it does to others. This is the underlying and painful context of American intergroup relations.

Discrimination Today

3-4 Describe how discrimination can be documented today.

Discrimination continues to be widespread in the United States. It sometimes results from prejudices held by individuals but, more significantly, it is found in institutional discrimination. We will look first at measuring discrimination in terms of income and then efforts that are being made to eliminate or at least reduce it.

Discrimination Hits the Wallet

How much discrimination is there? As in measuring prejudice, problems arise when trying to quantify discrimination. Measuring prejudice is hampered by the difficulties in assessing attitudes and by the need to take many factors into account. It is further limited by the initial challenge of identifying different treatment. A second difficulty of measuring discrimination is assigning a cost to discrimination.

An important measure of economic well-being for any household is their annual income and the wealth they have to draw upon in cases of emergency. **Income** refers to salaries, wages, and other money received; **wealth** is a more inclusive term that encompasses all of a person's material assets, including land and other types of property. We first consider income and then look at wealth later in this chapter.

Some tentative conclusions about discrimination can be made looking at income and wealth data. Figure 3.4 uses income data to show the vivid disparity in income between African Americans and Whites and also between men and women. This encompasses all full-time workers. White men, with a median income of $55,989, earn one-third more than Black men and almost twice what Hispanic women earn in wages.

Figure 3.4 Median Income by Race, Ethnicity, and Gender

Even at the very highest levels of schooling, the income gap remains between Whites and Blacks. Education also has little apparent effect on the income gap between male and female workers. Even a brief analysis reveals striking differences in earning power between White men and other groups in the United States. Furthermore, greater inequality is apparent for African American and Hispanic women.

Note: Data released in 2013 for income earned in 2012. Median income is from all sources and is limited to year-round, full-time workers at least 25 years old (American Indian data for 16 years or older). Data for White men and women are for non-Hispanics.

SOURCE: American Community Survey 2013a: Table B20017C; DeNavas-Walt, Proctor, and Smith 2013 PINC-03.

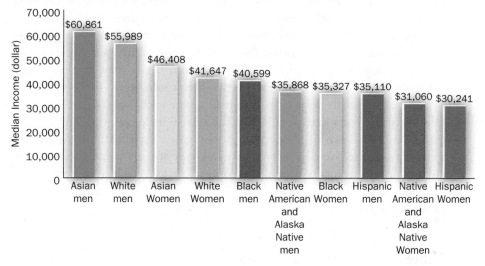

Yet Asian American men are at the top and edge out White males by almost $5,000 a year. Why do Asian American men earn so much if race serves as a barrier? The economic picture is not entirely positive. Some Asian American groups such as Laotians and Vietnamese have high levels of poverty. We might be drawn to the fact that Asian American income appears to slightly overtake that of Whites. However, a significant number of Asian Americans with advanced educations have high-earning jobs, which brings up the median income. However, as we will see, given their high levels of schooling, their incomes should be even higher.

Clearly, regardless of race or ethnicity, men outpace women in annual income. This disparity between the incomes of Black women and White men has remained unchanged over the more than 50 years during which such data have been tabulated. It illustrates yet another instance of the greater inequality experienced by minority women. Also, Figure 3.4 includes data only for full-time, year-round workers; it excludes homemakers and the unemployed. Even in this comparison, the deprivation of Blacks, Hispanics, and women is confirmed again.

Are these differences entirely the result of discrimination in employment? No. Individuals within the four groups are not equally prepared to compete for high-paying jobs. Past discrimination is a significant factor in a person's current social position. Taxpayers, predominantly White, were unwilling to subsidize the public education of African Americans and Hispanics at the same levels as White pupils. Even as these actions have changed, today's schools show the continuing results of this uneven spending pattern from the past. Education clearly is an appropriate variable to control.

In Table 3.1, median income is compared, holding education constant, which means that we can compare Blacks and Whites and men and women with approximately the same amount of formal schooling. More education means more money, but the disparity remains. The gap between races does narrow somewhat as education increases. However, both African Americans and women lag behind their more affluent counterparts. The contrast remains dramatic: Women with a master's degree typically receive $60,927, which means they earn more than $5,000 *less* than men who complete only a bachelor's degree.

Thinking over the long term, a woman with a bachelor's degree will work full-time three years to earn $150,000. The typical male can work a little more than 27 months, take over nine months off without pay, and still exceed the woman's earnings. Women, regardless of race, pay at every point. They are often hired at lower starting salaries in jobs comparable to those held by men. Salary increases come slower. And by their 30s, they rarely recover from even short maternity leaves.

Table 3.1 Median Income by Race and Sex, Holding Education Constant

Even at the very highest levels of schooling, the income gap remains between Whites and Blacks. Education also has little apparent effect on the income gap between male and female workers (income values in dollars).

	Race				Sex	
	White Families	Black Families	Asian Families	Hispanic Families	Male	Female
Total	72,404	41,737	80,046	41,970	50,955	39,777
High School						
Nongraduate	35,648	20,537	34,030	30,992	30,329	21,387
Graduate	55,037	32,075	48,734	39,145	40,351	30,406
College						
Associate Degree	71,633	48,813	70,110	55,580	50,961	37,321
Bachelor's degree	100,412	72,724	95,654	76,647	66,153	50,173
Master's degree	112,503	84,164	119,290	101,083	85,116	60,927
Doctorate degree	140,303	108,333	124,515	126,048	106,467	77,902

Note: Data released in 2013 for income earned in 2012. Figures are median income from all sources except capital gains. Included are public assistance payments, dividends, pensions, unemployment compensation, and so on. Incomes are for all workers 25 years of age and older with earnings. High school graduates include those with GEDs. Data for Whites are for White non-Hispanics. Family data for Hispanic doctorate-holders' families are author's estimate.

SOURCE: DeNavas-Walt, Proctor, and Smith 2013 FINC-01, PINC-03.

Note what happens to Asian American households. Although highly educated Asian Americans earn a lot of money, they trail well behind their White counterparts. With a doctorate degree holder in the family, the typical Asian American household earns an estimated $114,662, compared to $125,059 in a White household.

This is the picture today, but is it getting better? According to a Census Bureau report released in 2011, the answer is no. During the early years of the twenty-first century, Blacks were more likely to stay poor than Whites and those African Americans in the top rung of income were more likely to fall than their White counterparts among the wealthy. The inequality is dramatic and the trend is not diminishing (Hisnanick and Giefer 2011).

Now that education has been held constant, is the remaining gap caused by discrimination? Not necessarily. Table 3.1 uses only the amount of schooling, not its quality. Racial minorities are more likely to attend inadequately financed schools. Some efforts have been made to eliminate disparities between school districts in the amount of wealth available to tax for school support, but they have met with little success.

The inequality of educational opportunity may seem less important in explaining sex discrimination. Although women usually are not segregated from men, educational institutions encourage talented women to enter fields that pay less (nursing or elementary education) than other occupations that require similar amounts of training. Even when they do enter the same occupation, the earnings disparity persists. Even controlling for age, a study of census data showed that female physicians and surgeons earned 69 percent of what their male counterparts did. Looking at broad ranges of occupations, researchers in the last few years have attributed between one-quarter and one-third of the wage gap to discrimination rather than personal choices, skill preparation, and formal schooling (Reskin 2012; Weinberg 2004).

Eliminating Discrimination

Two main agents of social change work to reduce discrimination: voluntary associations organized to solve racial and ethnic problems and the federal government, including the courts. The two are closely related: Most efforts initiated by the government were urged by associations or organizations that represent minority groups, following vigorous protests by African Americans against racism. Resistance to social inequality by subordinate groups has been the key to change. Rarely has any government on its own initiative sought to end discrimination based on such criteria as race, ethnicity, and gender.

All racial and ethnic groups of any size are represented by private organizations that are, to some degree, trying to end discrimination. Some groups originated in the first half of the twentieth century, but most have been founded since World War II or have become significant forces in bringing about change only since then. These include church organizations, fraternal social groups, minor political parties, and legal defense funds, as well as more militant organizations operating under the scrutiny of law enforcement agencies. The purposes, membership, successes, and failures of these resistance organizations dedicated to eliminating discrimination are discussed throughout this book.

The judiciary, charged with interpreting laws and the U.S. Constitution, has a much longer history of involvement in the rights of racial, ethnic, and religious minorities. However, its early decisions protected the rights of the dominant group, as in the 1857 U.S. Supreme Court's *Dred Scott* decision, which ruled that slaves remained slaves even when living or traveling in states where slavery was illegal. Not until the 1940s did the Supreme Court revise earlier decisions and begin to grant African Americans the same rights as those held by Whites. The 1954 *Brown v. Board of Education* decision, which stated that "separate but equal" facilities—including education—were unconstitutional, heralded a new series of rulings, arguing that distinguishing between races in order to segregate was inherently unconstitutional.

The most important legislative effort to eradicate discrimination was the Civil Rights Act of 1964. This act led to the establishment of the Equal Employment Opportunity Commission (EEOC), which had the power to investigate complaints against employers and to recommend action to the Department of Justice. If the justice department sued and discrimination was found, then the court could order appropriate compensation. The act covered employment practices of all businesses with more than 25 employees and nearly all employment agencies and labor unions. A 1972 amendment broadened the coverage to employers with as few as 15 employees.

The Civil Rights Act of 1964 prohibited discrimination in public accommodations—that is, hotels, motels, restaurants, gasoline stations, and amusement parks. Publicly owned facilities such as parks, stadiums, and swimming pools were also prohibited from discriminating. Another important provision forbade discrimination in all federally supported programs and institutions such as hospitals, colleges, and road construction projects.

The Civil Rights Act of 1964 was not perfect. Since 1964, several acts and amendments to the original act have been added to cover the many areas of discrimination it left untouched, such as criminal justice and housing. Even in areas singled out for enforcement in the act, discrimination still occurs. Federal agencies charged with enforcement complain that they are underfunded or are denied wholehearted support by the White House. Also, regardless of how much the EEOC may want to act in a particular case, the person who alleges discrimination has to pursue the complaint over a long time that is marked by lengthy periods of inaction. Despite these efforts, devastating forms of discrimination persist. African Americans, Latinos, and others fall victim to **redlining**, or the pattern of discrimination against people trying to buy homes in minority and racially changing neighborhoods.

While overt discriminatory practices may have largely ended, home seekers are not treated alike. The race of the home seeker makes a difference. The

Department of Housing and Urban Development (HUD) issued a report based on testing 8,000 times in 28 metropolitan areas. Testers were matched gender and age, and presented themselves as equally well-qualified to rent or buy the advertised unit. Overall Blacks, Hispanics, and Asian Americans were all told about and shown fewer units than their White counterparts. HUD has done such studies since 1977 and the latest study shows a decline in the disparity in housing opportunities offered to minorities but the gap persists. Minority home seekers continue to be asked more questions about their finances, experience unkept appointments, are quoted higher rents for the same unit, and, in the case of home purchases, are expected to be prequalified for a loan. Discrimination against Blacks, Latinos, and Asians persists in housing even in a more subtle form from the days of the redlining (Turner et al. 2013).

People living in predominantly minority neighborhoods have found that companies with delivery services refuse to go to their area. In one case that attracted national attention in 1997, a Pizza Hut in Kansas City refused to deliver 40 pizzas to an honors program at a high school in an all-Black neighborhood. A Pizza Hut spokesperson called the neighborhood unsafe and said that almost every city has "restricted areas" to which the company will not deliver. This admission was particularly embarrassing because the high school already had a $170,000-a-year contract with Pizza Hut to deliver pizzas as a part of its school lunch program. Service redlining covers everything from parcel deliveries to repair people as well as food deliveries. The redlining continues to exist in cities throughout the United States (Fuller 1998; Rusk 2001; Schwartz 2001; Turner et al. 2002; Yinger 1995).

Although civil rights laws often have established rights for other minorities, the Supreme Court made them explicit in two 1987 decisions involving groups other than African Americans. In the first of the two cases, an Iraqi American professor asserted that he had been denied tenure because of his Arab origins; in the second, a Jewish congregation brought suit for damages in response to the defacement of its synagogue with derogatory symbols. The Supreme Court ruled unanimously that, in effect, any member of an ethnic minority might sue under federal prohibitions against discrimination. These decisions paved the way for almost all racial and ethnic groups to invoke the Civil Rights Act of 1964 (Taylor 1987).

A particularly insulting form of discrimination seemed finally to be on its way out in the late 1980s. Many social clubs had limitations that forbade membership to minorities, Jews, and women. For years, exclusive clubs argued that they were merely selecting friends, but, in fact, a principal function of these clubs is as a forum to transact business. Denial of membership meant more than the inability to attend a luncheon; it also seemed to exclude certain groups from part of the marketplace. In 1988, the Supreme Court ruled unanimously in *New York State Clubs Association v. City of New York* that states and cities might ban sex discrimination by large private clubs where business lunches and similar activities take place. Although the ruling does not apply to all clubs and leaves the issue

A setback in antidiscrimination lawsuits came when the Supreme Court told Lilly Ledbetter, in effect, that she was "too late." Ledbetter had been a supervisor for many years at the Gadsden, Alabama, Goodyear Tire Rubber plant when she realized that she was being paid $6,500 less per year than the lowest-paid male supervisor. The Court ruled that she must sue within 180 days of the initial discriminatory paycheck even though it had taken years before she even knew of the differential payment. Congress later enacted legislation eliminating the 180-day restriction.

of racial and ethnic barriers unresolved, it did chip away at the arbitrary exclusiveness of private groups (Steinhauer 2006; Taylor 1988).

Memberships and restrictive organizations remain perfectly legal. The rise to national attention of professional golfer Tiger Woods, of mixed Native American, African, and Asian ancestry, made the public aware that he would be prohibited from playing at a minimum of 23 golf courses by virtue of race. In 2002, women's groups tried unsuccessfully to have the golf champion speak out because the Master's and British Open were played on courses closed to women as members. Ten years later, the Augusta National Golf Club, home of the Masters, opened its membership to women (Martin, Dawsey, and McKay 2012; Scott 2003; Sherwood 2010).

Proving discrimination, even as outlined for generations in legislation, continues to be difficult. In the 2007 *Ledbetter v. Goodyear Tire and Rubber Co.* ruling, the Supreme Court affirmed that victims had to file a formal complaint within 180 days of the alleged discrimination. This set aside thousands of cases where employees learned their initial pay was lower to comparably employed White or male workers only after they had been in a job for years. Given the usual secrecy in workplaces around salaries, it would have made it difficult for potential cases of pay disparity to be effectively advanced. Two years later, Congress enacted the Lilly Ledbetter Fair Pay Act, which gives victims more time to file a lawsuit.

The inability of the Civil Rights Act, similar legislation, and court decisions to end discrimination does not result entirely from poor financial and political support, although it does play a role. The number of federal employees assigned to investigate and prosecute bias cases is insufficient. Many discriminatory practices, such as those described as institutional discrimination, are seldom subject to legal action.

Wealth Inequality: Discrimination's Legacy

3-5 Illustrate how wealth inequality is discrimination's legacy.

Discrimination that has occurred in the past carries into the present and future. African American and other minority groups have had less opportunity to accumulate assets such as homes, land, and savings that can insulate them, and later their children, from economic setbacks.

Wealth is a more inclusive term than income and encompasses all of a person's material assets, including land, stocks, and other types of property. Wealth allows one to live better; even modest assets provide insurance against the effects of job layoffs, natural disasters, and long-term illness, and they afford individuals much better interest rates when they need to borrow money. Wealth allows children to graduate from college with little or no debt. This reminds us that for many people, wealth is not always related to assets but also can be measured by indebtedness.

Studies document that the disparities in income we have seen are even greater when wealth is considered. In 2010, only 6 percent of homebuyers were African Americans and another 6 percent Latino. This is, unfortunately, to be expected, because if individuals experience lower incomes throughout their lives, they are less likely to be able to put anything aside for a down payment. They are more likely to have to pay for today's expenses rather than save for their future or their children's future.

In the "Research Focus," we consider findings regarding the relative assets among White, Black, and Latino Americans.

Research Focus

The Unequal Wealth Distribution

There is widespread consensus that African Americans typically have fewer assets and other wealth than Whites. However, recent research suggests that the gap is widening.

Using government data, a team of researchers at Brandeis University found that over two decades, the difference in wealth (excluding homes) grew from $20,000 less for the typical Black household to $95,000 less, as shown in Figure 3.5. This growing gap is the result of not only long-term economic effects but also recent policy changes such as lowering taxes on investment income and inheritances that benefit the more affluent, who are more likely to be White.

While the wealth gap has grown, so has debt. As indicated in Figure 3.6, among the least wealthy—the bottom 10 percent—the African American typically is $3,600 in debt, while the least wealthy White families are able to average $100 to the good. Other researchers have confirmed these findings and show further that the recession of the last few years has made the gaps even greater. A key to most people's wealth is home ownership and there is a long-standing fundamental gap in home ownership between Whites and minorities. The recent disaster in home loans has led many people to lose their homes—the most significant asset for most families—the proportion of Black homeowners who lost homes through foreclosure or bankruptcy is much higher than among White families.

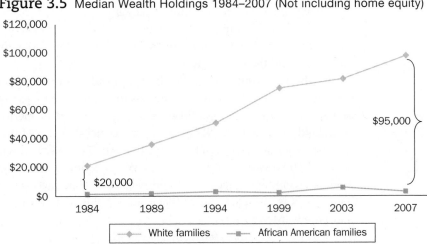

Figure 3.5 Median Wealth Holdings 1984–2007 (Not including home equity)

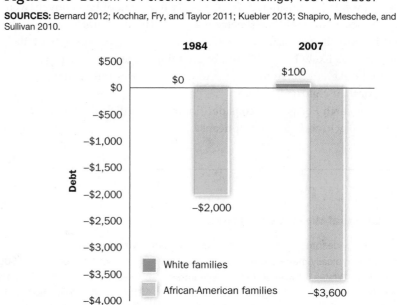

Figure 3.6 Bottom 10 Percent of Wealth Holdings, 1984 and 2007

SOURCES: Bernard 2012; Kochhar, Fry, and Taylor 2011; Kuebler 2013; Shapiro, Meschede, and Sullivan 2010.

The wealth gap continues. The economic slowdown of 2007 through 2009 has only increased the disparity between White households as a group and Black and Latino households. While the pace of wealth accumulation has varied, economists declared in 2013 that wealth disparity has increased steadily for 27 years. It is now approaching three decades of increased wealth of Whites compared to other households.

It is little wonder then that White children are more likely to surpass their parents' income than Black children. Furthermore, White children are more likely to move up the economic social class ladder than are Black children, who also are more likely to fall back in absolute terms. As adults, well-off Black Americans are less likely to have acquired knowledge from their parents about how to invest wisely and more likely will make "safe" economic decisions for the future of themselves and their children.

Wealth is not just money in the bank, but insurance against joblessness, homelessness, and ill health. On the positive side, wealth accumulation serves as a springboard to the middle class or higher. African American and Latinos households are much less likely to anticipate such a positive future.

A close analysis of wealth shows that African American families typically have $95,000 less in wealth than their White counterparts, even when households are comparably educated and employed. The median wealth of White households is 20 times that of Black households and 18 times that of Latino households (McKernan et al. 2013).

Environmental Justice

3-6 Discuss environmental justice.

Discrimination takes many forms and is not necessarily apparent, even when its impact can be far reaching. Take the example of Old Smokey, a massive incinerator shut down in 1970 in Miami after operating for 45 years in the segregated area that for a generation was cut out from public water and sewage systems leaving residents to rely on wells and outhouses. While older residents of the West Grove remember well the soiled laundry from the old incinerator days, recent revelations show a hazardous legacy.

Soil samples in the neighborhood reveal contamination from carcinogens like arsenic and heavy metals. The findings only became public in 2013 even though city officials knew two years earlier that a firefighting facility in the area had detected the dangerous levels. The environmental impact is now being closely examined given a cluster of cancer cases detected in West Grove (Madigan 2013).

The conflict perspective sees the case of the Miami neighborhood of West Grove as one in which pollution harms minority groups disproportionately. **Environmental justice** refers to the efforts to ensure that hazardous substances are controlled so that all communities receive protection regardless of race or socioeconomic circumstance. After the Environmental Protection Agency and other organizations documented discrimination in the location of hazardous waste sites, an executive order was issued in 1994 that requires all federal agencies to ensure that low-income and minority communities have access to better information about their environment and have an opportunity to participate in shaping government policies that affect their communities' health. Initial efforts

to implement the policy have met widespread opposition, including criticism from some proponents of economic development who argue that the guidelines unnecessarily delay or altogether block locating new industrial sites.

Low-income communities and areas with significant minority populations are more likely to be adjacent to waste sites, landfills, incinerators, and polluting factories than are affluent White communities. Studies in California show the higher probability that people of color live closer to sources of air pollution. Another study concluded that grade schools in Florida nearer to environmental hazards are disproportionately Black or Latino. People of color jeopardized by environmental problems also lack the resources and political muscle to do something about it (Pastor, Morello-Frosch, and Saad 2005; Pellow and Brehm 2013; Pellow and Brulle 2007; Stretesky and Lynch 2002).

Issues of environmental justice are not limited to metropolitan areas. Another continuing problem is abuse of Native American reservation land. Many American Indian leaders are concerned that tribal lands are too often regarded as toxic waste dumping grounds that go to the highest bidder. On the other hand, the economic devastation faced by some tribes in isolated areas has led one tribe in Utah to seek out becoming a depot for discarded nuclear waste (Jefferies 2007).

As with other aspects of discrimination, experts disagree. There is controversy within the scientific community over the potential hazards, and there is even some opposition within the subordinate communities being affected. This complexity of the issues in terms of social class and race is apparent; as some observers question the wisdom of an executive order that may slow economic development coming to areas in dire need of employment opportunities. On the other hand, some observers counter that such businesses typically employ only a few unskilled workers and make the environment less livable for those left behind. Despite such varying viewpoints, environmental justice is an excellent example of resistance and change in the 1990s that the civil rights workers of the 1950s could not have foreseen.

Affirmative Action

3-7   Explain affirmative action.

Affirmative action is the positive effort to recruit subordinate-group members, including women, for jobs, promotions, and educational opportunities. The phrase *affirmative action* first appeared in an executive order issued by President John F. Kennedy in 1961. The order called for contractors to "take affirmative action to ensure that applicants are employed, and that employees are treated during employment, without regard to their race, creed, color, or national origin." However, at that time, no enforcement procedures were specified. Six years later, the order was amended to prohibit discrimination on the basis of sex, but affirmative action was still defined vaguely.

Today, affirmative action has become a catchall term for racial preference programs and goals. It also has become a lightning rod for opposition to any programs that suggest special consideration of women or racial minorities.

Affirmative Action Explained

Affirmative action has been viewed as an important tool for reducing institutional discrimination. Whereas previous efforts were aimed at eliminating individual acts of discrimination, federal measures under the heading of affirmative action have been aimed at procedures that deny equal opportunities, even if they are not intended to be overtly discriminatory. This policy has been implemented to deal with both current discrimination and past discrimination, outlined earlier in this chapter.

Affirmative action has been aimed at institutional discrimination in areas such as the following:

- Height and weight requirements that are unnecessarily geared to the physical proportions of White men without regard to the actual characteristics needed to perform the job and that therefore exclude women and some minorities.
- Seniority rules, when applied to jobs historically held only by White men, that make more recently hired minorities and females more subject to layoff—the "last hired, first fired" employee—and less eligible for advancement.
- Nepotism-based membership policies of some unions that exclude those who are not relatives of members who, because of past employment practices, are usually White.
- Restrictive employment leave policies, coupled with prohibitions on part-time work or denials of fringe benefits to part-time workers, that make it difficult for the heads of single-parent families, most of whom are women, to get and keep jobs and also meet the needs of their families.
- Rules requiring that only English be spoken at the workplace, even when not a business necessity, which result in discriminatory employment practices toward people whose primary language is not English.
- Standardized academic tests or criteria geared to the cultural and educational norms of middle-class or White men when these are not relevant predictors of successful job performance.
- Preferences shown by law and medical schools in admitting children of wealthy and influential alumni, nearly all of whom are White.
- Credit policies of banks and lending institutions that prevent granting mortgages and loans in minority neighborhoods or that prevent granting credit to married women and others who have previously been denied the opportunity to build good credit histories in their own names.

Employers also have been cautioned against asking leading questions in interviews, for example, "Did you know you would be the first Black to supervise all Whites in that factory?" or "Does your husband mind your working on weekends?" Furthermore, the lack of minority-group or female employees may in itself represent evidence for a case of unlawful exclusion (Commission on Civil Rights 1981; see also Bohmer and Oka 2007).

The Legal Debate

How far can an employer go in encouraging women and minorities to apply for a job before it becomes unlawful discrimination against White men? Since the late 1970s, several bitterly debated cases on this difficult aspect of affirmative action have reached the U.S. Supreme Court. The most significant cases are summarized in Table 3.2.

In the 1978 *Bakke* case (*Regents of the University of California v. Bakke*), by a narrow 5–4 vote, the Court ordered the medical school of the University of California at Davis to admit Allan Bakke, a qualified White engineer who had originally been denied admission solely on the basis of his race. The justices ruled that the school had violated Bakke's constitutional rights by establishing a fixed quota system for minority students. However, the Court added that it was constitutional for universities to adopt flexible admission programs that use race as one factor in making decisions.

Colleges and universities responded with new policies designed to meet the *Bakke* ruling while broadening opportunities for traditionally underrepresented minority students. The Supreme Court heard arguments in *Fisher v. University of Texas at Austin* arguing that a White woman, Abigail Fisher, missed out on automatic admission under a Texas provision that extended admissions to the top 10 percent of a high school graduating class. While she was not in the top tenth, she contended that non-Whites who did not have comparable academic preparation were admitted and that the top 10 percent provision leaves any further racial consideration unnecessary. In 2013, the Court set aside a lower court's decision upholding the admissions policy arguing that the university must make a stronger case for race-based admissions policies. The ruling did not have any direct impact on any other institution's policies although other schools probably would re-examine their procedures in light of the *Fisher* decision. Given the various legal actions, further challenges to affirmative action can be expected.

So what has happened to minority enrolment? Since the African American and Latino college-age population is increasing, it makes analysis difficult. However, in states such as California, Florida, Michigan, and Texas, which have been barred from using race explicitly in admissions, Black and Latino enrolment has dropped. Sometimes pre-ban levels have begun to be approached after much maneuvering with new criteria but often these none-race-specific criteria have been called into question by opponents to affirmative action as well (Hoover 2013).

Table 3.2 Key Decisions on Affirmative Action

In a series of split and often very close decisions, the Supreme Court has expressed a variety of reservations in specific situations.

Year	Favorable (+) or Unfavorable (–) to Policy	Case	Vote	Ruling
1971	+	Griggs v. Duke Power Co.	9–0	Private employers must provide a remedy where minorities were denied opportunities, even if unintentional.
1978	–	Regents of the University of California v. Bakke	5–4	Prohibited holding a specific number of places for minorities in college admissions.
1979	+	United Steelworkers of America v. Weber	5–2	Okay for union to favor minorities in special training programs.
1984	–	Firefighters Local Union No. 1784 (Memphis, TN) v. Stotts	6–1	Seniority means recently hired minorities may be laid off first in staff reductions.
1986	+	International Association of Firefighters v. City of Cleveland	6–3	May promote minorities over more-senior Whites.
1986	+	New York City v. Sheet Metal	5–4	Approved specific quota of minority workers for union.
1987	+	United States v. Paradise	5–4	Endorsed quotas for promotions of state troopers.
1987	+	Johnson v. Transportation Agency, Santa Clara, CA	6–3	Approved preference in hiring for minorities and women over better-qualified men and Whites.
1989	–	Richmond v. Croson Company	6–3	Ruled a 30 percent set-aside program for minority contractors unconstitutional.
1989	–	Martin v. Wilks	5–4	Ruled Whites may bring reverse discrimination claims against Court-approved affirmative action plans.
1990	+	Metro Broadcasting v. FCC	5–4	Supported federal programs aimed at increasing minority ownership of broadcast licenses.
1995	–	Adarand Constructors Inc. v. Peña	5–4	Benefits based on race are constitutional only if narrowly defined to accomplish a compelling interest.
1996	–	Texas v. Hopwood	*	Let stand a lower court decision covering Louisiana, Mississippi, and Texas that race could not be used in college admissions.
2003	+	Grutter v. Bollinger	5–4	Race can be a limited factor in admissions at the University of Michigan Law School.
2003	–	Gratz v. Bollinger	6–3	Cannot use a strict formula awarding advantage based on race for admissions to the University of Michigan.
2009	–	Ricci v. DeStefano	5–4	May not disregard a promotion test because Blacks failed to qualify for advancement.
2013	–	Davis v. University of Texas at Austin	7–1	The college must show compelling evidence that racial preferences are justified as one of the admissions criteria.

*U.S. Court of Appeals Fifth Circuit decision.

Has affirmative action actually helped alleviate employment inequality on the basis of race and gender? This question is difficult to answer, given the complexity of the labor market and the fact that other anti-discrimination measures are in place, but it does appear that affirmative action has had a significant impact in the sectors where it has been applied. Sociologist Barbara Reskin (2012) reviewed available studies looking at workforce composition in terms of race and gender in light of affirmative action policies. She found that gains in minority employment could be attributed to affirmative action policies. This includes firms mandated to follow affirmative action guidelines and those that took them on voluntarily. There is also evidence that some earnings gains can be attributed to affirmative action. Economists M. V. Lee Badgett and Heidi Hartmann (1995), reviewing 26 other research studies, came to similar conclusions: Affirmative action and other federal compliance programs have had a modest impact, but it is difficult to assess, given larger economic changes such as recessions or the rapid increase in women in the paid labor force.

Reverse Discrimination

3-8 Analyze reverse discrimination.

Although researchers debated the merit of affirmative action, the public—particularly Whites but also some affluent African Americans and Hispanics—questioned the wisdom of the program. Particularly strident were the charges of reverse discrimination: that government actions cause better-qualified White men to be bypassed in favor of women and minority men. **Reverse discrimination** is an emotional term, because it conjures up the notion that somehow women and minorities will subject White men in the United States to the same treatment received by minorities during the last three centuries. Such cases are not unknown, but they are uncommon.

Does affirmative action represent an overdue just solution to a centuries-old problem or an undeserved outright reward for the current generation?

Increasingly, critics of affirmative action call for color-blind policies that would end affirmative action and, they argue, allow all people to be judged fairly. However, will that end institutional practices that favored Whites? For example, according to the latest data, 40 percent of applicants who are children of Harvard's alumni, who are almost all White, are admitted to the university, compared to 11 percent of nonalumni children.

By contrast, at the competitive California Institute of Technology, which specifically does not use legacy preferences, only 1.5 percent of students are children of alumni. Ironically, studies show that students who are children of alumni are far more likely than either minority students or athletes to run into academic trouble (Kahlenberg 2010; Massey and Mooney 2007; Pincus 2003, 2008).

Is it possible to have color-blind policies prevail in the United States in the twenty-first century? Supporters of affirmative action contend that as long as businesses rely on informal social networks, personal recommendations, and family ties, White men will have a distinct advantage built on generations of being in positions of power. Furthermore, an end to affirmative action should also mean an end to the many programs that give advantages to certain businesses, homeowners, veterans, farmers, and others. Most of these preference holders are White.

Consequently, by the 1990s and into the twenty-first century, affirmative action had emerged as an increasingly important issue in state and national political campaigns. As noted earlier, in 2003, the Supreme Court reviewed the admission policies at the University of Michigan, which may favor racial minorities (see Table 3.2). In 2006, Michigan citizens, by a 58 percent margin, voted to restrict all their state universities from using affirmative action in their admissions policies. Generally, discussions have focused on the use of quotas in hiring practices. Supporters of affirmative action argue that hiring goals establish "floors" for minority inclusion but do not exclude truly qualified candidates from any group. Opponents insist that these "targets" are, in fact, quotas that lead to reverse discrimination (Lewin 2006; Mack 1996).

The State of California, in particular, was a battleground for this controversial issue. The California Civil Rights Initiative (Proposition 209) was placed on the ballot in 1996 as a referendum to amend the state constitution and prohibit any programs that give preference to women and minorities for college admission, employment, promotion, or government contracts. Overall, 54 percent of the voters backed the state proposition.

In 2009, the Supreme Court ruled 5–4 in the *Ricci v. DeStefano* case in favor of White firefighters. Many observers felt this outcome recognized reverse racism. In 2003, in New Haven, Connecticut, firefighters took an examination to identify possible promotions but no African Americans taking the test qualified to be eligible for advancement. Rather than select all White (including one Hispanic) firefighters, the city threw out the test results. The qualifying firefighters sued that they were victims of discrimination and the Court eventually concurred.

The decision was limited in its applications because the justices seemed to say that possible test bias could be considered in the design stage of a test, but others saw it as "impeding" the use of race in hiring even advantaged minorities.

The Glass Ceiling

3-9 **Put into your own words the glass ceiling.**

We have discussed racial and ethnic groups primarily as if they have uniformly failed to keep pace with Whites. Although this notion is accurate, tens of thousands of people of color have matched and even exceeded Whites in terms of income. For example, in 2012, more than 395,000 Black households and over 541,000 Hispanic households earned more than $200,000. What can we say about financially better-off members of subordinate groups in the United States (DeNavas-Walt, Proctor, and Smith 2013 Table HINC-03)?

Prejudice does not necessarily end with wealth. Black newspaper columnist De Wayne Wickham (1993) wrote of the subtle racism he had experienced. He heard a White clerk in a supermarket ask a White customer whether she knew the price of an item the computer would not scan; when the problem occurred while the clerk was ringing up Wickham's groceries, she called for a price check. Affluent subordinate-group members routinely report being blocked as they move toward the first-class section aboard airplanes or seek service in upscale stores. Another journalist, Ellis Cose (1993), has called these insults the soul-destroying slights to affluent minorities that lead to the "rage of a privileged class."

Discrimination persists for even educated and qualified people from the best family backgrounds. As subordinate-group members are able to compete successfully, they sometimes encounter attitudinal or organizational bias that prevents them from reaching their full potential. They have confronted what has come to be called the **glass ceiling**. This refers to the barrier that blocks the promotion of a qualified worker because of gender or minority membership (see Figure 3.7). Often, people entering nontraditional areas of employment become marginalized and are made to feel uncomfortable, much like the situation of immigrants who feel like they are part of two cultures, as we discussed in Chapter 1.

Reasons for glass ceilings are as many as the occurrences. It may be that one Black or one woman vice president is regarded as enough, so the second potential candidate faces a block to movement up through management. Decision makers may be concerned that their clientele will not trust them if they have too many people of color or may worry that a talented woman could become overwhelmed with her duties as a mother and wife and thus perform poorly in the workplace.

Concern about women and minorities climbing a broken ladder led to the formation in 1991 of the Glass Ceiling Commission, with the U.S. secretary of

Figure 3.7 Glass Ceilings and Glass Walls

Women and minority men are moving up in corporations but encounter glass ceilings that block entry to top positions. In addition, they face glass walls that block lateral moves to areas from which executives are promoted. These barriers contribute to women and minority men not moving into the ultimate decision-making positions in the nation's corporate giants.

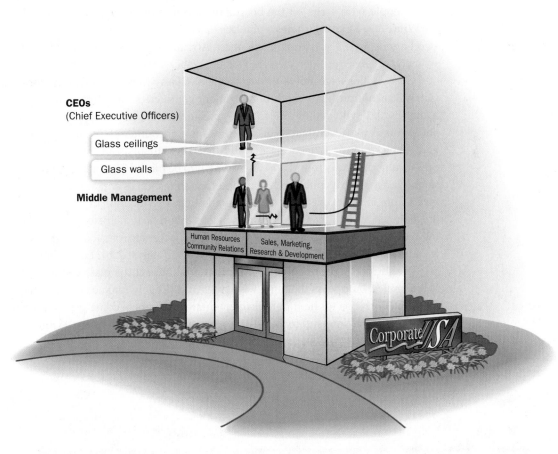

labor chairing the 21-member group. Initially, it regarded the following as some of the glass ceiling barriers:

- Lack of management commitment to establishing systems, policies, and practices for achieving workplace diversity and upward mobility
- Pay inequities for work of equal or comparable value
- Sex-, race-, and ethnicity-based stereotyping and harassment
- Unfair recruitment practices
- Lack of family-friendly workplace policies
- "Parent-track" policies that discourage parental leave policies
- Limited opportunities for advancement to decision-making positions

This significant underrepresentation of women and minority males in managerial positions results in large part from the presence of glass ceilings. Sociologist Max Weber wrote more than a century ago that the privileged class monopolizes the purchase of high-priced consumer goods and wields the power to grant or withhold opportunity from others. To grasp just how White and male the membership of this elite group is, consider the following: 71 percent of the 1,219 people who serve on the boards of directors of *Fortune* 100 corporations are White non-Hispanic males. For every 82 White men on these boards, there are two Latinos, two Asian Americans, three African Americans, and eleven White women (Alliance for Board Diversity 2009; Weber 1947).

Glass ceilings are not the only barriers. Glass walls also block minorities. Catalyst, a nonprofit research organization, conducted interviews in 1992 and again in 2001 with senior and middle managers from larger corporations. The study found that even before glass ceilings are encountered, women and racial and ethnic minorities face **glass walls** that keep them from moving laterally. Specifically, the study found that women tend to be placed in staff or support positions in areas such as public relations and human resources and are often directed away from jobs in core areas such as marketing, production, and sales. Women are assigned to and, therefore, trapped in jobs that reflect their stereotypical helping nature and encounter glass walls that cut off access to jobs that might lead to broader experience and advancement (Bjerk 2008; Catalyst 2001; Lopez 1992).

Researchers have documented a differential impact the glass ceiling has on White males. It appears that men who enter traditionally female occupations are more likely to rise to the top. Male elementary teachers become principals, and male nurses become supervisors. The **glass escalator** refers to the White male

Spectrum of Intergroup Relations

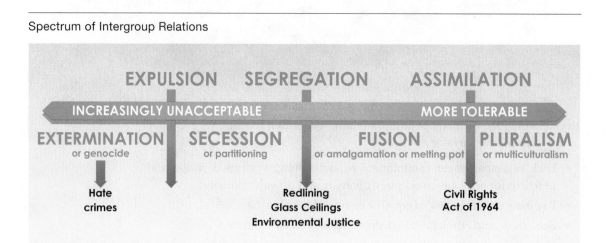

advantage experienced in occupations dominated by women. Whereas females may become tokens when they enter traditionally male occupations, men are more likely to be advantaged when they move out of sex-typical jobs. In summary, women and minority men confront a glass ceiling that limits upward mobility and glass walls that reduce their ability to move into fast-track jobs leading to the highest reaches of the corporate executive suite. Meanwhile, White men who do choose to enter female-dominated occupations are often rewarded with promotions and positions of responsibility coveted by their fellow female workers (Budig 2002; Cognard-Black 2004).

Conclusion

What is it like to experience discrimination over and over again? Not just an occasional slight or a possible instance of discrimination but constantly seeing yourself dealt with differently because of race, ethnicity, or gender? W. E. B. Du Bois (1903: 9) wrote in his classic *The Souls of Black Folks*, "To be a poor man is hard, but to be a poor race in a land of dollars is the very bottom of hardships." Not all members of racial and ethnic minorities, much less all women, are poor, of course, but virtually all can recall instances where they were treated as second-class citizens, not necessarily by White men, but even by members of their own group or by other women.

One job advertisement read "African Americans and Arabians tend to clash with me so that won't work out." Sounds like it was from your grandfather's era? Actually, it appeared on the popular Craigslist website in 2006 and is just one example of how explicit discrimination thrives even in the digital age. Similar charges have been made concerning "no minorities" wording in housing advertisements. Courts have not held Craigslist responsible and accepted the website's argument that it cannot screen out all racism in online advertising. Nonetheless, Craigslist finally posted in 2012 a policy forbidding ads that violated state or federal laws ensuring equal access to housing (American Financial Resources 2012; Oliveri 2009).

Discrimination takes its toll, whether or not a person who is discriminated against is part of the informal economy or looking for a job on the Internet. Even members of minority groups who are not today overtly discriminated against continue to fall victim to past discrimination. We also have identified the costs of discrimination to members of the privileged group.

From the conflict perspective, it is not surprising to find the widespread presence of the informal economy proposed by the dual labor market model and even an underclass. Derrick Bell (1994), an African American law professor, has made the sobering assertion that "racism is permanent." He contends that the attitudes of dominant Whites prevail, and society is willing to advance programs on behalf of subordinate groups only when they coincide with needs as perceived by those Whites.

The surveys presented in Chapter 2 show gradual acceptance of the earliest efforts to eliminate discrimination, but that support is failing as color-blind racism takes hold, especially as it relates to affirmative action. Indeed, concerns about doing something about alleged reverse discrimination are as likely to be voiced as concerns about racial or gender discrimination or glass ceilings and glass walls.

Institutional discrimination remains a formidable challenge in the United States. Attempts to reduce discrimination by attacking institutional discrimination have met with staunch resistance. Partly as a result of this outcry from some of the public, especially White Americans, the federal government gradually deemphasized its affirmative action efforts, beginning in the 1980s and continuing into the twenty-first century. Most of the material in this chapter has been about racial groups, especially Black and White Americans. It would be easy to see intergroup hostility as a racial phenomenon, but that would be incorrect. Throughout the history of the United States, relations between some White groups have been characterized by resentment and violence. The next two chapters examine the ongoing legacy of immigration and the nature and relations of White ethnic groups.

Summary

1. Discrimination is likely to result in feeling of relative deprivation, not necessarily absolute deprivation.
2. Hate crimes highlight hostility that culminates in a criminal offense.
3. Institutional discrimination results from the normal operations of a society.
4. Discrimination in hiring is documented through job-testing experiments.
5. Inequality continues to be apparent in the analysis of annual incomes, controlling for the amount of education attained and wealth, and even in the absence of environmental justice.

6. Presidential executive orders, legislative acts, and judicial decisions have all played a part in reducing discrimination.
7. For over 60 years, affirmative action as a remedy to inequality has been a hotly contested issue, with its critics contending it amounts to reverse discrimination.
8. Upwardly mobile professional women and minority males may encounter a glass ceiling and be thwarted in their efforts by glass walls to become more attractive candidates for advancement.

Key Terms

absolute deprivation, p. 79
affirmative action, p. 96
discrimination, p. 78
environmental justice, p. 95
glass ceiling, p. 102
glass escalator, p. 104

glass wall, p. 104
hate crime, p. 79
income, p. 86
institutional discrimination, p. 84
redlining, p. 90

relative deprivation, p. 79
reverse discrimination, p. 100
wealth, p. 86

Review Questions

1. Why might people feel disadvantaged even though their incomes are rising and their housing circumstances have improved?

2. How do hate crimes differ from other types of felony crimes?

3. Why does institutional discrimination sometimes seem less objectionable than individual discrimination?

4. In what way might national income data point to discrimination?

5. What is wealth disparity among racial and ethnic groups and what is the trend in this disparity?

6. Explain how the concept of environmental justice relates to understanding racial and ethnic groups.

7. Why are questions raised about affirmative action even though inequality persists?

8. Describe what is meant by reverse discrimination.

9. Distinguish among glass ceilings, glass walls, and glass escalators. How do they differ from more obvious forms of discrimination in employment?

Critical Thinking

1. What are the purposes of hate crimes? Do you think they serve those purposes?

2. Discrimination can take many forms. Select a case of discrimination that you think almost everyone would agree is wrong. Then describe another incident in which the alleged discrimination was subtler. Who is likely to condemn and who is likely to overlook such situations?

3. Discuss the social implications that wealth disparity between racial and ethnic groups has for social mobility.

4. Analyze what is meant by "environmental justice can be understood in terms of institutional discrimination."

5. Resistance is a continuing theme of intergroup race relations. Discrimination implies the oppression of a group, but how can discrimination also unify the oppressed group to resist such unequal treatment? How can acceptance, or integration, for example, weaken the sense of solidarity within a group?

6. Voluntary associations such as the National Association for the Advancement of Colored People (NAACP) and government units such as the courts have been important vehicles for bringing about a measure of social justice. In what ways can the private sector—corporations and businesses—also work to bring about an end to discrimination?

Chapter 4
Immigration

PATTERNS OF IMMIGRATION TO THE UNITED STATES

   4-1 Summarize the general patterns of immigration to the United States.

EARLY IMMIGRATION

   4-2 Characterize how immigration was controlled in the nineteenth century.

RESTRICTIONIST SENTIMENT INCREASES

   4-3 Describe how restrictionist sentiment increased in the twentieth century.

CONTEMPORARY SOCIAL CONCERNS

4-4 Identify the concerns about immigration policy today.

ILLEGAL IMMIGRATION

4-5 Discuss the scope of and issues related to illegal immigration.

PATH TO CITIZENSHIP: NATURALIZATION

4-6 Outline the process of naturalization.

WOMEN AND IMMIGRATION

4-7 Understand the special role of women in immigration.

THE GLOBAL ECONOMY AND IMMIGRATION

4-8 Illustrate the relationship of globalization with respect to immigrants.

THE ENVIRONMENT AND IMMIGRATION

4-9 Interpret how immigration is related to the environment.

REFUGEES

4-10 Restate the United States' policies toward refugees.

The story of Alfredo the immigrant is not typical, but then every immigrant who comes to the United States has a unique story. Alfredo Quiñoes-Hinojosa came to the United States as an illegal immigrant in 1987 at the age of nineteen. Caught the first time, he succeeded the second time on the same day. (The majority of immigrants apprehended at the border have been caught previously.) One of six children, Alfredo had frequently come across the border from his native Mexico to work as a farmhand pulling weeds in the fields to help support his five younger brothers and sisters. Eventually, he settled with relatives in Stockton, California. He tried other jobs: sweeping floors, shoeing horses, and soldering metal. He learned English and eventually applied and was accepted to the local San Joaquin Delta College.

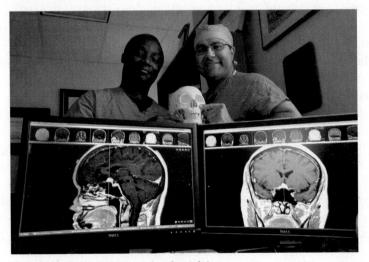

Dr. Alfredo Quiñoes-Hinojosa (on the right)

His next big step was when he accepted an offer to study at the University of California at Berkeley. Alfredo dreamed of becoming a doctor, and nothing was going to stop him.

After graduating from Berkeley, Alfredo was accepted to Harvard Medical School, where he graduated with honors, but he also became a citizen along the way.

While Quĩnoes-Hinojosa, and later his parents, had entered the United States as an undocumented worker, under an amnesty provision passed under President Reagan, he was able to secure a green card legally allowing him to work and continue his education. In 1997, he became a U.S. citizen.

Today, married with three children, he heads the Brain Tumor Surgery Program at Johns Hopkins Medical Center and is actively engaged in research as to the causes of brain cancer. It has not been easy. His hands now perform brain surgery, but they bear the scars of farmwork. He endured prejudice: People strongly suggested he change his name to something easier to pronounce. While reluctant to speak out in the immigration debate, he recognizes that many people today want to exclude from the United States people exactly like he was fewer than 30 years ago (Cave 2011; Gupta 2012; Quĩnoes-Hinojosa with Rivas 2011; Ramos 2010).

The world is now a global network. The core and periphery countries, described in world systems theory (see page 27 in Chapter 1), link not only commercial goods but also families and workers across political borders. Social forces that cause people to emigrate are complex. The most important have been economic, such as the case of Alfredo Quĩnoes-Hinojosa: financial failure in the old country and expectations of higher incomes and standards of living in the new land. Other factors include dislike of new political regimes in their native lands, being victims of racial or religious bigotry, and a desire to reunite families. All these factors push people from their homelands and pull them to other nations such as the United States. Immigration into the United States, in particular, has been facilitated by cheap ocean transportation and by other countries' removal of restrictions on emigration.

Scholars of immigration often point to *push* and *pull factors*. For example, economic difficulties, religious or ethnic persecution, and political unrest may push individuals from their homelands. Immigration to a particular nation, the pull factors, may be a result of perceptions of a better life ahead or a desire to join a community of their fellow nationals already established abroad.

A potent factor contributing to immigration anywhere in the world is chain immigration. **Chain immigration** refers to an immigrant who sponsors several other immigrants who, on their arrival, may sponsor still more. Laws that favor people desiring to enter a given country who already have relatives there or someone who can vouch for them financially may facilitate this sponsorship. But probably the most important aspect of chain immigration is that immigrants anticipate knowing someone who can help them adjust to their new surroundings and find a new job, place to live, and even the kinds of foods that are familiar to them. Later in this chapter, we revisit the social impact of worldwide immigration.

Patterns of Immigration to the United States

4-1 Summarize the general patterns of immigration to the United States.

Immigration to the United States has three unmistakable patterns: (1) the number of immigrants has fluctuated dramatically over time largely because of government policy changes; (2) settlement has not been uniform across the country but centered in certain regions and cities; and (3) the immigrants' countries of origin have changed over time. First, we look at the historical picture of immigrant numbers.

Vast numbers of immigrants have come to the United States. Figure 4.1 indicates the high but fluctuating number of immigrants who arrived during every decade from the 1820s through the beginning of the twenty-first century. The United States received the largest number of legal immigrants during the first decade of the 1900s; that number likely will be surpassed in the first decade of

Figure 4.1 Legal Immigration to the United States, 1820–2020

SOURCE: Office of Immigration Statistics 2013 and author's estimates for projection out to 2020.

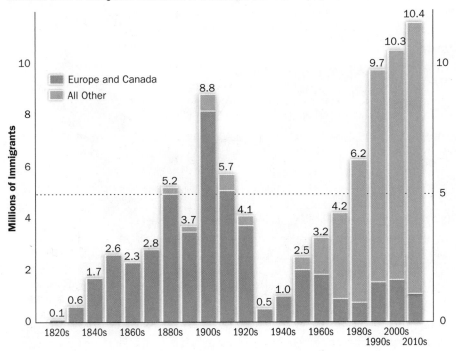

the twenty-first century. However, the country was much smaller in the period from 1900 through 1910, so the numerical impact was even greater then.

Immigrants to this country have not always received a friendly reception. Open bloodshed, restrictive laws, and the eventual return of almost one-third of immigrants and their children to their home countries attest to some Americans' uneasy feelings toward strangers who want to settle here. Generally surveys show immigration viewed negatively but with some ambivalence. Opinion polls in the United States beginning in 1965 through 2013 have never shown more than 23 percent of the public in favor of more immigration, and usually about 35 to 40 percent want less, but the trend over the last decade has been slowly moving to welcoming *more* immigrants. Nationally border enforcement remains a concern, but support for deporting illegal immigrants already here has declined (Jones and Saad 2013; Muste 2013).

Before considering the sweep of past immigration policies, let us consider today's immigrant population. About 13 percent of the nation's people are foreign-born—a level not reached since the 1920s. As recently as 1979, this proportion was just 4.7 percent. By global comparisons, the foreign-born population

Figure 4.2 Foreign-Born Population in the United States

SOURCE: Grieco et al. 2012: 4.

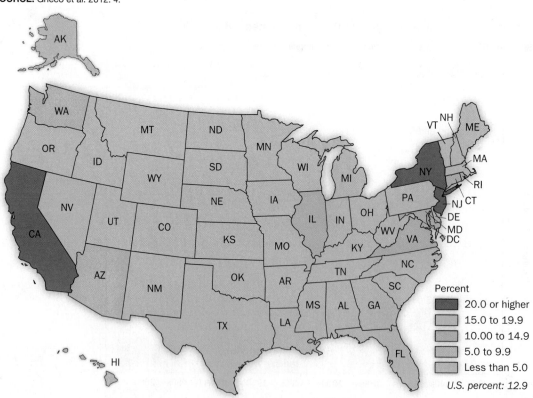

Percent
- 20.0 or higher
- 15.0 to 19.9
- 10.00 to 14.9
- 5.0 to 9.9
- Less than 5.0

U.S. percent: 12.9

in the United States is large but not unusual. Whereas most industrial countries have a foreign population of around 5 percent, Canada's foreign population is 19 percent and Australia's is 25 percent.

As noted earlier, immigrants have not settled evenly across the nation. As shown in the map in Figure 4.2, six states—California, New York, Texas, Florida, New Jersey, and Illinois—account for two-thirds of the nation's total foreign-born population but less than 40 percent of the nation's total population.

Cities in these states are the destinations of the foreign-born population. Almost half (43.3 percent) live in the central city of a metropolitan area, compared with about one-quarter (27 percent) of the nation's population. More than one-third of residents in the cities of Miami, Los Angeles, San Francisco, San Jose, and New York are now foreign-born.

The source countries of immigrants have changed. First, settlers came from Europe, then Latin America, and, now, increasingly, Asia. The majority of today's 38.5 million foreign-born people are from Latin America rather than Europe, as was the case through the 1950s. Primarily, they are from Central America and, more specifically, Mexico. By contrast, Europeans, who dominated the early settlement of the United States, now account for fewer than one in seven of the foreign-born today. The changing patterns of immigration have continued into the twenty-first century. Beginning in 2010, the annual immigration from Asia exceeded the level of annual immigration from Latin America for the first time (Grieco et al. 2012; Pew Social and Demographic Trends 2012; Semple 2012).

Early Immigration

4-2 **Characterize how immigration was controlled in the nineteenth century.**

Settlers, the first immigrants to the Western Hemisphere, soon followed the European explorers of North America. The Spanish founded St. Augustine, Florida, in 1565, and the English founded Jamestown, Virginia, in 1607. Protestants from England emerged from the colonial period as the dominant force numerically, politically, and socially. The English accounted for 60 percent of the 3 million White Americans in 1790. Although exact statistics are lacking for the early years of the United States, the English were soon outnumbered by other nationalities as the numbers of Scotch-Irish and Germans, in particular, swelled. However, the English colonists maintained their dominant position, as Chapter 5 examines.

Throughout American history, immigration policy has been politically controversial. The policies of the English king, George III, were criticized in the U.S. Declaration of Independence for obstructing immigration to the colonies. Toward the end of the nineteenth century, the American republic itself was criticized for enacting immigration restrictions. In the beginning, however, the country encouraged immigration. Legislation initially fixed the residence requirement for naturalization at five years, although briefly, under the Alien Act of 1798, it was 14 years, and so-called dangerous people could be expelled. Despite this brief harshness, immigration was unregulated through most of the 1800s, and naturalization was easily available. Until 1870, naturalization was limited to "free white persons" (Calavita 2007).

Although some people hold the mistaken belief that concern about immigration is something new, some people also assume that immigrants to the United States rarely reconsider their decision to come to a new country. Analysis of available records, beginning in the early 1900s, suggests that about 35 percent of all immigrants to the United States eventually emigrated back to their home country. The proportion varies, with the figures for some countries being much higher, but the overall pattern is clear: About one in three immigrants to this nation eventually choose to return home (Wyman 1993).

The relative absence of federal legislation from 1790 to 1881 does not mean that all new arrivals were welcomed. **Xenophobia** (the fear or hatred of strangers or foreigners) led naturally to **nativism** (beliefs and policies favoring native-born citizens over immigrants). Although the term *nativism* has largely been used to describe nineteenth-century sentiments, anti-immigration views and organized movements have continued into the twenty-first century. Political scientist Samuel P. Huntington (1993, 1996) articulated the continuing immigration as a "clash of civilizations" that could be remedied only by significantly reducing legal immigration, not to mention closing the border to illegal arrivals. His view, which enjoys support, is that the fundamental world conflicts of the new century are cultural in nature rather than ideological or even economic (Citrin et al. 2007; Schaefer 2008b).

The most dramatic outbreak of nativism in the nineteenth century was aimed at the Chinese. If any doubt remained by the mid-1800s that the United States could harmoniously accommodate all and was some sort of melting pot, debate on the Chinese Exclusion Act negatively ended that doubt.

The Anti-Chinese Movement

Before 1851, official records show that only 46 Chinese had immigrated to the United States. Over the next 30 years, more than 200,000 came to this country, lured by the discovery of gold and the opening of job opportunities in the West. Overcrowding, drought, and warfare in China also encouraged them to take a chance in the United States. Another important factor was improved oceanic transportation; it was cheaper to travel from Hong Kong to San Francisco than from Chicago to San Francisco. The frontier communities of the West, particularly in California, looked on the Chinese as a valuable resource to fill manual jobs. As early as 1854, so many Chinese wanted to emigrate that ships had difficulty handling the volume.

In the 1860s, railroad work provided the greatest demand for Chinese labor until the Union Pacific and Central Pacific railroads were joined at Promontory

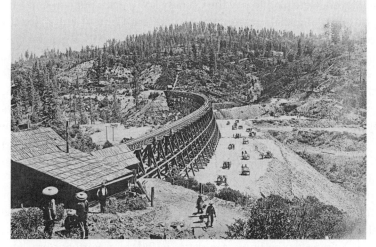

Chinese workers, such as these pictured in 1844, played a major role in building railroads in the West.

Summit, Utah, in 1869. The Union Pacific relied primarily on Irish laborers, but 90 percent of the Central Pacific's labor force was Chinese because Whites generally refused to do the backbreaking work over the Western terrain. Despite the contribution of the Chinese, White workers physically prevented them from attending the driving of the golden spike to mark the joining of the two railroads.

With the dangerous railroad work largely completed, people began to rethink the wisdom of encouraging Chinese to immigrate to do the work no one else would do. Reflecting their xenophobia, White settlers found the Chinese immigrants, their customs, and religion difficult to understand. Indeed, few people tried to understand these immigrants from Asia. Although they had had no firsthand contact with Chinese Americans, Easterners and legislators soon jumped on the anti-Chinese bandwagon as they read sensationalized accounts of the lifestyle of the new arrivals.

Even before the Chinese immigrated, stereotypes of them and their customs were prevalent. American traders returning from China, European diplomats, and Protestant missionaries consistently emphasized the exotic and sinister aspects of life in China. **Sinophobes**, people who fear anything associated with China, appealed to the racist theory developed during the slavery controversy that non-Europeans were subhuman. Americans also were becoming more conscious of biological inheritance and disease, so it was not hard to conjure up fears of alien genes and germs. The only real challenge the anti-Chinese movement faced was convincing people that the negative consequences of unrestricted Chinese immigration outweighed any possible economic gain. Earlier, racial prejudice was subordinated to industrial dependence on Chinese labor for the work that Whites shunned, but acceptance of the Chinese was short-lived. The fear of the "yellow peril" overwhelmed any desire to know more about Asian peoples and their customs (Takaki 1998).

Employers were glad to pay the Chinese low wages, but non-Chinese laborers began directing their resentment against the Chinese rather than against their compatriots' willingness to exploit the Chinese. Only a generation earlier, the same concerns were felt about the Irish, but with the Chinese, the hostility reached new heights because of another factor.

Although many arguments were voiced, racial fears motivated the anti-Chinese movement. Race was the critical issue. The labor market fears were largely unfounded, and most advocates of restrictions at that time knew that. There was no possibility of the Chinese immigrating in numbers that would match those of Europeans at that time, so it is difficult to find any explanation other than racism for their fears (Winant 1994).

From the sociological perspective of conflict theory, we can explain how the Chinese immigrants were welcomed only when their labor was necessary to fuel growth in the United States. When that labor was no longer necessary, the welcome mat for the immigrants was withdrawn. Furthermore, as conflict theorists point out, restrictions were not applied evenly: Americans focused on a specific nationality (the Chinese) to reduce the number of foreign workers in the nation. Because decision making at that time rested in the hands of the descendants of European immigrants, the steps taken were most likely to be directed against the least powerful: immigrants from China who, unlike Europeans seeking entry, had few allies among legislators and other policymakers.

In 1882, Congress enacted the Chinese Exclusion Act, which outlawed Chinese immigration for ten years. It also explicitly denied naturalization rights to the Chinese in the United States; that is, they were not allowed to become citizens. There was little debate in Congress, and discussion concentrated on how to best handle suspending Chinese immigration. No allowance was made for spouses and children to be reunited with their husbands and fathers in the United States. Only brief visits of Chinese government officials, teachers, tourists, and merchants were exempted.

The rest of the nineteenth century saw the remaining loopholes allowing Chinese immigration closed. Beginning in 1884, Chinese laborers could not enter the United States from any foreign place, a ban that also lasted ten years. Two years later, the Statue of Liberty was dedicated, with a poem by Emma Lazarus inscribed on its base. To the Chinese, the poem welcoming the tired, the poor, and the huddled masses must have seemed a hollow mockery.

In 1892, Congress extended the Exclusion Act for another ten years and added that Chinese laborers had to obtain certificates of residence within a year or face deportation. After the turn of the century, the Exclusion Act was extended again. With immigration restrictions, like many other laws, the ill effects last generations. Judy Chu, born of Chinese immigrants, was first elected to Congress in 2009 from suburban Los Angeles. A psychology professor and school board member before going to Washington, she was keenly aware of the toll that one of the most restrictive immigration laws ever passed in the United States had on Chinese Americans. In "Speaking Out," we hear the congresswoman's case for

Speaking Out

Chinese Exclusion Act of 1882

Judy Chu

A century ago, the Chinese came here in search of a better life; but they faced harsh conditions, particularly in the Halls of Congress. Congress passed numerous laws to restrict Chinese Americans, starting from the 1882 Chinese Exclusion Act, to stop the Chinese from immigrating, from becoming naturalized citizens, and from ever having the right to vote.

These were the only such laws to target a specific ethnic group. The Chinese were the only residents that had to carry papers on them at all times. They were often harassed and detained. If they couldn't produce the proper documents, authorities threw them into prison or out of the country, regardless of their citizenship status. Political cartoons and hateful banners... were hung in towns and cities and printed in papers. At that time of this hateful law, the Chinese were called racial slurs, were spat upon in the streets, and even brutally murdered.

Only after China became an ally of the United States in World War II was this law repealed in 1943, 60 years after its passage. Congress has never formally acknowledged it as incompatible with America's founding principles.

That is why, as the first Chinese American woman elected to Congress, and whose grandfather was a victim of this law, I stand on the very floor where the Chinese Exclusion Act was passed and announce that I have introduced a resolution calling for a formal acknowledgment and expression of regret for the Chinese exclusion laws.

When the exclusion laws were first introduced, there was a great deal of debate in Congress over their merits. The U.S. had just abolished slavery. The 14th and 15th Amendments had recently been ratified. Slavery had been defeated, and freedom seemed more certain. The national atmosphere led many in Congress to stand up against the discriminatory anti-Chinese laws. But over the years, those standing for justice almost all disappeared. By the time 1882 came around, Members of Congress were fighting over who deserved the most credit for getting the most discriminatory laws passed and standing against the "Mongolian horde."....

But there were a brave few, a small minority who fought hard against prejudice and principles of freedom. One such man was Senator George Frisbie Hoar, whose statue now stands proudly in the Capitol. He stood up to all of the Chinese exclusion laws and voted against each. He said in 1904 when the laws were made permanent, "I cannot agree with the principle that this legislation or any legislation on the subject rests. All races, all colors, all nationalities contain persons entitled to be recognized everywhere as equals of other men. I am bound to record my protest, if I stand alone."

And stand alone he did. The final vote against the Chinese in the Senate was 76–1. What Senator Hoar stood up for is what I am asking Congress to stand up for today: that all people, no matter the color of their skin, or the nation of origin, are the equals of every other man or woman.

America came to be what it is today through immigrants who came from all corners of the world. Chinese immigrants were amongst them. They sought a place to live that was founded upon liberty and equality. They came in search of the American Dream—that if you worked hard, you could build a good life. It is why my grandfather came to the United States.

But when the Chinese Exclusion Act was passed, the truths that this Nation holds as self-evident—that all are endowed with the inalienable rights of life, liberty and the pursuit of happiness—were discounted by the very ones elected to uphold them.

And so for a generation of our ancestors, like my grandfather, who were told for six decades by the U.S. government that the land of the free wasn't open to them, it is long past time that Congress officially and formally acknowledges these ugly laws that targeted Chinese immigrants, and express sincere regret for these actions.

With my resolution, Congress will acknowledge the injustice of the Chinese Exclusion Act, express regret for the lives it destroyed, and make sure that the prejudice that stained our Nation is never repeated again. And it will demonstrate that today is a different day and that today we stand side by side for a stronger America.

SOURCE: Chu 2011.

---

a resolution apologizing for the passage of the Chinese Exclusion Act. In 2012, Congress passed the resolution unanimously. This marked only the fourth official apology in the last 25 years—the other three were slavery, the internment of Japanese Americans during World War II, and mistreatment of native Hawaiians and the overthrow of their rule of the islands (Chu 2011; Nahm 2012).

Restrictionist Sentiment Increases

4-3   Describe how restrictionist sentiment increased in the twentieth century.

As Congress closed the door to Chinese immigration, the debate on restricting immigration turned in new directions. Prodded by growing anti-Japanese feelings, the United States entered into the so-called gentlemen's agreement, which was completed in 1908. Japan agreed to halt further immigration to the United States, and the United States agreed to end discrimination against the Japanese who had already arrived. The immigration ended, but anti-Japanese feelings continued. Americans were growing uneasy that the "new immigrants" would overwhelm the culture established by the "old immigrants." The earlier immigrants, if not Anglo-Saxon, were from similar groups such as the Scandinavians, the Swiss, and the French Huguenots. These people were more experienced in democratic political practices and had a greater affinity with the dominant Anglo-Saxon culture. By the end of the nineteenth century, however, more and more immigrants were neither English speaking nor Protestant and came from dramatically different cultures.

The National Origin System

Beginning in 1921, a series of measures was enacted that marked a new era in American immigration policy. Whatever the legal language, the measures were drawn up to block the growing immigration from Southern Europe (from Italy and Greece, for example) and also to block all Asian immigrants by establishing a zero quota for them.

ELLIS ISLAND
Although it was not opened until 1892, New York Harbor's Ellis Island—the country's first federal immigration facility—quickly became the symbol of all migrant streams to the United States. By the time it closed in late 1954, it had processed 17 million immigrants. Today, their descendants number over 100 million Americans.

To understand the effect of the national origin system on immigration, it is necessary to clarify the quota system. Quotas were deliberately weighted to favor immigration from Northern Europe. Because of the ethnic composition of the country in 1920, the quotas placed severe restrictions on immigration from the rest of Europe and other parts of the world. Immigration from the Western Hemisphere (i.e., Canada, Mexico, Central and South America, and the Caribbean) continued unrestricted. The quota for each nation was set at 3 percent of the number of people descended from each nationality recorded in the 1920 census. Once the statistical manipulations were completed, almost 70 percent of the quota for the Eastern Hemisphere went to just three countries: Great Britain, Ireland, and Germany.

The absurdities of the system soon became obvious, but it was nevertheless continued. British immigration had fallen sharply, so most of its quota of 65,000 went unfilled. However, the openings could not be transferred, even though countries such as Italy, with a quota of only 6,000, had 200,000 people who wanted to enter. However one rationalizes the purpose behind the act, the result was obvious: Any English person, regardless of skill and whether related to anyone already here, could enter the country more easily than, say, a Greek doctor whose children were American citizens. The quota for Greece was 305, with the backlog of people wanting to come reaching 100,000.

By the end of the 1920s, annual immigration had dropped to one-fourth of its pre–World War I level. The worldwide economic depression of the 1930s decreased immigration still further. A brief upsurge in immigration just before World War II reflected the flight of Europeans from the oppression of expanding

Nazi Germany. The war virtually ended transatlantic immigration. The era of the great European migration to the United States had been legislated out of existence.

The Immigration and Nationality Act

The national origin system was abandoned with the passage of the 1965 Immigration and Nationality Act (also called the Hart-Cellar Act), signed into law by President Lyndon B. Johnson at the foot of the Statue of Liberty. The primary goals of the act were to reunite families and to protect the American labor market. The act also initiated restrictions on immigration from Latin America. After the act, immigration increased by one-third, but the act's influence was primarily on the composition rather than the size of immigration. The sources of immigrants now included Italy, Greece, Portugal, Mexico, the Philippines, the West Indies, and South America.

The lasting effect is apparent when we compare the changing sources of immigration over the last 190 years, as shown in Figure 4.3. The most recent period shows that Asian and Latin American immigrants combined to account for 78 percent of the people who were permitted entry. This contrasts sharply with early immigration, which was dominated by arrivals from Europe.

The nature of immigration laws is exceedingly complex and is subjected to frequent, often minor, adjustments. From 2000 to 2010, between 840,000 and 1,270,000 people were legally admitted each year. For 2010, people were admitted for the following reasons:

- Relatives of citizens   57%
- Relatives of legal residents   9%
- Employment based   14%
- Refugees/people seeking political asylum   13%
- Diversity (lottery among applications from
  nations historically sending few immigrants)   5%
- Other   2%

Overall, two-thirds of immigrants come to join their families, one-seventh because of skills needed in the United States, and another one-seventh because of special refugee status. However, it would be a mistake for thinking family reunions are easy to accomplish. Because there are limits on how many people can enter legally each year for any one country, backlogs exist for such nations as China, India, Mexico, and Philippines. So, for example, as of 2013, there was a *13-year* backlog for adult children from the Philippines to join their American citizen parents. Similarly, there was a *17-year* backlog for the Mexican brothers and sisters of American citizens to join their siblings (Martin and Yankay 2013; Preston 2013b).

Figure 4.3 Legal Immigrants Admitted to the United States by Region of Last Residence, 1820–2012

SOURCE: Office of Immigration Statistics 2013.

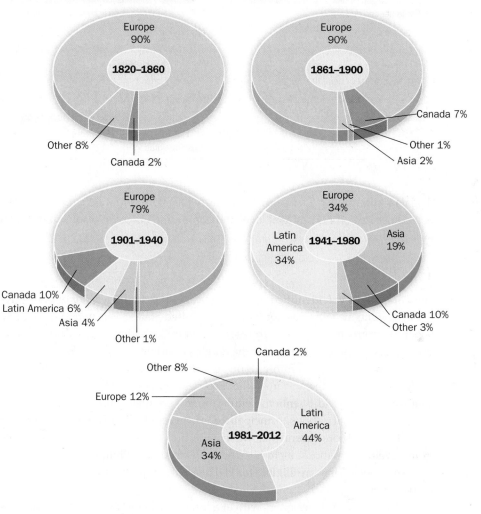

Contemporary Social Concerns

4-4   Identify the concerns about immigration policy today.

Although our current immigration policies are less restrictive than other nations', they are the subjects of great debate. Table 4.1 summarizes the benefits and concerns regarding immigration to the United States. We now consider six continuing criticisms relating to our immigration policy: the brain drain, population growth, mixed status, English language acquisition, economic impact, and

Table 4.1 Immigration Benefits and Concerns

Potential Benefits	Areas of Concern
Provide needed skills	Drain needed resources from home country
Contribute to taxes	Send money home
May come with substantial capital to start business	Less-skilled immigrants compete with already disadvantaged residents
Maintain growth of consumer market	Population growth
Diversify the population (intangible gain)	Language differences
Maintain ties with countries throughout the world	May complicate foreign policy by lobbying the government
	Illegal immigration

illegal immigration. All five, but particularly illegal immigration, have provoked heated debates on the national level and continuing efforts to resolve them with new policies.

The Brain Drain

How often have you identified your science or mathematics teacher or your physician as someone who was not born in the United States? This nation has clearly benefited from attracting human resources from throughout the world, but this phenomenon has had its price for the nations of origin.

Brain drain is the immigration to the United States of skilled workers, professionals, and technicians who are desperately needed by their home countries. In the mid-twentieth century, many scientists and other professionals from industrial nations, principally Germany and Great Britain, came to the United States. More recently, however, the brain drain has pulled emigrants from developing nations, including India, Pakistan, the Philippines, and several African nations. They are eligible for H-1B visas that qualify them for permanent work permits.

Currently 65,000 foreigners with at a least a bachelor's degree and a specialized skill receive the H-1B visa. Another 20,000 such visas go to foreign nationals with advanced degrees from U.S. universities. In these cases, a person comes to the United States on a student visa, secures a degree, say in engineering, and then may apply for the H-1B.

More than one out of four physicians (27 percent) in the United States are foreign-born and play a critical role in serving areas with too few doctors. Thousands of doctors have sought to enter the United States, pulled by the economic opportunity. Persons born in India, the Philippines, and China account for the largest groups of foreign-born physicians. The pay differential is so great that, beginning in 2004, when foreign physicians were no longer favored with entry to the United States, physicians in the Philippines retrained as nurses so that they could immigrate to the United States where, employed as nurses, they would make four times what they would as doctors in the Philippines. By 2010, one-third of the foreign-born workers employed as registered nurses were born in the Philippines (McCabe 2012; *New York Times* 2005).

Many foreign students say they plan to return home. Fortunately for the United States, many do not and make their talents available in the United States. One study showed that the majority of foreign students receiving their doctorates in the sciences and engineering remain here four years later. Critics note, however, that this foreign supply means that the United States overlooks its own minority scholars and relies on students from overseas. Currently, a foreign citizen receives a doctorate in the United States for every doctorate earned by an African American or Latino. More encouragement must be given to African Americans and Latinos to enter high-tech career paths.

Conflict theorists see the current brain drain as yet another symptom of the unequal distribution of world resources. In their view, it is ironic that the United States gives foreign aid to improve the technical resources of African and Asian countries while maintaining an immigration policy that encourages professionals in such nations to migrate to our shores. These very countries have unacceptable public health conditions and need native scientists, educators, technicians, and other professionals. In addition, by relying on foreign talent, the United States is not encouraging native members of subordinate groups to enter these desirable fields of employment (National Center for Education Statistics 2013: Table 307; Pearson 2006; Wessel 2001; West 2010).

Population Growth

The United States, like a few other industrial nations, continues to accept large numbers of permanent immigrants and refugees. Although such immigration has increased since the passage of the 1965 Immigration and Nationality Act, the nation's birth rate has decreased. Consequently, the contribution of immigration to population growth has become more significant. As citizen "baby boomers" age, the country has increasingly depended on the economically younger population fueled by immigrants (Meyers 2007).

Immigration, legal and illegal, is projected to account for nearly 50 percent of the nation's growth from 2005 to 2050 with the children and grandchildren of immigrants accounting for another 35 percent. To some observers, the United States is already overpopulated. Environmentalists have weighed in on the immigration issue, questioning immigration's possible negative impact on the nation's natural resources. We consider that aspect of the immigration debate later in this chapter. Thus far, the majority of environmentalists have indicated a desire to keep a neutral position rather than enter the politically charged immigration debate (Kotkin 2010; Livingston and Cohn 2012).

The patterns of uneven settlement by immigrants in the United States are expected to continue, so future immigrants' impact on population growth will be felt much more in certain areas, for example, California and New York rather than Wyoming or West Virginia. Although immigration and population growth may be viewed as national concerns, their impact is localized in certain areas, such as Southern California and large urban centers nationwide (Camarota and Jensenius 2009; Passel and Cohn 2009).

Mixed-Status Families

Little is simple when it comes to immigration. This is particularly true regarding the challenge of the estimated 9 million people living in mixed status families. **Mixed status** refers to families in which one or more members are citizens and one or more are noncitizens. This especially becomes problematic when the noncitizens are illegal or undocumented immigrants.

The problem of mixed status emerges on two levels. On the macro level, when policy debates are made about issues that seem clear to many people—such as whether illegal immigrants should be allowed to attend state colleges or whether illegal immigrants should be immediately deported—the complicating factor of mixed-status families quickly emerges. On the micro level, the daily toll on members of mixed-status households is difficult. Often, the legal resident or even the U.S. citizen in a household finds daily life limited for fear of revealing the undocumented status of a parent or brother or even a son.

About three-quarters of illegal immigrants' children were born in the United States and thus are citizens. This means that perhaps half of all adult illegal immigrants have a citizen in their immediate family. This proportion has grown in recent years. Therefore, some of the issues facing illegal immigrants, whom we discuss later, also affect the citizens in the families because they avoid bringing attention to themselves for fear of revealing the illegal status of their mother or father. Immigration issues aside, one can only begin to imagine the additional pressure this places upon mixed-status families beyond the usual ones of balancing work and home, school, and children moving through adolescent to adulthood (Gonzalez 2009; Gonzales 2011; Passel and Cohn 2009; Pew Hispanic Center 2011b).

Language Barriers

For many people in the United States, the most visible aspects of immigration are non–English speakers, businesses with foreign-language storefronts, and even familiar stores assuring potential customers that their employees speak Spanish or Polish or Chinese or another foreign language. Non–English speakers cluster in certain states, but bilingualism attracts nationwide passions. The release in 2006 of "Nuestro Himno," the Spanish-language version of "The Star-Spangled Banner," led to a strong reaction, with 69 percent of people saying it was appropriate to be sung only in English. Yet at least one congressman who decried the Spanish version sang the anthem himself in English with incorrect lyrics (Carroll 2006; Koch 2006).

About 21 percent of the population speaks a language other than English at home, as shown in Figure 4.4. Indeed, 39 different languages are spoken at home by at least 90,000 residents. Spanish accounts for 62 percent of the foreign language speakers at home. As of 2011, about half of the 61 million people speaking a foreign language at home abroad spoke English less than "very well."

Figure 4.4 Ten Languages Most Frequently Spoken at Home, Other Than English and Spanish

By comparison, of 291 million people over five years of age, 231 million only speak English at home, 38 million Spanish, and about 22 million some other language.

SOURCE: Data for 2011 in Ryan 2013: 3.

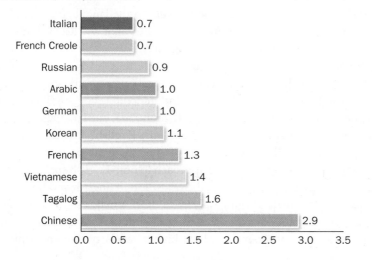

Since 1980, the largest growth has been in speakers of Spanish, Chinese, Korean, Vietnamese, Tagalog, Russian, and Persian. The largest decreases have all been in European-based languages such as Italian, Greek, German, Yiddish, and Polish (Ryan 2013).

The myth of Anglo superiority has rested in part on language differences. (The term *Anglo* in the following text means all non-Hispanics but primarily Whites.) First, the criteria for economic and social achievement usually include proficiency in English. By such standards, Spanish-speaking pupils are judged less able to compete until they learn English. Second, many Anglos believe that Spanish is not an asset occupationally. Only recently, as government agencies belatedly began serving Latino people and as businesses recognized the growing Latino consumer market, have Anglos recognized that knowing Spanish is not only useful but also necessary to carry out certain tasks.

Until the last 40 years, a conscious effort was made to devalue Spanish and other languages and to discourage the use of foreign languages in schools. In the case of Spanish, this practice was built on a pattern of segregating Hispanic schoolchildren from Anglos. In the recent past in the Southwest, Mexican Americans were assigned to Mexican schools to keep Anglo schools all-White. These Mexican schools, created through de jure school segregation resulting from residential segregation, were substantially underfunded compared with the Anglo public schools. Legal action against such schools dates back to 1945, but it was not until 1970 that the U.S. Supreme Court ruled, in *Cisneros v. Corpus Christi Independent School District*, that segregation of Mexican Americans was unconstitutional. Appeals delayed implementation of that decision, and not until September 1975 was the de jure plan forcibly overturned in Corpus Christi, Texas (Commission on Civil Rights 1976).

Is it essential that English be the sole language of instruction in schools in the United States? **Bilingualism** is the use of two or more languages in places of work or educational facilities and accords each language equal legitimacy. Thus, a program of **bilingual education** may instruct children in their native language (such as Spanish) while gradually introducing them to the language of the dominant society (English). If such a program also is bicultural, it will teach children about the culture of both linguistic groups. Bilingual education allows students to learn academic material in their own language while they learn a second language. Proponents believe that, ideally, bilingual education programs should also allow English-speaking pupils to be bilingual, but generally they are directed only at making non–English speakers proficient in more than one language.

Do bilingual programs help children learn English? It is difficult to reach firm conclusions on the effectiveness of the bilingual programs in general because they vary so widely in their approach to non–English speaking children. The programs differ in the length of the transition to English and how long they allow students to remain in bilingual classrooms. A major study analyzed more than three decades of research, combining 17 different studies, and found that bilingual education programs produce higher levels of student achievement in reading. The most successful are paired bilingual programs—those offering ongoing instruction in a native language and English at different times of the day (Slavin and Cheung 2003; Soltero 2008).

Attacks on bilingualism in voting and education have taken several forms and have even broadened to question the appropriateness of U.S. residents using any language other than English. Federal policy has become more restrictive. Local schools have been given more authority to determine appropriate methods of instruction; they also have been forced to provide more of their own funding for bilingual education. Adding to the difficulty is that increasingly school districts outside the central city in suburbs and rural agricultural areas face the challenge of serving non–English speaking schoolchildren.

In the United States, as of 2013, 30 states have made English their official language. Repeated efforts have been made to introduce a constitutional amendment declaring English as the nation's official language. Even such an action would not completely outlaw bilingual or multilingual government services. It would, however, require that such services be called for specifically as in the Voting Rights Act of 1965, which requires voting information to be available in multiple languages (U.S. English 2013).

The Economic Impact

There is much public and scholarly debate about the economic effects of immigration, both legal and illegal. Varied, conflicting conclusions have resulted from research ranging from case studies of Korean immigrants' dominance among New York City greengrocers to mobility studies charting the progress of all immigrants and their children. The confusion results in part from the different methods of analysis. For example, the studies do not always include political refugees, who generally are less prepared than other refugees to become assimilated. Sometimes, the research focuses only on economic effects, such as whether people are employed or are on welfare; in other cases, it also considers cultural factors such as knowledge of English.

Perhaps the most significant factor in determining the economic impact of immigration is whether a study examines the national impact of immigration or only its effects on a local area. Overall, we can conclude from the research that immigrants adapt well and are an asset to the local economy. In some areas, heavy immigration may drain a community's resources. However, it can also revitalize a local economy. Marginally employed workers, most of whom are either themselves immigrants or African Americans, often experience a negative impact by new arrivals. With or without immigration, competition for low-paying jobs in the United States is high, and those who gain the most from this competition are the employers and the consumers who want to keep prices down (Steinberg 2005; Zimmerman 2008).

There is no one portrait, or even a dozen portraits, of the typical situation that describes the economic role of immigrants in the United States. Similarly,

Research Focus

The Hispanic Dairyland

Dairyland Wisconsin invokes images of rolling hills and pastures, black and white Holstein cows, and roadside shops selling cheese. But now an indispensable part of this portrayal is the important role played by Latino workers.

Just since the beginning of the twenty-first century, immigrant workers, almost entirely Hispanic and largely Mexican, have become the majority of laborers on large dairy farms and overall at least 40 percent of all hired dairy employees on the more than 14,000 dairy farms in Wisconsin. Latinos working in agriculture is not new—nationally they accounted in 2012 for 24 percent of all employed persons in animal and crop production—but their rapid presence in dairy farming is a recent twenty-first century phenomenon. Dairy farmers turned to immigrant workers when they found it difficult to locate U.S.-born workers who were "reliable," to use their often-expressed criteria. Dairy farms have also grown larger, requiring additional milking shifts and more workhands.

As one typical dairy farmer with 150 cows said in 2009,

> So as our last two children entered high school, and I realized that soon I would have no family labor to rely on, we moved our farm to all hired labor. I have not been able to hire an American citizen since 1997. I have tried! The way I see it, if we didn't have Hispanics to rely on for a work force, I don't believe I could continue farming. (Harrison, Lloyd, and O'Kane 2009: 2–3)

The important role that Latinos now play on dairy farms is not limited to the Midwest but is repeated in places like California, Texas, New York state, and Vermont, which also used to depend on local workers.

The use of immigrant labor on dairy farms is an example of **occupational segregation**. This refers to the concentration of one particular group of people to a particular job. In this case we see occupational segregation with respect to Latinos, largely male, to the more manual labor on these farms. They are not involved in caring for the herd, distribution of the product, or managing equipment maintenance, much less owning the farm. They are limited to the "milking parlors" or the large barns where cows are milked. The Latinos work as "milkers," typically hooking the cows to hoses; "pushers," getting the cows in and out of the salon; or "cleaners," scraping manure from the parlors. Cows are milked two to three times a day, every day, so the labor demand is continuous.

The low-level jobs are now often even described as "Mexican" work, regardless of the nationality of the laborer, even though little more than a decade or two ago it was all done by family or local workers. So associated are Latinos with this hard labor that farm operators now speak of the U.S.-born workers as being too weak to do the immigrant labor. Hispanic laborers are so well-regarded for working the long hours at tough work that when a worker seems reluctant to do it, they are derisively referred to as now being "Americanized" in a reference to the local people unwilling to do labor in the milk parlors. Occupation segregation is growing so well-defined that now Latinos are seen as suited for the job and unsatisfactory for any more skilled and higher paying work on the farm. For the workers, their "success" as milkers has led to chain migration to the area through family and friendship networks as more and more workers are needed.

Pay is about $9 an hour as of 2013 with few non-wage benefits, and jobs are year-round, but this often means working at split intervals in the same day totaling 55 to 60 hours a week. Even though they may work for several years on the same farm, there is little interest in training the workers to do more highly skilled labor. The farm owners recognize that many of these workers may be illegal and do not wish to "invest" in their future. From the workers' standpoint, they rarely complain, fearing that their illegal status or that of their friends and family members, even if they themselves are legal, may be disclosed. Given that they labor in rural areas doing work that no one else wants to do, there is little incentive to investigate their legal status and dairy farms are rarely investigated.

Dairy farms represent a very small aspect of Latino life in the United States but for dairy farmers,

Latinos are all important. Therefore, through agriculture lobbying organizations, farm operators and owners are well heard on any immigration bill that may jeopardize their continuing to access their "reliable," if illegal, workforce.

SOURCES: Campion 2013; Department of Agriculture 2010; Dorschner 2013; Harrison and Lloyd 2012; Jordan 2009; Kohli 2013.

there are many explanations for whey unauthorized immigration persists. In the "Research Focus," we show that labor on a dairy farm has been dominated by Latino workers, many of them undocumented.

The impact of immigration on African Americans deserves special attention. Given that African Americans are a large minority and many continue to be in the underclass, many people, including some Blacks themselves, perceive immigrants as advancing at the expense of the African American community. There is evidence that in the lowest paid jobs—for example, workers in chicken-processing plants—wages have dropped with the availability of unskilled immigrants to perform them, and Blacks have left these jobs for good. Many of these African Americans do not necessarily move to better or even equivalent jobs. This pattern is repeated in other relatively low-paying, undesirable employment sectors, so Blacks are not alone in being impacted; but given other job opportunities, the impact is longer lasting (Borjas, Grogger, and Hanson 2006; Holzer 2008).

About 70 percent of illegal immigrant workers pay taxes of one type or another. Many of them do not file to receive entitled refunds or benefits. For example, in 2005, the Social Security Administration identified thousands of unauthorized workers contributing about $7 billion to the fund but that could not be credited properly. Supporters of immigration reform point to increased tax revenue and even more net financial benefits to all local governments if illegal immigrants move toward legal residency (Institute on Taxation and Economic Policy 2013; Lipman 2008; Porter 2005).

Social science studies generally contradict many of the negative stereotypes about the economic impact of immigration. A variety of recent studies found that immigrants are a net economic gain for the population in times of economic boom as well as in periods of recession. But despite national gains, in some areas and for some groups, immigration may be an economic burden or create unwanted competition for jobs (Kochhar 2006).

What about the immigrants themselves? Considering contemporary immigrants as a group, we can make the following conclusions in Table 4.2. They represent a mix of successes and challenges to adaptation. These positive trends diverge among specific immigrant groups, with Asian immigrants doing better than European immigrants, who do better than Latino immigrants (Capps, Leighton, and Fix 2002; Farkas 2003; Myers, Pitkin, and Park 2004; Zimmerman 2008).

Table 4.2 Immigrant Adaptation to the USA

Less Encouraging	Positive Signs
• Although immigrants have lower divorce rates and are less likely to form single-parent households than natives, their rates equal or exceed these rates by the second generation. • Children in immigrant families tend to be healthier than U.S.-born children, but the advantage declines. We consider this in greater detail later in this chapter. • Immigrant children attend schools that are disproportionately attended by other poor children and students with limited English proficiency, so they are ethnically, economically, and linguistically isolated.	• Immigrant families and, more broadly, noncitizen households are more likely to be on public assistance, but their time on public assistance is less and they receive fewer benefits. This is even true when considering special restrictions that may apply to noncitizens. • Second-generation immigrants (i.e., children of immigrants) are overall doing as well as or better than White non-Hispanic natives in educational attainment, labor force participation, wages, and household income. • Immigrants overwhelmingly (65 percent) continue to see learning English as an ethical obligation of all immigrants.

One economic aspect of immigration that has received increasing attention is the role of **remittances**, or the monies that immigrants return to their countries of origin. The amounts are significant and measure in the hundreds of millions of dollars flowing from the United States to a number of countries where they provide substantial support for families and even venture capital for new businesses. Although some observers express concern over this outflow of money, others counter that it probably represents a small price to pay for the human capital that the United States is able to use in the form of the immigrants themselves. Immigrants in the United States send annually about $31 billion to their home countries and worldwide remittances bring about $530 billion to all the world's countries, easily surpassing all other forms of foreign aid. While this cash inflow is integral to the economies of many nations, it also means that during the global economic recession that occurred recently, this resource dropped off significantly (World Bank 2013a, 2013b).

The concern about immigration today is both understandable and perplexing. The nation has always been uneasy about new arrivals, especially those who are different from the more affluent and the policymakers. In most of the 1990s, we had paradoxical concerns about immigrants hurting the economy despite strong economic growth. With the economic downturn beginning in 2008, it was clear that low-skilled immigrants (legal or illegal) took the hardest hit and, as a result, remittances immediately declined.

Illegal Immigration

4-5 **Discuss the scope of and issues related to illegal immigration.**

The most bitterly debated aspect of U.S. immigration policy has been the control of illegal or undocumented immigrants. These immigrants and their families come to the United States in search of higher-paying jobs than their

The immigration debates range from loosening to tightening the flow of immigrants, whether illegal immigrants who came here as children and went to school should be allowed a pathway to citizenship (the proposed DREAM Act), and whether states such as Arizona have overstepped their bounds in trying to identify illegal immigrants by empowering any person stopped or arrested if they have reason to believe they have immigrated illegally.

home countries can provide. While some people contend there are differences in their meaning, we will use the terms *illegal*, *undocumented*, or *unauthorized* interchangeably to refer to people who have entered the country without the proper documents as well as people who entered legally as students or tourists but then remained illegally.

Because by definition illegal immigrants are in the country illegally, the exact number of these undocumented or unauthorized workers is subject to estimates and disputes. Based on the best available information in late 2013, more than 11.7 million illegal or unauthorized immigrants live in the United States. This compares with about 3.5 million in 1990 and a peak of 12.2 million in 2007. With employment opportunities drying up during the economic downturn beginning in 2008, significantly fewer people tried to enter illegally, and many unauthorized immigrants returned to their countries (Passel, Cohn, and Gonzalez-Barrera 2013).

The public has tied illegal immigrants, and even legal immigrants, to almost every social problem in the nation. They become the scapegoats for unemployment; they are labeled "drug runners" and, especially since September 11, 2001, "terrorists." Arrest, detention, and deportation of illegal immigrants greatly increased. Their vital economic and cultural contribution to the United States is generally overlooked, as it has been for more than a hundred years. Considering it from the perspective of the immigrant, the possibility of apprehension and punishment are not significant determents. However, the decision to enter illegally is affected by the assessment of the employment possibilities in the home country and, as we will see later, the dangers of border crossing (Ryo 2013).

There are significant costs for aliens—that is, foreign-born noncitizens—and for other citizens. Civil rights advocates have expressed concern that the procedures used to apprehend and deport people are discriminatory and deprive many aliens of their legal rights. American citizens of Hispanic or Asian origin, some of whom were born in the United States, may be greeted with prejudice and distrust, as if their names automatically imply that they are illegal immigrants. Furthermore, these citizens and legal residents of the United States may be unable to find work because employers wrongly believe that their documents are forged.

In the context of this illegal immigration, Congress approved the Immigration Reform and Control Act of 1986 (IRCA) after debating it for nearly a decade. The act marked a historic change in immigration policy compared with earlier laws, as summarized in Table 4.3. Amnesty was granted to 2.7 million illegal immigrants who could document that they had established long-term residency in the United States. Under the IRCA, hiring illegal aliens became illegal, and employers became subject to fines and even prison sentences. Little workplace enforcement occurred for years, but beginning in 2009, federal agents concentrated on auditing large employers rather than raiding workplaces (Massey and Pren 2012; Siegal 2013).

Many illegal immigrants continue to live in fear and hiding, subject to even more severe harassment and discrimination than before. From a conflict perspective, these immigrants, primarily poor and Hispanic or Asian, are being firmly lodged at the bottom of the nation's social and economic hierarchies. However, from a functionalist perspective, employers, by paying low wages, are able to produce goods and services that are profitable for industry and more affordable

Table 4.3 Major Immigration Policies

Policy	Target Group	Impact
Chinese Exclusion Act, 1882	Chinese	Effectively ended all Chinese immigration for more than 60 years
National origin system, 1921	Southern Europeans	Reduced overall immigration and significantly reduced likely immigration from Greece and Italy
Immigration and Nationality Act, 1965 (Hart-Cellar Act)	Western Hemisphere and the less skilled	Facilitated entry of skilled workers and relatives of U.S. residents
Immigration Reform and Control Act of 1986	Illegal immigrants	Modest reduction of illegal immigration
Illegal Immigration Reform and Immigrant Responsibility Act of 1996	Illegal immigrants	Greater border surveillance and increased scrutiny of legal immigrants seeking benefits

to consumers. Despite the poor working conditions often experienced by illegal immigrants, they continue to come because it is still in their best economic interest to work here in disadvantaged positions rather than seek wage labor unsuccessfully in their home countries.

Illegal aliens or undocumented workers are not necessarily transient. One estimate indicates 63 percent had been here for at least ten years. Many have established homes, families, and networks with relatives and friends in the United States whose legal status might differ. These are the mixed-status households noted earlier. For the most part, their lives are not much different from legal residents, except when they seek services that require documentation proving citizenship status (Pew Hispanic Center 2011a).

Policymakers continue to avoid the only real way to stop illegal immigration: discourage employment opportunities. This has certainly been the approach in recent years. The Immigration and Customs Enforcement (ICE) notifies major companies that it will soon audit its employment records looking for illegal immigrants. If found, civil and criminal penalties can be levied against the business. The workers themselves are subject to deportation. This has led corporations such as American Apparel and Chipotle Mexican Grill to look more closely at and fire hundreds of employees lacking sufficient documentation. In 2012, about 410,000 people had been deported, a similar number to the year before—this is equivalent to deporting the people of San Diego during a two-year period (Migration News 2012b; Preston 2013a).

The public often thinks in terms of controlling illegal immigration through greater surveillance at the border. After the terrorist attacks of September 11, 2001, greater control of border traffic took on a new sense of urgency, even though almost all the hijackers had entered the United States legally. It also is very difficult to secure the vast boundaries that mark the United States on land and sea. The cost of the federal government's attempt to police the nation's borders and locate illegal immigrants is sizable. The federal government spends $18 billion annually with costs of proposed enhancements of border security ranging from fencing to drones easily reaching another $4.5 billion (*Economist* 2013a; Preston 2013a).

Numerous civil rights groups and migrant advocacy organizations have expressed alarm regarding people who cross into the United States illegally and perish in the attempt. Some die in deserts, in isolated canyons, and while concealed in containers or locked in trucks during smuggling attempts. Several hundred die annually in the Southwest by seeking ever more dangerous crossing points because border control has increased. However, this toll has received so little attention that one journalist likened it to several jumbo jets crashing between Los Angeles and Phoenix every year without anyone giving it much notice. Approximately 2,269 immigrant deaths were recorded from October 1999 through March 2012. The immigration policy debate was largely absent from the 2008 and 2012 presidential races and was replaced by concerns over the economy (Del Olmo 2003; Helmore 2013).

An immigration-related issue that began being raised recently has been concern over illegal immigrants' children who are born here and thus regarded as citizens at birth. Public opinion polls reveal that about half of the population has concerns regarding these children. Some people want to alter the Fourteenth Amendment to revise the "birthright citizenship" that was intended for children of slaves but has long been interpreted to cover anyone born in the United States regardless of their parents' legal status. While such a movement is unlikely to succeed, it is yet another example of a relatively minor issue that sidetracks any substantive discussion of immigration reform (Gomez 2010).

So what is the future of immigration reform? It is unlikely to be resolved in any satisfying way because the issues are complex and are wrapped up in economic interests, humanitarian concerns, party politics, constitutional rights, and even foreign policy. Alongside immigration policy is how the nation is to accommodate people escaping political and religious persecution.

Path to Citizenship: Naturalization

4-6 Outline the process of naturalization.

In **naturalization**, citizenship is conferred on a person after birth, a process that has been outlined by Congress and extends to foreigners the same benefits given to native-born U.S. citizens. Naturalized citizens, however, cannot serve as president.

Until the 1970s, most people who were naturalized had been born in Europe. Reflecting changing patterns of immigration, Asia and Latin America are now the largest sources of new citizens. In fact, the number of naturalized citizens from Mexico has come close to matching those from all of Europe. In recent years, the number of new citizens going through the naturalization process has been close to 1 million a year (Baker 2009).

To become a naturalized U.S. citizen, a person must meet the following general conditions:

- be 18 years of age;
- have continually resided in the United States for at least five years (three years for the spouses of U.S. citizens);
- have good moral character as determined by the absence of conviction of selected criminal offenses;
- be able to read, write, speak, and understand words of ordinary usage in the English language; and
- pass a test in U.S. government and history administered orally in English.

Table 4.4 offers the types of questions immigrants face on the citizenship test. This is a sample of the actual questions used; you must get six out of ten correct to pass. If a person fails, he or she can immediately retake it with different questions. If failed a second time, typically the person must wait 90 days to retake the test. As of 2013, the fee for applying for citizenship is $680, compared with $95 in 1998.

Although we often picture the United States as having a very insular, nativistic attitude toward foreigners living here, the country has a rather liberal policy toward people maintaining the citizenship of their old countries. Although most countries do not allow people to maintain dual (or even multiple) citizenships, the United States does not forbid it. Dual citizenship is most common when a person goes through naturalization after already being a citizen of another country or is a U.S.-born citizen and goes through the process of becoming a citizen of another country—for example, after marrying a foreigner (Department of State 2013).

Table 4.4 So You Want to Be a Citizen?

Try these sample questions from the naturalization test (answers below).

1. What do the stripes on the flag represent?
2. How many amendments are there to the Constitution?
3. Who is the chief justice of the Supreme Court?
4. Who was president during World War I?
5. What do we call the first 10 amendments to the Constitution?
6. What are two rights in the Declaration of Independence?
7. Name one right or freedom from the First Amendment.
8. When was the Constitution written?

Answers: (1) The first 13 states; (2) 27; (3) John Roberts; (4) Woodrow Wilson; (5) Bill of Rights; (6) life, liberty, and the pursuit of happiness; (7) The rights are freedom of speech, religion, assembly, and press, and freedom to petition the government; (8) 1787.

SOURCE: Department of Homeland Security 2013.

The continuing debate about immigration reform often includes calls for some type of "amnesty" or pathway to citizenship for illegal immigrants. Details in proposals vary but usually include proof of long-term residence in the USA, absence of criminal activity, and willingness to accept a waiting period before actual citizenship can occur. Critics of such proposals question the wisdom of "rewarding illegals" but also argue that if legal residency is acquired than their relatives will also apply for legal residency. Current policy, as noted earlier, has created long waiting periods for those abroad trying to join their relatives, but surveys also show that, as in 1986 when some type of amnesty was offered, not all qualified illegal immigrants will seek legal status. For example, in recent years only 46 percent of Hispanic immigrants eligible to naturalize have chosen to become citizens, compared with 71 percent of non-Hispanic immigrants. Typical difficulties with the English language and the costs of application serve as a barrier to the path to citizenship. Other special one-time programs since 1986 also show only about half taking advantage of naturalization (Lopez and Gonzalez-Barrera 2013).

Women and Immigration

4-7 Understand the special role of women in immigration.

Immigration is presented as if all immigrants are similar, with the only distinctions being made concerning point of origin, education, and employment prospects. Another significant distinction is whether immigrants travel with or without their families. We often think that historical immigrants to the United States were males in search of work. Men dominate much of the labor migration

Immigration is a challenge to all family members. But immigrant women must navigate a new culture and a new country not only for themselves but also for their children, such as in this household in Colorado.

worldwide, but because of the diversified labor force in the United States and some policies that facilitate relatives coming, immigration to the United States generally has been fairly balanced. Actually, most immigration historically appears to be families. For example, from 1870 through 1940, men entering the United States exceeded women by only about 10 to 20 percent. Since 1950, women immigrants have actually exceeded men by a modest amount (Gibson and Jung 2006).

The second-class status women normally experience in society is reflected in immigration. Most dramatically, women citizens who married immigrants who were not citizens actually lost their U.S. citizenship from 1907 through 1922 with few exceptions. However, this policy did not apply to men (Johnson 2004).

Immigrant women face not only all the challenges faced by immigrant men but also additional ones. Typically, they have the responsibility of navigating the new society when it comes to services for their family and, in particular, their children. Many new immigrants view the United States as a dangerous place to raise a family and therefore remain particularly vigilant of what happens in their children's lives.

Male immigrants are more likely to be consumed with work, leaving the women to navigate the bureaucratic morass of city services, schools, medical facilities, and even everyday concerns such as stores and markets. Immigrant women are often reluctant to seek outside help, whether they are in need of special services for medical purposes or they are victims of domestic violence. Yet immigrant women are more likely to be the liaison for the household, including adult men, to community associations and religious organizations (Hondagneu-Sotelo 2003; Jones 2008).

Women play a critical role in overseeing the household; for immigrant women, the added pressures of being in a new country and trying to move ahead in a different culture heighten this social role.

The Global Economy and Immigration

4-8 Illustrate the relationship of globalization with respect to immigrants.

Immigration is defined by political boundaries that bring the movement of peoples crossing borders to the attention of government authorities and their policies. Within the United States, people may move their residence, but they are not immigrating. For residents in the member nations of the European Union, free movement of people within the union is also protected.

Yet, increasingly, people recognize the need to think beyond national borders and national identity. As noted in Chapter 1, **globalization** is the worldwide integration of government policies, cultures, social movements, and financial markets through trade, movement of people, and the exchange of ideas. In this global framework, even immigrants are less likely to think of themselves as residents of only one country. For generations, immigrants have used foreign-language newspapers to keep in touch with events in their home countries. Today, cable channels carry news and variety programs from their home countries, and the Internet offers immediate access to the homeland and kinfolk thousands of miles away.

Although it helps in bringing the world together, globalization has also highlighted the dramatic economic inequalities between nations. Today, people in North America, Europe, and Japan consume 32 times more resources than the billions of people in developing nations. Thanks to tourism, media, and other aspects of globalization, the people of less-affluent countries are aware of such affluent lifestyles and, of course, often aspire to enjoy them (Diamond 2003).

Transnationals are immigrants who sustain multiple social relationships that link their societies of origin and settlement. Immigrants from the Dominican Republic, for example, not only identify themselves with Americans but also maintain very close ties to their Caribbean homeland. They return for visits, send remittances, and host extended stays of relatives and friends. Back in the Dominican Republic, villages reflect these close ties, as shown in billboards promoting special long-distance services to the United States and by the presence of household appliances sent by relatives. The volume of remittances worldwide is easily the most reliable source of foreign money going to poor countries, far outstripping foreign aid programs.

The presence of transnationals would be yet another example of pluralism, as illustrated in the Spectrum of Intergroup Relations. Since transnationals move back and forth, it is not unusual for any given moment that different generations of the same family will find themselves residing in different countries (Foner and Dreby 2011).

The growing number of transnationals, as well as immigration in general, directly reflects the world systems analysis we considered in Chapter 1. Transnationals are not new, but the ability to communicate and transfer resources makes the immigration experience today different from that of the nineteenth century. The sharp contrast between the industrial "have" nations and the developing "have-not" nations only encourages movement across borders. The industrial haves gain benefits from such movement even when they seem to discourage it. The back-and-forth movement only serves to increase globalization and help create informal social networks between people who seek a better life and those already enjoying increased prosperity.

The transnationals themselves maintain a multithreaded relationship between friends and relatives in the United Sates, their home country, and perhaps other countries where relatives and friends have resettled. Besides the economic impact of remittances described above, scholars are increasingly giving attention to "social remittances" that include ideas, social norms, and practices (religious and secular) throughout this global social network (Levitt and Jaworsky 2007).

The Environment and Immigration

4-9 **Interpret how immigration is related to the environment.**

At the beginning of the twenty-first century, the public expressed growing concern on a variety of environmental issues, from water quality to global warming. As with so many other aspects of life, the environment and immigration are tightly linked.

First, environmental factors are behind a significant amount of world migration. Famine, typhoons, rising sea levels, expanding deserts, chronic water shortages, earthquakes, and so forth lead to cross-border migration. One estimate suggests up to 200 million people may move due to environmental factors between 2005 and 2050. **Environmental refugees** are people forced to leave their communities because of natural disasters, or the effects of climate change and global warming. A particularly deadly aspect of this forced movement is that overwhelmingly the migration is by vulnerable poor people to developing countries ill-suited to accept the arrivals (International Organization for Migration 2009; Meyers 2005; Stern 2007).

Second, some environmentalists favor reducing or even ending U.S. population growth by imposing a much more restrictive immigration policy. The respected environmentalist group Sierra Club debated for several years whether to take an official position favoring restricting immigration. Thus far, the majority of the club's members have indicated a desire to keep a neutral position rather than enter the politically charged immigration debate.

Yet others still contend for the United States to finally address environmental problems at home and become global environmental citizens and for the United States to stop population growth. Critics of this environmentalist approach counter that we should focus on consumption, not population (Barringer 2004; CaFaro and Staples 2009; National Public Radio 2013).

Refugees

4-10 Restate the United States' policies toward refugees.

Refugees are people who live outside their country of citizenship for fear of political or religious persecution. Approximately 11 million refugees exist worldwide, enough to populate an entire "nation." That nation of refugees is larger than Belgium, Sweden, or Cuba. The United States has touted itself as a haven for political refugees. However, political refugees have not always received an unqualified welcome.

The United States makes the largest financial contribution of any nation to worldwide assistance programs. As such, it resettles between 56,000 and 73,000 refugees annually and has hosted over 1 million refugees between 1990 and 2008. Following 9/11, procedures have become much more cumbersome for foreigners to acquire refugee status and gain entry to the United States. Many other much smaller and poorer nations have received much larger numbers of refugees, with Jordan, Iran, and Pakistan hosting more than 1 million refugees each (Martin and Yankay 2013; United Nations High Commission on Refugees 2008).

The United States, insulated by distance from wars and famines in Europe and Asia, has been able to be selective about which and how many refugees are welcomed. Since the arrival of refugees uprooted by World War II through the 1980s, the United States allowed three groups of refugees to enter in numbers greater than regulations would ordinarily permit: Hungarians, Cubans, and Southeast Asians.

Despite periodic public opposition, the U.S. government is officially committed to accepting refugees from other nations. In Table 4.5, we consider the major sources of refugees. According to the United Nations treaty on refugees, which our government ratified in 1968, countries are obliged to refrain from forcibly returning people to territories where their lives or liberty might be endangered. However, it is not always clear whether a person is fleeing for his or her personal safety or to escape poverty. Although people in the latter category may be of humanitarian interest, they do not meet the official definition of refugees and are subject to deportation.

Refugees are people who are granted the right to enter a country while still residing abroad. **Asylees** are foreigners who have already entered the United States and seek protection because of persecution or a well-founded fear of persecution in their home country. This persecution may be based on the individual's race, religion, nationality, membership in a particular social group, or political opinion. Asylees are eligible to adjust to lawful permanent resident status after one year of continuous presence in the United States. Asylum is granted to about 12,000 people annually.

Because asylees, by definition, are already here, they are either granted legal entry or returned to their home country. The practice of deporting people who are fleeing poverty has been the subject of criticism. The United States has a long tradition of facilitating the arrival of people leaving Communist nations, such as the Cubans. Mexicans who are refugees from poverty, Liberians fleeing civil war,

Table 4.5 Top Sources of Refugees

2000		2012	
1. Bosnia-Herzegovina	22,699	Bhutan	15,070
2. Yugoslavia (former)	14,280	Burma	14,160
3. Vietnam	9,622	Iraq	12,163
4. Ukraine	8,649	Somalia	4,911
5. Russia	4,386	Cuba	2,920
Total Refugees from All Countries:	85,076		58,179

SOURCE: Martin and Yankay 2013: 3.

and Haitians running from despotic rule are not similarly welcomed. The plight of Haitians is of particular concern.

Haitians began fleeing their country, often on small boats, in the 1980s. The U.S. Coast Guard intercepted many Haitians at sea, saving some of these boat people from death in their rickety and overcrowded wooden vessels. The Haitians said they feared detentions, torture, and execution if they remained in Haiti. Yet both Republican and Democratic administrations viewed most Haitian exiles as economic migrants rather than political refugees and opposed granting them asylum and permission to enter the United States. Once apprehended, the Haitians are returned. In 1993, the U.S. Supreme Court, by an 8–1 vote, upheld the government's right to intercept Haitian refugees at sea and return them to their homeland without asylum hearings.

The devastating 2010 earthquake in Haiti made the government reconsider this policy. Indeed, the United States halted deportations of 30,000 Haitians that were about to occur for at least 18 months. The moratorium also applied to the more than 100,000 Haitians believed to be living in the United States. As more residents of Haiti with U.S. citizenship or dual citizenship arrived from the island nation in the aftermath of the earthquake, the Haitian community increased. Despite continuing obstacles, the Haitian American community exhibits pride in those who have succeeded, from a Haitian American Florida state legislator and professional athletes to hip-hop musician Wyclef Jean. In fact, the initial earthquake refugees tended to come from the Haitian middle class or higher. Some even expressed annoyance at the quality of the public schools their children attended in America compared to the private ones in Haiti (Buchanan, Albert, and Beaulieu 2010; Office of Immigration Statistics 2013; Preston 2010; Winerip 2011).

Like all other immigrants, Muslim Americans incorporate U.S. traditions into their daily lives. Here Girl Scout troop leader Farheen Hakeem (right) prepares hot dogs that are halal—that is, dietary acceptable—during a Girl Scout outing in Minneapolis. Most of these troop members are Somali immigrants or their children.

New foreign military campaigns often bring new refugee issues. Large movements of Iraqis throughout the country and the region accompanied the occupation of Iraq, beginning in 2003. It is hoped that most will return home, but some want to relocate to the United States. As was true in Vietnam, many Iraqis who aided the U.S.-led mission have increasingly sought refuge in the West, fearing for their safety if they remain in Iraq or even in the Middle East. Gradually, the United States has begun to offer refugee status to Iraqis; some 39,000 arrived from 2010 through 2012 to create an Iraqi American community of 93,000. The diverse landscape of the United States has taken on yet another nationality group in large numbers (Asi and Beaulieu 2013; Martin and Yankay 2013).

Conclusion

The immigrant presence in the United States can often be heard on the streets and the workplace as people speak in different languages; check out your radio. As of 2011, radio stations broadcast in 35 languages other than English, including Albanian, Creole, Welsh, Yiddish, and Oji—a language spoken in Ghana. The Internet in 2013 expanded it to over 90 languages via online radio stations aimed at the USA (Keen 2011; Omniglot 2013).

Throughout the history of the United States, as we have seen, there has been intense debate over the nation's policies that bring the immigrants who speak these and other languages to the country. In a sense, this debate reflects the deep value conflicts in the U.S. culture and parallels the "American dilemma" identified by Swedish social economist Gunnar Myrdal (1944). One strand of our culture—epitomized by the words "Give us your tired, your poor, your huddled masses"—has emphasized egalitarian principles and a desire to help people in their time of need. One could hardly have anticipated at the time the Statue of Liberty was dedicated in 1886 that more than a century later Barack Obama, the son of a Kenyan immigrant, would be elected president of the United States.

At the same time, however, hostility to potential immigrants and refugees—whether the Chinese in the 1880s, European Jews in the 1930s and 1940s, or Mexicans, Haitians, and Arabs today—reflects not only racial, ethnic, and religious prejudice but also a desire to maintain the dominant culture of the in-group by keeping out those viewed as outsiders. The conflict between these cultural values is central to the American dilemma of the twenty-first century.

The current debate about immigration is highly charged and emotional. Some people see it in economic terms, whereas others see the new arrivals as a challenge to the very culture of our society. Clearly, the general perception is that immigration presents a problem rather than a promise for the future.

Today's concern about immigrants follows generations of people coming to settle in the United States. This immigration in the past produced a very

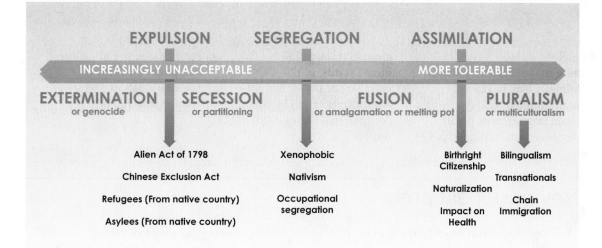

diverse country in terms of both nationality and religion, even before the immigration of the last 60 years. Therefore, the majority of Americans today are not descended from the English, and Protestants are just more than half of all worshipers. This diversity of religious and ethnic groups is examined in Chapter 5.

Summary

1. Immigration to the United States has changed over time from unrestricted to restricted, with the sending nations now in Latin America and Asia rather than Europe.
2. Immigration began being regulated by the United States in the nineteenth century; the first significant restriction was the Chinese Exclusion Act in 1882.
3. Subsequent legislation through the national origins system favored Northern and Western Europeans. Not until 1965 were quotas by nation largely lifted.
4. Issues including the brain drain, population growth, mixed-status households, English-language acquisition, and economic impact influence contemporary immigration policy.
5. Often more of a concern than legal immigration has been the continuing presence of a large number of illegal immigrants.
6. Naturalization is a complex process that is still pursued by those abroad as well as by unauthorized immigrants.
7. While immigrant men may typically dominate the workers, women play a critical role in the household formation and increasingly in the workforce.
8. The worldwide integration of societies has been facilitated by transnationals who sustain multiple social relationships across borders.
9. Environment affects and, in turn, is influenced by global immigration.
10. Refugees present a special challenge to policymakers who balance humanitarian values against an unwillingness to accept all those who are fleeing poverty and political unrest.

Key Terms

asylees, p. 140
bilingual education, p. 126
bilingualism, p. 126
brain drain, p. 122
chain immigration, p. 110
environmental refugees, p. 139

globalization, p. 137
mixed status, p. 124
nativism, p. 114
naturalization, p. 134
occupational segregation, p. 128
refugees, p. 139

remittances, p. 130
sinophobes, p. 115
transnationals, p. 138
xenophobia, p. 114

Review Questions

1. How would you describe the general patterns of immigration?
2. What were the social and economic issues when public opinion mounted against Chinese immigration to the United States?
3. How did restrictionist immigration policies develop in the twentieth century?
4. What are the contemporary social concerns about legal immigration today?
5. What are the main issues surrounding illegal immigration?
6. How can one become a naturalized citizen?
7. How do women play a critical role in global immigration?
8. How are the physical environment and immigration interrelated?
9. How is globalization furthered by immigration?
10. What principles appear to guide U.S. refugee policy?

Critical Thinking

1. What are the functions and dysfunctions of immigration?
2. Ultimately, what do you think is the major concern people have about contemporary immigration to the United States: the numbers of immigrants, their legal status, or their nationality?
3. What challenge does the presence of people in the United States speaking languages other than English present for them? For schools? For the workplace? For you?
4. What is your family's immigrant root story? Consider how your ancestors arrived in the United States and also how other immigrant groups have shaped your family's past.

Chapter 5
Ethnicity and Religion

STUDYING WHITENESS

5-1 Understand what is meant by "Whiteness."

REDISCOVERING ETHNICITY

5-2 Describe how people rediscover ethnicity.

THE GERMAN AMERICANS

5-3 Recall the German American experience.

THE IRISH AMERICANS

5-4 Identify the major periods of the Irish American immigration.

THE ITALIAN AMERICANS

5-5 Put into your own words the Italian American experience.

THE POLISH AMERICANS

5-6 Restate the Polish American immigration story.

RELIGIOUS PLURALISM

5-7 State what is meant by religious pluralism.

CONCLUSION

5-8 Interpret how the courts have ruled on religion.

When China and the United States established diplomatic relations in 1868, Chinese were allowed to legally immigrate to the United States. Most settled in California but some made their way to New York City and settled around Mott Street just south of Canal Street. Italians began immigrating in large numbers about the same time, settling in several areas including along Mulberry Street one street over from Mott but north of Canal. For 150 years Italian and Chinese Americans lived in adjoining densely populated neighborhoods.

By 1940, Little Italy was a tourist destination as was neighboring Chinatown. A decade later few Italians immigrated and those already in Little Italy began to move out. A few years later the Chinese community and its Chinatown expanded and by 1980 the population had surpassed that of San Francisco.

The character of Little Italy changed. In 1950, half of the residents were Italian American, with 20 percent of those born in Italy. By 2000 it was only 6 percent Italian American with very few born in Italy. Ten years later the proportion of Italian Americans had edged down to 5 percent with not a single Italian-born resident living in Little Italy. While the area along Mulberry remained a powerful symbol to ethnic Italians, today it is defined not as a place to live but by two elements: one is food, as represented by 50 or so restaurants and cafes as well as an occasional bakery, and the other is religion.

Going to church? The Zion English Lutheran Church established in 1801 became in 1853 the Church of the Transfiguration, as the Catholic Church took over the facility to serve the poor Irish. By 1891, it served the Italian neighborhood, but a couple of generations later Chinese Catholics began to attend and now its congregation is almost entirely Chinese with masses offered in English, Mandarin, and Cantonese.

Looking for the Chinese American Planning Council? Its offices are in Little Italy. Looking for the Museum of Chinese in America? Little Italy. By 2010, the 38-block area of Little Italy and Chinatown were listed in a single historic district on the National Register of Historic Places. So is it, "Arrivederci, Little Italy"?

Not yet. Near the Church of the Transfiguration, an annual 11-day festival of San Gennaro takes over several blocks and honors the Patron Saint of Naples— the point of origin for many of the Italian immigrants. The festival's climactic parade runs on both Mott and Mulberry Streets, where most of the residents are Chinese. Some follow Catholicism but others are of the Protestant, Buddhist, and Daoist faiths.

The changing nature of ethnicity in America's cities was underscored when the 2010 Census showed not a single Italian-born person living in New York City's Little Italy. While many people of Italian descent resided there, one was much more likely to find Chinese-born people than people of any other nationality.

Yes, the Italian Americans express concern over the visible Chinese American presence, but often they work with their ethnic neighbors to maintain an Italian presence. What really worries the Italian and even the much more numerous Chinese Americans about losing their ethnic neighborhood and religious institutions? It is the encroachment of boutiques, fancy little restaurants prepared to pay higher rents, and the dreaded arrival of a Starbucks. There is no negotiating the maintenance of ethnic ties with these agents of social change, so the Italian and Chinese Americans work together. For example, the two groups organized the annual Marco Polo Day, now in its fifth year, which honors the explorer from Venice who journeyed in the thirteenth century through Central Asia to China (Guest 2003; Krase 2006; National Park Service 2009, 2012; Roberts 2011; Tonelli 2004; Two Bridges 2013).

It's May, ready for the National Day of Prayer? Congress formalized this observance in 1952. While 83 percent of people in the United States indicate there is a God who answers prayers, the increasing diversity of believers makes even the observance of this event increasingly contentious. What kind of praying? Some more ecumenical prayers (no reference to Jesus Christ, for example, or even to a supreme being) affront many. Specific Biblical, Talmudic, or Qur'anic references have limited appeals across a nation tolerant of so many faiths. So are we too religious or not religious enough (Grossman 2010)?

One's religious or ethnic experience is unlikely to be identical to the next person, so it is this diversity that we consider in this chapter. Also, with this diversity we consider how one goes about "fitting in" to a new society. First, we will consider the social canvas against which this diversity is painted—Whiteness.

Studying Whiteness

5.1 Understand what is meant by "Whiteness."

Race is socially constructed, as we learned in Chapter 1. Sometimes we define race in a clear-cut manner. A descendant of a Pilgrim is White, for example. But sometimes race is more ambiguous: Children of an African American and Vietnamese American union are biracial, mixed, or whatever they come to be seen by others. Our recognition that race is socially constructed has sparked a renewed interest in what it means to be White in the United States. Two aspects of the White race are useful to consider: the historical creation of Whiteness and how contemporary White people reflect on their racial identity.

When the English immigrants established themselves as the political founders of the United States, they also came to define what it meant to be White. Other groups that today are regarded as White—such as Irish, Germans, Norwegians, or Swedes—were not always considered White in the eyes of the English. Differences in language and religious worship as well as past allegiance to a king in Europe different from the English monarch meant these groups were seen not so much as Whites in the Western Hemisphere but more as nationals of their home country who happened to reside in North America.

The old distrust in Europe, where, for example, the English viewed the Irish as socially and culturally inferior, continued on this side of the Atlantic Ocean. Writing from England, Karl Marx reported that the average English worker looked down on the Irish the way poor Whites in the U.S. South looked down on Black people (Ignatiev 1994, 1995; Roediger 1994).

As European immigrants and their descendants assimilated to the English and distanced themselves from other oppressed groups such as American Indians and African Americans, they came to be viewed as White rather than as part of a particular "alien" culture. Writer Noel Ignatiev (1994: 84), contrasting being White with being Polish, argues, "Whiteness is nothing but an expression of race privilege." This strong statement argues that being White, as opposed to being Black or Asian, is characterized by being a member of the dominant group. Whiteness, although it may often be invisible, is aggressively embraced and defended (Giroux 1997).

White people do not think of themselves as a race or have a conscious racial identity. A White racial identity emerges only when filling out a form asking for self-designation of race or when Whites are culturally or socially surrounded by people who are not White.

Many immigrants who were not "White on arrival" had to "become White" in a process long forgotten by today's White Americans. The long-documented transparent racial divide that engulfed the South during slavery let us ignore how Whiteness was constructed.

Therefore, contemporary White Americans give little thought to "being White." Consequently, there is little interest in studying "Whiteness" or considering "being White" except that it is "not being Black." Unlike non-Whites, who are much more likely to interact with Whites, take orders from Whites, and see Whites as leading figures in the mass media, Whites enjoy not being reminded of their Whiteness.

Unlike racial minorities, Whites downplay the importance of their racial identity, although they are willing to receive the advantages that come from being White. This means that advocating a "color-blind" or "race-neutral" outlook permits the privilege of Whiteness to prevail (Bonilla-Silva 2002; Feagin and Cobas 2008; Yancey 2003).

New scholarly interest seeks to view Whiteness but not from the vantage point of a White supremacist. Rather, focusing on White people as a race or on what it means today to be White goes beyond any definition that implies superiority over non-Whites. It also is recognized that "being White" is not the same experience for all Whites, any more than "being Asian American" or "being Black" is the same for all Asian Americans or all Blacks. Historian Noel Ignatiev observes that studying Whiteness is a necessary stage to the "abolition of whiteness"—just as, in Marxist analysis, class-consciousness is a necessary stage to the abolition of class. By confronting Whiteness, society grasps the all-encompassing power that accompanies socially constructed race (Lewis 2004; McKinney 2003; Roediger 2006).

White privilege, introduced in Chapter 2, refers to the rights granted as a benefit or favor of being White and can be an element of Whiteness. However, of course, many Whites consciously minimize exercising this privilege. Admittedly, it is difficult when a White person is more likely than not to see national leaders, celebrities, and role models who also are White. For every Barack Obama, there are hundreds of movers and shakers who are White. For example, many White people champion the cause of the HBCUs (historically Black colleges and universities), conveniently ignoring that their presence is due to the existence of thousands of HWCUs (historically White colleges and universities) (Bonilla-Silva 2012).

When race is articulated or emphasized for Whites, it is more likely to be seen as threatening to Whites than allowing them to embrace their own race or national roots with pride. Behavioral economists Michael Norton and Samuel Sommers (2011) found that Whites view race as a zero-sum game—that is, decreases in bias against African Americans over the last 60 years are associated with increases in what they perceive as bias against Whites. While still seeing anti-Black bias as greater today than anti-White feeling in society, their analysis shows that, in the minds of the White respondents, the two biases are coming closer together. Black respondents also saw a marked decline in anti-Black bias during the same period but perceived only a modest increase in anti-White feelings. While Norton and Sommers's research deals only with perception of reality, it does suggest that race, and not just that of non-Whites, influences one's perception of society.

Rediscovering Ethnicity

5.2 **Describe how people rediscover ethnicity.**

Robert Park (1950: 205), a prominent early sociologist, wrote in 1913, "a Pole, Lithuanian, or Norwegian cannot be distinguished, in the second generation, from an American, born of native parents." At one time, sociologists saw the end of ethnicity as nearly a foregone conclusion. W. Lloyd Warner and Leo Srole (1945) wrote in their often-cited *Yankee City* series that the future of ethnic groups seemed to be limited in the United States and that they would be quickly absorbed. Oscar Handlin's *The Uprooted* (1951) told of the destruction of immigrant values and their replacement by American culture. Although Handlin was among the pioneers in investigating ethnicity, assimilation was the dominant theme in his work.

Many writers have shown almost a fervent hope that ethnicity would vanish. For some time, sociologists treated the persistence of ethnicity as dysfunctional because it meant continuing old values that interfered with the allegedly superior new values. For example, holding on to one's language delayed entry into the larger labor market and the upward social mobility it afforded. Ethnicity was expected to disappear not only because of assimilation but also because aspirations to higher social class and status demanded that it vanish. It was assumed that one could not be ethnic and middle class, much less affluent.

Blended Identity

The process of being an ethnic to an ethnic who is a part of a larger society leads to what has been termed a **blended identity**. This is a self-image and worldview that is a combination of religious faith, cultural background based on nationality, and the status of being a resident of the United States.

Consider the example of a Pakistani American. As shown in Figure 5.1, Muslims often find their daily activities defined by their faith, their nationality, and their status as American, however defined in terms of citizenship. Younger Muslims especially can move freely among the different identities. In Chicago, Muslim college students perform hip-hop in Arabic with lyrics like "La ilaha ila Allah" ("There is no God but Allah"). In Fremont, California, high school Muslim girls and some of their non-Muslim girlfriends hold an alternative prom, decked out in silken gowns, dancing to both 50 Cent and Arabic music, dining on lasagna, but pausing at sunset to face toward Mecca and pray (Abdo 2004a; Mostofi 2003).

Multiple identities along ethnic, racial, and national lines can lead to confusion between how one sees themselves. In any ethnic or immigrant community, divisions arise over who can truly be counted as a member of the community. Sociologist Gary David (2003, 2007) developed the concept of the **deficit model of ethnic identity**. This states that others view one's identity as a factor of subtracting away characteristics corresponding to some ideal ethnic type. Each factor

Figure 5.1 Blended Identity of Muslim Americans

Muslim Americans, as shown in this illustration representing the life/experience of a Pakistani Muslim living in the United States, form their identity by bringing together three different identities: their faith, their homeland, and the United States.

SOURCE: Prepared by Schaefer

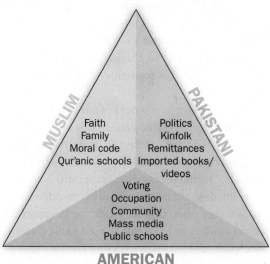

encompassing a perfect ethnic identity missing from a person's background or identity leads the person to be viewed by others as more assimilated and less ethnic. In the case of Arab Americans, if they are unable to speak Arabic, then they are less Arab to some people; if they are married to non-Arabs, then they are less ethnic; if they have never been to the home country, then they are less ethnic. Depending on one's perspective, an Arab American can come to regard another Arab American as either "too American" or "too Arab." Arab American organizations, magazines, and associations may seek to cater to the entire Arab American community, but, more likely, cater to certain segments based on nationality, religion, and degree of assimilation.

The Third-Generation Principle

Historian Marcus Hansen's (1952) **principle of third-generation interest** was an early exception to the assimilationist approach to White ethnic groups. Simply stated, Hansen maintained that in the third generation—the grandchildren of the original immigrants—ethnic interest and awareness would increase. According to Hansen, "What the son wishes to forget, the grandson wishes to remember."

Hansen's principle has been tested several times since it was first put forth. John Goering (1971), in interviewing Irish and Italian Catholics, found that ethnicity was more important to members of the third generation than to the immigrants themselves. Similarly, Mary Waters (1990)—in her interviews of White ethnics living in suburban areas of San Jose, California, and Philadelphia,

Pennsylvania—observed that many grandchildren wanted to study their ancestors' language, even though it would be a foreign language to them. They also expressed interest in learning more of their ethnic group's history and a desire to visit their homeland.

Social scientists in the past were quick to minimize the ethnic awareness of blue-collar workers. In fact, ethnicity was viewed as merely another aspect of White ethnics' alleged racist nature, an allegation examined later in this chapter. Curiously, the same intellectuals and journalists who bent over backward to understand the growing solidarity of Blacks, Hispanics, and Native Americans refused to give White ethnics the academic attention they deserved (Kivisto 2008; Wrong 1972).

The new assertiveness of ethnicity is not limited to Whites of European descent. Many members of third and successive generations of Asian and Latin American immigrants are showing renewed interest in their native languages. The very languages they avoided or even scorned themselves as children, they now want to learn as young adults. "Heritage language" programs have become increasingly common. Even when the descendants may easily communicate in their native language in everyday life, they often find they lack the language tools necessary for more sophisticated vocabulary or to be able to read easily (Nawa 2011).

Ethnic Paradox

While many nearly assimilated Whites are rediscovering their ethnicity (i.e., the principle of third-generation interest), others are at least publicly acknowledging their ethnicity from time to time (i.e., symbolic ethnicity). Yet research confirms that preserving elements of one's ethnicity may advance economic success and further societal acceptance.

Ethnic paradox refers to the maintenance of one's ethnic ties in a manner that can assist with assimilation with larger society. Immigrant youth as well as adults who maintain their ethnicity tend to have more success as indicated by health measures, educational attainment, and lower incidence of behavioral problems such as delinquency and truancy.

Researchers typically measure ethnic maintenance by facility in the mother language (not just conversational or "street" use) and living with others of the same ethnic background. These clear ethnic ties are not an automatic recipe for success. For example, residing with co-ethnics can lead to exploitation such as in neighborhoods where people steer those of their own ethnicity into dead-end, poor-paying, and even unhealthy working conditions. Yet for many ethnics, enclaves offer a refuge, sort of a halfway house, between two different cultures. Language maintenance, as noted in the previous chapter, is often critical to being literate and comfortable with English (Desmond and Kubrin 2009).

In "Speaking Out," sociologist Tomás Jiménez at Stanford University considers the role that new people arriving has played in the United States in shaping the nation's identity and how immigrants manage life in a new society.

Speaking Out

The Next Americans

How immigrants and their descendants see themselves will change over time, and they will simultaneously transform many aspects of what it means to be an American. This is undoubtedly an uncomfortable process, fraught with tension between newcomers and established Americans that can occasionally become explosive. But the real issue is whether the United States can provide opportunities for upward mobility so that immigrants can, in turn, fortify what is most essential to our nation's identity.

Tomás Jiménez

History is instructive on whether immigrants will create a messy patchwork of ethnicities in the U.S. About a century ago, a tide of Southern and Eastern European immigrants arriving on our shores raised fears similar to those we hear today. Then, as now, Americans worried that the newcomers were destroying American identity. Many were certain that Catholic immigrants would help the pope rule the United States from Rome, and that immigrants from Southern Europe would contaminate the American gene pool.

None of this came to pass, of course. The pope has no political say in American affairs, the United States is still a capitalist democracy, and there is nothing wrong with the American gene pool. The fact that these fears never materialized are often cited as proof that European-origin immigrants and their descendants successfully assimilated into an American societal monolith.

However, as sociologists Richard Alba and Victor Nee point out, much of the American identity, as we know it today, was shaped by previous waves of immigrants. For instance, they note that the Christian tradition of the Christmas tree and the leisure Sunday made their way into the American mainstream because German immigrants and their descendants brought these traditions with them. Where religion was concerned, Protestantism was the clear marker of the nonsecular mainstream. But because of the assimilation of millions of Jews and Catholics, we today commonly refer to an American "Judeo-Christian tradition," a far more encompassing notion of American religious identity than the one envisioned in the past....

Even in Los Angeles County, where 36 percent of the population is foreign-born and more than half speak a language other than English at home, English is not losing out in the long run. According to a recent study by social scientists Rubén Rumbaut, Douglas Massey, and Frank Bean, published in the *Population and Development Review,* the use of non-English languages virtually disappears among nearly all U.S.-born children of immigrants in the country. Spanish shows more staying power among the U.S.-born children and grandchildren of Mexican immigrants, which is not surprising given that the size of the Spanish-speaking population provides near-ubiquitous access to the language. But the survival of Spanish among U.S.-born descendants of Mexican immigrants does not come at the expense of their ability to speak English and, more strikingly, English overwhelms Spanish-language use among the grandchildren of these immigrants.

An equally telling sign of how much immigrants and their children are becoming "American" is how different they have become from those in their ethnic homelands. Virtually all of today's immigrants stay connected to their countries of origin. They send money to family members who remain behind. Relatively inexpensive air, rail, and bus travel and the availability of cheap telecommunication and e-mail enable them to stay in constant contact, and dual citizenship allows their political voices to be heard from abroad. These enduring ties might lead to the conclusion that continuity between here and there threatens loyalty to the Stars and Stripes.

But ask any immigrant or their children about a recent visit to their country of origin, and they are likely to tell you how American they felt. The family and friends they visit quickly recognize the prodigal children's tastes for American styles, their American accents, and their declining cultural familiarity with life in the ethnic homeland—all telltale signs that they've Americanized. As sociologist David Fitzgerald puts it, their assimilation into American society entails a good deal of "dissimilation" from the countries the immigrants left behind.

American identity is absorbing something quite significant from immigrants and being changed by them. Language, food, entertainment, and holiday traditions are palpable aspects of American culture on which immigrants today, as in the past, are leaving their mark. Our everyday lexicon is sprinkled with Spanish words. We are now just as likely to grab a burrito as a burger. Hip-hop is tinged with South Asian rhythms. And Chinese New Year and Cinco de Mayo are taking their places alongside St. Patrick's Day as widely celebrated American ethnic holidays.

SOURCE: Jiménez 2007.

Symbolic Ethnicity

Observers comment on both the evidence of assimilation and the signs of ethnic identity that support a pluralistic view of society. How can both be possible?

First, the visible evidence of **symbolic ethnicity** might lead us to exaggerate the persistence of ethnic ties among White Americans. According to sociologist Herbert Gans (1979), ethnicity today increasingly involves symbols of ethnicity, such as eating ethnic food, acknowledging ceremonial holidays such as St. Patrick's Day, and supporting specific political issues or issues confronting the old country. One example was the push in 1998 by Irish Americans to convince state legislatures to make it compulsory that public schools teach about the Irish potato famine—a significant factor in immigration to the United States. This symbolic ethnicity may be more visible, but this type of ethnic heritage does not interfere with what people do, read, or say, or even whom they befriend or marry. By one analysis, only an estimated 7 percent of White non-Hispanics self-express a significant sense of ethnicity (Scully 2012; Torkelson and Hartmann 2010).

The ethnicity of the twenty-first century, as embraced by English-speaking Whites, is largely symbolic. It does not include active involvement in ethnic activities or participation in ethnic-related organizations. In fact, sizable proportions of White ethnics have gained large-scale entry into almost all clubs, cliques, and fraternal groups. Such acceptance is a key indicator of assimilation. Ethnicity has become increasingly peripheral to the lives of members of the ethnic group. Although today's White ethnics may not relinquish their ethnic identity, other identities become more important.

Second, the ethnicity that exists may be more a result of living in the United States than importing practices from the past or the old country. Many so-called ethnic foods or celebrations, for example, began in the United States. The persistence of ethnic consciousness, then, may not depend on foreign birth, a distinctive language, and a unique way of life. Instead, it may reflect the experiences in the United States of a unique group that developed a cultural tradition distinct from that of the mainstream. For example, in Poland, the *szlachta*, or landed gentry, rarely mixed socially with the peasant class. In the United States, however, even with those associations still fresh, *szlachta* and peasants interacted together in social organizations as they settled in concentrated communities segregated physically and socially from others (Lopata 1994; Winter 2008).

Third, maintaining ethnicity can be a critical step toward successful assimilation. This ethnicity paradox facilitates full entry into the dominant culture. The ethnic community may give its members not only a useful financial boost but also the psychological strength and positive self-esteem that will allow them to compete effectively in a larger society. Thus, we may witness people participating actively in their ethnic enclave while trying to cross the bridge into the wider community (Lal 1995).

Therefore, ethnicity gives continuity with the past in the form of an effective or emotional tie. The significance of this sense of belonging cannot be emphasized enough. Whether reinforced by distinctive behavior or by what Milton Gordon (1964) called a sense of *peoplehood*, ethnicity is an effective, functional source of cohesion. Proximity to fellow ethnics is not necessary for a person to maintain social cohesion and in-group identity. Fraternal organizations or sports-related groups can preserve associations between ethnics who are separated geographically. Members of ethnic groups may even maintain feelings of in-group solidarity after leaving ethnic communities in the central cities for the suburban fringe.

The German Americans

5.3   **Recall the German American experience.**

Germany is the largest single source of ancestry of people in the United States today, even exceeding the continents of either Africa or Asia. Yet except in a few big-city neighborhood enclaves, the explicit presence of German culture seems largely relegated to bratwurst, pretzels, and Kris Kringle.

Settlement Patterns

In the late 1700s, the newly formed United States experienced the arrival of a number of religious dissenters from Germany (such as the Amish) who were attracted by the proclamation of religious freedom as well as prospects for economic advancement. At the time of the American Revolution, immigrants from Germany accounted for about one in eight White residents. German colonial subjects split their loyalty between the revolutionaries and the British, but were united in their optimistic view of the opportunities the New World would present.

Although Pennsylvania was the center of early settlements, German Americans, like virtually all other Europeans, moved out west (Ohio, Michigan, and beyond), where land was abundant. In many isolated communities, they

Figure 5.2 Immigration from Germany, Ireland, Italy, and Poland

Note: Immigration after 1925 from Northern Ireland is not included. No separate data is included for Poland from 1900 to 1920.

SOURCE: Office of Immigration Statistics 2009: Table 2.

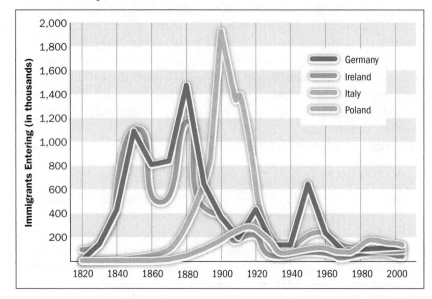

established churches and parochial schools, and, in some instances, ethnic enclaves that in selected areas spoke of creating "New Germanys."

Beginning in the 1830s through 1890, Germans represented at least one-quarter of the immigrants, ensuring their destiny in the settlement of the United States (see Figure 5.2). Their major urban presence was in Milwaukee, Chicago, Cleveland, Detroit, and Cincinnati.

Early in the history of America, German immigrant cultural influence was apparent. Although the new United States never voted on making German the national language, publications of the proceedings of the Continental Congress were published in German and English. Yet even in those early years, the fear of foreigners—that is, non-Anglos—prevented German, even temporarily, from ever getting equal footing with English.

German Americans, then perhaps representing 10 percent of the population, established bilingual programs in many public schools, but the rise of Germany as a military foe in the twentieth century ended that movement (Harzig 2008; Nelsen 1973).

Twenty-First-Century German America

In 1901, the German-American National Alliance (Deutsche-Amerikanischer National-Bund) was founded to speak for all Germans in the United States, especially urban Protestant middle-class German Americans. As time passed,

Anti-German sentiment spread in the United States during World War I, escalating dramatically after the United States entered the war in April 1917. A wave of verbal and physical attacks on German Americans was accompanied by a campaign to repress German culture. In this photograph from 1917, a group of children stand in front of an anti-German sign posted in Chicago. As the sign suggests, some people in the United States questioned the loyalty of their German American neighbors.

it sought to commemorate the contributions to the nation's development but also sought to block Prohibition. With the rise of German military power, many German Americans sought to argue for U.S. neutrality. But these efforts ended quickly, and the organization actually disbanded after the United States declared war on Germany in 1917.

With World War I and especially the rise of the Nazi era and the war years of the 1930s and 1940s, most German Americans sought to distance themselves from the politics in their homeland. There were anti-German incidents of harassment and intimidation. About 11,000 German Americans (out of 5 million) were interned, but the stigmatization did not come close to that felt by Japanese Americans. By comparison, many more German Americans enlisted and played important roles (none more so than Dwight Eisenhower, whose ancestors immigrated to Pennsylvania from Germany in 1741).

German Americans made the group transition into core society. Indeed, Horace Kallen, who popularized the term *pluralism,* held up German America as a success in finding a place in the United States. With the end of wartime tensions, German Americans moved from having multiple identities that included being somewhat marginalized as "Germans" to an identity of "American" and, less explicitly, White (Carlson 2003; Kazal 2004; Krammer 1997).

By the latter half of the twentieth century, the animosity toward Germany seemed a part of the distant past. Germany and its people became emblematic of stalwart friends of the United States, as reflected with appearances beginning with John F. Kennedy in Berlin in 1963 and Ronald Reagan in 1987. Both spoke of the U.S. commitment to uniting Germany, and presidential candidate Barack Obama in 2008 spoke in Berlin of a united Europe.

In the last ten years, immigration from Germany, a country of 82 million, has fluctuated between 6,000 and 10,000 annually. The steady immigration for decades placed Germany in the 2000 Census as the tenth-largest source of foreign-born residents, with more than 700,000 (only about 170,000 behind Cuba and Korea). Yet the broad dispersion of these immigrants and their bilingual capability means the numbers are insufficient to create (or re-create) a German cultural presence. Rather, today's German American community is characterized by postwar and historical ties that have long since overshadowed the lingering bitterness of World Wars I and II (Harzig 2008; Office of Immigration Statistics 2012).

Famous German Americans include industrialist John D. Rockefeller, General John Pershing, baseball players Babe Ruth and Lou Gehrig, celebrity Paris Hilton, and actors Clark Gable and Katherine Heigl.

The Irish Americans

5.4   Identify the major periods of the Irish American immigration.

The Irish presence in the United States stretches back to the 1600s and reflects a diversity based on time of entry, settlement area, and religion. Irish Americans have been visible both in a positive way in terms of playing a central role in American life and in a negative way at certain historical periods, being victimized like so many other immigrant groups.

Irish Immigration

The Roman Catholics among the early immigrants were a diverse group. Some were extensions of the privileged classes seeking even greater prosperity. Protestant settlers of all national backgrounds including those coming from Ireland were united in their hatred of Catholicism. In most of the colonies, Catholics could not practice their faith openly and either struggled inwardly or converted to Anglicanism. Other Roman Catholics and some Protestants came from Europe as an alternative to prison or after signing articles of indenture and arriving bound to labor for periods of customarily three to five years and sometimes as long as seven years (Meagher 2005).

The American Revolution temporarily stopped the flow of immigration, but deteriorating economic conditions in Ireland soon spurred even greater movement to North America. British officials, by making passage to the newly formed republic of the United States expensive, diverted many immigrants to British North America (Canada). Yet the numbers to the United States remained significant and, although still primarily Protestant, drew from a broader spectrum of Ireland both economically and geographically.

Many people mistakenly overlook this early immigration and begin with Irish immigration during the Great Famine. Yet the Irish were the largest group after the English among immigrants during the colonial period. The historical emphasis on the famine immigrants is understandable, given the role it played in Ireland and its impetus for the massive transfer of population from Ireland to the United States.

In 1845, a fungus wiped out the potato crop of Ireland, as well as that of much of Western Europe and even coastal America. Potatoes were particularly central to the lives of the Irish, and the devastating starvation did not begin to recede until 1851. Mortality was high, especially among the poor and in the more agricultural areas of the island. Predictably, to escape catastrophe, some 2 million Irish fled mostly to England, but then many continued on to the United States. From 1841 through 1890, more than 3.2 million Irish arrived in the United States (Figure 5.2).

This new migration fleeing the old country was much more likely to consist of families rather than single men. The arrival of entire households and extended kinship networks increased significantly the rapid formation of Irish social organizations in the United States. This large influx of immigrants led to the creation of ethnic neighborhoods called Little Italy such as described in the beginning of the chapter, complete with parochial schools and parish churches serving as focal points. Fraternal organizations such as the Ancient Order of Hibernians, corner saloons, local political organizations, and Irish nationalist groups seeking the ouster of Britain from Ireland rounded out neighborhood social life.

Even in the best of times, the lives of the famine Irish would have been challenging in the United States, but they arrived at a very difficult time. Nativist— that is, anti-Catholic and anti-immigrant—movements were already emerging and being embraced by politicians. Antagonism was not limited to harsh words. From 1834 to 1854, mob violence against Catholics across the country led to death, the burning of a Boston convent, the destruction of a Catholic church and the homes of Catholics, and the use of Marines and state militia to bring peace to American cities as far west as St. Louis.

In retrospect, the reception given to the Irish is not difficult to understand. Many immigrated after the potato crop failure and famine in Ireland. They fled not so much to a better life as from almost certain death. The Irish Catholics brought with them a celibate clergy, who struck the New England aristocracy as strange and reawakened old religious hatreds. The Irish were worse than Blacks, according to the dominant Whites, because unlike the slaves and even the freed Blacks, who "knew their place," the Irish did not suffer their maltreatment in silence. Employers balanced minorities by judiciously mixing immigrant groups to prevent unified action by the laborers. For the most part, nativist efforts only led the foreign born to emphasize their ties to Europe.

Mostly of peasant backgrounds, the arriving Irish were ill prepared to compete successfully for jobs in the city. Their children found it much easier to improve their occupational status over that of their fathers as well as experienced upward mobility in their own lifetimes (Miller 2014: 268–270).

Becoming White

Ireland had a long antislavery tradition, including practices that prohibited Irish trade in English slaves. Some 60,000 Irish signed an address in 1841, petitioning Irish Americans to join the abolitionist movement in the United States. Many Irish Americans already opposed to slavery applauded the appeal, but they were soon drowned out by fellow immigrants who denounced or questioned the authenticity of the petition.

The Irish immigrants, subjected to derision and menial jobs, sought to separate themselves from the even lower classes, particularly Black Americans and especially the slaves. It was not altogether clear that the Irish were "White" during the antebellum period. Irish character was rigidly cast in negative racial typology. Although the shared experiences of oppression could have led Irish Americans to ally with Black Americans, they grasped for Whiteness at the margins of their lives in the United States. Direct competition was not common between the two groups. For example, in 1855, Irish immigrants made up 87 percent of New York City's unskilled laborers, whereas free Blacks accounted for only 3 percent (Greeley 1981; Ignatiev 1995; Roediger 1994).

As Irish immigration continued in the latter part of the nineteenth century until Irish independence in 1921, they began to see themselves favorably in comparison to the initial waves of Italian, Polish, and Slovak Roman Catholic immigrants. The Irish Americans began to assume more leadership positions in politics and labor unions. Loyalty to the church still played a major role. By 1910, the priesthood was the professional occupation of choice for second-generation men. Irish women were more likely than their German and English immigrant counterparts to become schoolteachers. In time, Irish Americans' occupational profiles diversified, and they began to experience slow advancement and gradually were welcomed into the White working class as their identity as "White" overcame any status as "immigrant."

With mobility came social class distinctions within Irish America. The immigrants and their children who began to move into the more affluent urban areas were derogatorily referred to as the "lace-curtain Irish." The lower-class Irish immigrants they left behind, meanwhile, were referred to as the "shanty Irish." But as immigration from Ireland slowed and upward mobility quickened, fewer and fewer Irish qualified as the poor cousins of their predecessors.

For the Irish American man, the priesthood was viewed as a desirable and respected occupation. Irish Americans furthermore played a leadership role in the Roman Catholic Church in the United States. The Irish dominance persisted long after other ethnic groups swelled the ranks of the faithful (Fallows 1979; Lee and Bean 2007; Lee and Casey 2006).

The Contemporary Picture

By 2010, 35.6 million people identified themselves as having Irish ancestry—second only to German ancestry and more than five times the current population of Ireland itself. Massachusetts has the largest concentration of Irish Americans, with 24 percent of the state indicating Irish ancestry.

Irish immigration today is relatively slight, accounting for perhaps one out of 1,000 legal arrivals until because of tough economic times it climbed to 2,800 in 2010. About 122,000 people in the United States were born in Ireland. Today's Irish American typically enjoys the symbolic ethnicity of food, dance, and music. Gaelic language instruction is limited to fewer than 30 colleges. Visibility as a collective ethnic group is greatest with the annual St. Patrick's Day celebrations, when everyone seems to be Irish, or with the occasional fervent nationalism aimed at curtailing Great Britain's role in Northern Ireland. Yet some stereotypes remain concerning excessive drinking despite available data indicating that alcoholism rates are no higher and sometimes lower among people of Irish ancestry compared to descendants of other European immigrant groups (Bureau of the Census 2011b; Chazan and Tomson 2011).

For many Irish American participants in a St. Patrick's Day parade, this is their most visible expression of symbolic ethnicity during the entire year.

St. Patrick's Day celebrations, as noted previously, offer an example of how ethnic identity evolves over time. The Feast of St. Patrick has a long history, but public celebrations with parties, concerts, and parades originated in the United States, which were then exported to Ireland in the latter part of the twentieth century. Even today, the large Irish American population often defines what is authentic Irish globally. For example, participants in Irish step dancing in the United States have developed such clout in international competitions that they have come to define many aspects of cultural expression, much to the consternation of the Irish in Ireland (Bureau of the Census 2009b; Hassrick 2007).

Well-known Irish Americans can be found in all arenas of American society, including celebrity chef Bobby Flay, songwriter and musician Kurt Cobain, comedian Conan O'Brien, and author Frank McCourt, as well as the political dynasties of the Kennedys in Massachusetts and the Daleys in Chicago. Reflecting growing rates of intermarriage, Irish America also includes singer Mariah Carey (her mother Irish and her father African American and Venezuelan).

The Irish were the first immigrant group to encounter prolonged organized resistance. However, strengthened by continued immigration, facility with the English language, building on strong community and family networks, and familiarity with representative politics, Irish Americans became an integral part of the United States.

The Italian Americans

5.5   Put into your own words the Italian American experience.

Although each European country's immigration to the United States has created its own social history, the case of Italians, though not typical of every nationality, offers insight into the White ethnic experience. Italians immigrated even during the colonial period, coming from what was a highly differentiated land, because Italian states did not unify as one nation and escaped foreign domination until 1848.

Early Immigration

From the beginning Italian Americans played prominent roles during the American Revolution and the early days of the republic. Mass immigration began in the 1880s, peaking in the first 20 years of the twentieth century, when Italians accounted for one-fourth of European immigration (refer to Figure 5.2).

Italian immigration was concentrated not only in time but also by geography. The majority of the immigrants were landless peasants from rural southern Italy, the Mezzogiorno. Although many people in the United States assume that Italians are a nationality with a single culture, this is not true either culturally or economically. The Italian people recognize multiple geographic divisions reflecting sharp cultural distinctions. These divisions were brought with the immigrants to the New World.

Many Italians, especially in the early years of mass immigration in the nineteenth century, received their jobs through an ethnic labor contractor, the padrone. Similar arrangements have been used by Asian, Hispanic, and Greek immigrants, where the labor contractors, most often immigrants, have mastered sufficient English to mediate for their compatriots. Exploitation was common within the padrone system through kickbacks, provision of inadequate housing, and withholding of wages. By World War I, 90 percent of Italian girls and 99 percent of Italian boys in New York City were leaving school at age 14 to work, but by that time, Italian Americans were sufficiently fluent in English to seek out work on their own, and the padrone system had disappeared. Still, by comparison to the Irish, the Italians in the United States were slower to accept formal schooling as essential to success (Sassler 2006).

Along with manual labor, the Catholic Church was a very important part of Italian Americans' lives at that time. Yet they found little comfort in a Catholic Church dominated by an earlier immigrant group: the Irish. The traditions were different; weekly attendance for Italian Americans was overshadowed by the religious aspects of the feste (or festivals) held throughout the year in honor of saints (the Irish viewed the feste as practically a form of paganism). These initial adjustment problems were overcome with the establishment of ethnic parishes, a pattern repeated by other non-Irish immigrant groups. Thus, parishes would be staffed by Italian priests, sometimes imported for that purpose. Although the hierarchy of the Church adjusted more slowly, Italian Americans were increasingly able to feel at home in their local parish church. Today, more than 70 percent of Italian Americans identify themselves as Roman Catholics (Luconi 2001).

Over the first few generations in the United States, Italian Americans rose up through the social classes largely by acquiring skills in low-skilled occupations rather than acquiring advanced degrees and entering professions. Eventually they began to achieve success in wine and fruit growing as well as entrepreneurs of retail outlets in the urban northeast and Midwest (Llosa 2013).

Constructing Identity

As assimilation proceeded, Italian Americans began to construct a social identity as a nationality group rather than viewing themselves in terms of their village or province. As shown in Figure 5.3, over time, Italian Americans shed old identities for new ones. As immigration from Italy declined, the descendants' ties became more nationalistic. This move from local or regional to national identity was followed by Irish and Greek Americans. The changing identity of Italian Americans reflected the treatment they received in the United States, whereas non-Italians did not make those regional distinctions. However, they were not treated well. For example, in turn-of-the-century New Orleans, Italian Americans established special ties with the Black community because both groups were marginalized in Southern society. Gradually, Italian Americans became White and enjoyed all the privileges that came with it. Today, it would be inconceivable to imagine

Figure 5.3 Constructing Social Identity among Italian Immigrants

Over time, Italian Americans moved from seeing themselves in terms of their provincial or village identity to their national identity, and then they successfully became indistinguishable from other Whites.

SOURCE: Prepared by Schaefer

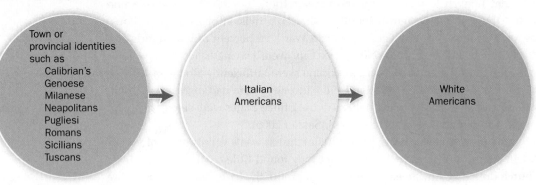

that Italian Americans of New Orleans would reach out to the African American community as their natural allies on social and political issues (Guglielmo and Salerno 2003; Luconi 2001; Steinberg 2007: 126).

A controversial aspect of the Italian American experience involves organized crime, as typified by Al Capone (1899–1947). Arriving in U.S. society in the bottom layers, Italians lived in decaying, crime-ridden neighborhoods. For a small segment of these immigrants, crime was a significant means of upward social mobility. In effect, entering and leading criminal activity was one aspect of assimilation, though not a positive one. Complaints linking ethnicity and crime actually began in colonial times with talk about the criminally inclined Irish and Germans, and they continue with contemporary stereotyping of groups such as Colombian drug dealers and Vietnamese street gangs. Yet the image of Italians as criminals has persisted from Prohibition-era gangsters to the view of mob families today. As noted earlier, it is not at all surprising that groups have been organized to counter such negative images.

The fact that Italians often are characterized as criminal, even in the mass media, is another example of what we have called respectable bigotry toward White ethnics. The persistence of linking Italians, or any other minority group, with crime probably is attributable to attempts to explain a problem by citing a single cause: the presence of perceived undesirables. Many Italian Americans still see their image tied to old stereotypes. A 2001 survey of Italian American teenagers found that 39 percent felt the media presented their ethnic group as criminal or gang members and 34 percent as restaurant workers (Girardelli 2004; IAAMS 2009; National Italian American Foundation 2006; Parrillo 2008).

The immigration of Italians was slowed by the national origins system, described in Chapter 4. As Italian Americans settled permanently, the mutual aid societies that had grown up in the 1920s to provide basic social services began to dissolve. More slowly, education came to be valued by Italian Americans as a means of upward mobility. Even becoming more educated did not ward off prejudice, however. In 1930, for example, President Herbert Hoover rebuked Fiorello La Guardia, then an Italian American member of Congress from New York City, stating that "the Italians are predominantly our murderers and bootleggers" and recommending that La Guardia "go back to where you belong" because, "like a lot of other foreign spawn, you do not appreciate this country which supports you and tolerates you" (Baltzell 1964: 30).

Although U.S. troops, including 500,000 Italian Americans, battled Italy during World War II, some hatred and sporadic violence emerged against Italian Americans and their property. However, they were not limited to actions against individuals. Italian Americans were even confined by the federal government in specific areas of California by virtue of their ethnicity alone, and 10,000 were relocated from coastal areas. In addition, 1,800 Italian Americans who were citizens of Italy were placed in an internment camp in Montana. The internees were eventually freed on Columbus Day 1942 as President Roosevelt lobbied the Italian American community to gain full support for the impending land invasion of Italy (Department of Justice 2001; Fox 1990).

In the "Research Focus" we consider how social scientists examine the economic experience of these early Italian immigrants and their children in the United States and compare it to how Mexican immigrants are faring today.

The Contemporary Picture

In politics, Italian Americans have been more successful, at least at the local level, where family and community ties can be translated into votes. However, political success did not come easily because many Italian immigrants anticipated returning to their homeland and did not always take neighborhood politics seriously. It was even more difficult for Italian Americans to break into national politics.

For many people the six seasons of MTVs Jersey Shore represented sheer entertainment, but for some in the Italian American community it stigmatized the Italian American working class as engaged in outrageous behavior.

Research Focus

Immigrants: Yesterday and Today

Anyone thinking about the future of today's immigrants might reflect back on the experiences of those who came a century ago. It is widely agreed that, despite difficult times and often harsh treatment by those already here, the immigrants of the late nineteenth and early twentieth century ultimately fared well. Certainly their descendants are doing well today. So can we generalize from this experience to today's immigrants?

Sociologist Joel Perlmann and other scholars have considered the experience of immigrants from Southern, Central, and Eastern Europe who were predominantly low-skilled workers. A significant number were Italian and Polish. Based on his analysis and that of other sociologists, we find that these earlier immigrant workers earned typically only between 60 and 88 percent in wages as that of nonimmigrant Whites in the same occupational groups.

Contrary to an often commonly held belief, these immigrants did not end up in well-paying jobs in manufacturing that led them into the middle class in their own lifetimes. Rather, they firmly remained working class until after World War II. Upward mobility occurred across generations typically, not within the lifetimes of the arriving Italian, Polish, and other Southern, Central, and Eastern European immigrants. This would mean economic parity took about three or four generations and not a decade as some writers have romantically portrayed it.

Taking these data, Perlmann looks at contemporary Mexican immigrants. In many ways the deck is stacked against this current immigrant group, which is by far the largest. Unlike their European counterparts of a century ago, many arrivals from Mexico (about 55 percent) are having to labor as illegal immigrants, which obviously curtail the opportunities available to them and their family members. Today's second-generation Mexicans in the United States are lagging further behind in education compared to the general population than were the comparable generation of the turn-of-the century European immigrants.

The education gap among today's Latinos does not facilitate upward mobility. This is particularly challenging given the much greater importance that formal schooling has today for economic success compared to a century ago.

Language acquisition does not appear to be an issue, even given the large concentrations of Spanish-speaking neighborhoods that might seem to work against Hispanics becoming fluent English speakers. Although 23 percent of Hispanic immigrants as a group speak English very well, the percentage of these immigrants who are fluent in English rises to 88 percent among their U.S.-born children and then to 94 percent in the third generation.

It is early to make firm direct comparisons because the second-generation Mexican American is just coming of age, much less having full labor force experience and creating their own families. Although the complete entry of today's immigrants into the economy is likely to come based on analysis of the situation today, comparisons to White ethnics suggests that it may take the immigrants longer by at least an additional generation.

SOURCES: Bean and Stevens 2003; Camarota 2007a; Dickson 2006; Hakimzadeh and Cohn 2007; Katz, Stern, and Fader 2007; Perlmann 2005; Portes 2006; Portes and Rumbaut 2006.

Not until 1962 was an Italian American named to a cabinet-level position. Geraldine Ferraro's nomination as the Democratic vice presidential candidate in 1984 was every bit as much an achievement for Italian Americans as it was for women. The opposition to the nomination of Judge Samuel Alito to the Supreme Court in 2006 struck many as bordering on anti–Italian American sentiments in the manner the opposition was advanced. Numerous critics used the phrase

"Judge Scalito" in obvious reference to the sitting Italian American on the Court, Justice Antonio Scalia (Cornacchia and Nelson 1992).

While as a group Italian Americans are firmly a part of middle America, they frequently continue to be associated with crime. In 2009, three New Jersey mayors were indicted for corruption and not all of them were Italian. At the core of the scandal were five Syrian American rabbis, yet newspapers quickly dubbed it "New Jersey's 'Italian' Problem." MTV's successful reality show *Jersey Shore*, which seems to focus on drinking, hot tubbing, and brawling stars, did not help. Stereotypes and labeling do not go away and truth is no antidote (Cohen 2010a; McGurn 2009).

There is no paucity of famous Italian Americans. They include athletes such as Joe DiMaggio, politician Rudolph Giuliani, film director Francis Ford Coppola, singer Madonna, comedian Jay Leno, writer Mario Puzo, actor Leonardo DiCaprio, chef Rachel Ray, and auto racing legend Mario Andretti.

Italian Americans still remain the seventh-largest immigrant group. Just how ethnically conscious is the Italian American community? Although the number is declining, 700,000 Americans speak Italian at home. Only eight languages are spoken more frequently at home: Spanish, Chinese, Tagalog (Philippines), Vietnamese, Korean, Russian, German, Arabic, Russian, and French Creole. For the 17-plus million Italian Americans, however, the language tie to their culture is absent, and, depending on their degree of assimilation, only traces of symbolic ethnicity may remain. As we saw in the chapter opener describing Little Italy in New York City, Italian ethnic enclaves throughout North America are more and more limited to a cluster of Italian restaurants and bakeries. In a later section, we look at the role that language plays for many immigrants and their children (Ryan 2013: 3).

The Polish Americans

5.6 **Restate the Polish American immigration story.**

Immigrants from Poland have had experiences similar to those of the Irish and Italians. They had to overcome economic problems and personal hardships just to make the journey. Once in the United States, they found themselves often assigned to the jobs many citizens had not wanted to do. They had to adjust to a new language and a familiar yet different culture. And always they were looking back to the family members left behind who either wanted to join them in the United States or, in contrast, never wanted them to leave in the first place.

Like other arrivals, many Poles sought improvement in their lives, a migration that was known as Za Chlebem (For Bread). The Poles who came were, at different times, more likely than many other European immigrants to see themselves as forced immigrants and were often described by, and themselves adopted, the terminology directly reflecting their social roles—exiles, refugees, displaced persons, or émigrés. The primary force for this exodus was the changing political status of Poland through most of the nineteenth and twentieth centuries, which was as turbulent as the lives of the new arrivals.

Early Immigration

Polish immigrants were among the settlers at Jamestown, Virginia, in 1608, to help develop the colony's timber industry, but it was the Poles who came later in that century who made a lasting mark. The successful exploits of Polish immigrants such as cavalry officer Casimir Pulaski and military engineer Thaddeus Kosciuszko are still commemorated today in communities with large Polish American populations. As we can see in Figure 5.2, it was not until the 1890s that Polish immigration was significant in comparison to some other European arrivals. Admittedly, it is difficult to exactly document the size of this immigration because at various historical periods Poland or parts of the country became part of Austria-Hungary, Germany (Prussia), and the Soviet Union so that the migrants were not officially coming from a nation called "Poland."

Many of the Polish immigrants were adjusting not only to a new culture but also to a more urban way of life. Sociologists William I. Thomas and Florian Znaniecki, in their classic study *The Polish Peasant in Europe and America* ([1918] 1996), traced the path from rural Poland to urban America. Many of the peasants did not necessarily come directly to the United States but first traveled through other European countries. This pattern is not unique and reminds us that, even today, many immigrants have crossed several countries, sometimes establishing themselves for a period of time before finally settling in the United States (Abbott and Egloff 2008).

Like the Germans, Italians, and Irish, Poles arrived at the large port cities of the East Coast but, unlike the other immigrant groups, they were more likely to settle in cities further inland or work in mines in Pennsylvania. In such areas, they would join kinfolk or acquaintances through the process of chain migration (described in the previous chapter).

The reference to coal mining as an occupation reflects the continuing tendency of immigrants to work in jobs avoided by most U.S. citizens because they paid little, were dangerous, or both. For example, in September 1897, a group of miners in Lattimer, Pennsylvania, marched to demand safer working conditions and an end to special taxes placed only on foreign-born workers. In the ensuing confrontation with local officials, police officers shot at the protesters, killing 19 people, most of who were Polish, the others Lithuanians and Slovaks (Duszak 1997).

Polonia

With growing numbers, the emergence of Polonia (meaning Polish communities outside of Poland) became more common in cities throughout the Midwest. Male immigrants who came alone often took shelter through a system of inexpensive boarding houses called *tryzmanie bortnków* (brother keeping), which allowed the new arrival to save money and send it back to Poland to support his family. These funds eventually provided the financial means necessary to bring family members over, adding to the size of Polonia in cities such as Buffalo, Cleveland, Detroit, Milwaukee, Pittsburgh, and, above all, Chicago, where the population of Poles was second only to Warsaw, Poland.

Religion has played an important role among Polish immigrants and their descendants. Most of the Polish immigrants who came to the United States before World War I were Roman Catholic. They quickly established their own parishes where new arrivals could feel welcome. Although religious services at that time were in the Latin language, as they had been in Poland, the many service organizations around the parish, not to mention the Catholic schools, kept the immigrants steeped in the Polish language and the latest happenings back home. Jewish Poles began immigrating during the first part of the twentieth century to escape the growing hostility they felt in Europe, which culminated in the Holocaust. Their numbers swelled greatly until movement from Poland stopped with the invasion of Poland by Germany in 1939; it resumed after the war.

Although the Jewish–Catholic distinction may be the most obvious distinguishing factor among Polish Americans, there are other divisions as well. Regional subgroups such as the Kashubes, the Górali, and the Mazurians have often carried great significance. Some Poles emigrated from areas where German was actually the language of origin.

As with other immigrant groups, Polish Americans could make use of a rich structure of voluntary self-help associations that were already well established by the 1890s. Not all organizations smoothly cut across different generations of Polish immigrants. For example, the Poles who came immediately after World War II as political refugees fleeing Soviet domination were quite different in their outlook than the descendants of the economic refugees from the turn of the century. These kinds of tensions in an immigrant community are not unusual, even if they go unnoticed by the casual observer who lumps all immigrants of the same nationality together (Jaroszyn'ska-Kirchmann 2004).

Like many other newcomers, Poles have been stigmatized as outsiders and also stereotyped as simple and uncultured—the typical biased view of working-class White ethnics. Their struggles in manual occupations placed them in direct competition with other White ethnics and African Americans, which occasionally led to labor disputes and longer-term tense and emotional rivalries. "Polish jokes" continue now to have a remarkable shelf life in casual conversation well into the twenty-first century. Jewish Poles suffer the added indignities of anti-Semitism (Dolan and Stotsky 1997).

The Contemporary Picture

Today, Polonia in the United States is nearly 10 million. Although this may not seem significant in a country of more than 300 million, we need to recall that today Poland itself has a population of only about 39 million. Whether it was

Polish American actress Scarlett Johansonn reflects the multiple ethnic roots of many Americans today. Born in New York City, her father is a Danish immigrant and her mother is a U.S.-born Jew whose parents came from Poland and Belarus, then part of the former Soviet Union. She reports celebrating both Hanukkah and Christmas and holds both American and Danish citizenship.

to support the efforts of Lech Walesa, the Solidarity movement leader who confronted the Soviet Union in the 1980s, or to celebrate the elevation of Karol Józef Wojtyla as Pope John Paul II in 1978, Polish Americans are a central part of the global Polish community.

Many Polish Americans have retained little of their rich cultural traditions and may barely acknowledge even symbolic ethnicity. Data released in 2013 show about 600,000 whose primary language is Polish—a decline from over 800,000 in 1980. For those still immersed in Polonia, their lives revolve around many of the same religious and social institutions that were the center of Polonia a century ago. For example, 54 Roman Catholic churches in the metropolitan Chicago area still offer Polish-language masses. Although in many of these parishes there may be only one service in Polish serving a declining number of celebrants, a few traditional "Polish" churches still have Polish-speaking priests in residence. Even with the decline in Polish-language service, the Roman Catholic Church actively recruits Pole seminarians, although now English-language training is often emphasized.

In the latter part of the twentieth century, some of the voluntary associations relocated or built satellite centers to serve the outlying Polish American populations. To sustain their activities financially, these social organizations also reached out of the central cities in order to tap into the financial resources of suburban Poles. Increasingly, people of Polish descent also have now made their way into the same social networks populated by German, Irish, Italian, and other ethnic Americans (Bukowczyk 2007; Erdmans 1998, 2006; Lopata 1994; Mocha 1998; Polzin 1973; Shin and Kominski 2010; Stone 2006).

Except for immigrants who fled persecution in their homelands, immigration typically has back-and-forth movement. In the early years of the twenty-first century, there was an identifiable movement of Polish Americans from Polonia to Poland, especially as economic opportunity improved in the home country. One estimate of returnees places it at 50,000 from 2004, when Poland entered the European Union, to 2009, which is a significant number in absolute numbers but is relatively small given the magnitude of the Polish American community (Hundley 2009; Mastony 2013).

Among the many Polish Americans well known or remembered today are home designer Martha (Kostyra) Stewart, comedian Jack Benny (Benjamin

Kubelsky), guitarist Richie Sambora of the rock group Bon Jovi, actress Scarlett Johansson, entertainer Liberace, *Wheel of Fortune* host Pat Sajak, baseball star Stan Musial, football star Mike Ditka, novelist Joseph Conrad (Józef Korzeniowski), singer Bobby Vinton (Stanley Ventula, Jr.), polio vaccine pioneer Albert Sabin, and motion picture director Stanley Kubrick.

Religious Pluralism

5.7   **State what is meant by religious pluralism.**

Religion plays a fundamental role in society and affects even those who do not practice or even believe in organized religion. **Religion** refers to a unified system of sacred beliefs and practices that encompass elements beyond everyday life that inspire awe, respect, and even fear (Durkheim [1912] 2001).

In popular speech, the term *pluralism* has often been used in the United States to refer explicitly to religion. Although certain faiths figure more prominently in the worship scene, the United States has a history of greater religious tolerance than most other nations. Today, religious bodies number more than 1,500 in the United States and range from the more than 66 million members of the Roman Catholic Church to sects with fewer than 1,000 adherents. In every region of the country, religion is being expressed in greater variety, whether it be the Latinization of Catholicism and some Christian faiths or the de-Europeanizing of some established Protestant faiths, as with Asian Americans, or the de-Christianizing of the overall religious landscape with Muslims, Buddhists, Hindus, Sikhs, and others (Roof 2007).

The Greek Orthodox Church is one of 25 Christian faiths with at least a million members.

How do we view the United States in terms of religion? Increasingly, the United States has a non-Christian presence. In 1900, an estimated 96 percent of the nation was Christian; slightly more than 1 percent was nonreligious, and approximately 3 percent held other faiths. In 2013, it was estimated that the nation was 74 percent Christian, 17 percent nonreligious, and another 9 percent all other faiths. The United States has a long Jewish tradition, and Muslims number close to 5 million. A smaller but also growing number of people adhere to such Eastern faiths as Hinduism, Buddhism, Confucianism, and Taoism (Newport 2011).

Sociologists use the word **denomination** for a large, organized religion that is not linked officially with the state or government. By far, the largest

Table 5.1 Churches with More Than a Million Members

Denomination Name	Inclusive Membership
Roman Catholic Church	68,503,456
Southern Baptist Convention	16,160,088
United Methodist Church	7,774,931
Church of Jesus Christ of Latter-Day Saints	6,058,907
Church of God in Christ	5,499,875
National Baptist Convention, U.S.A., Inc.	5,000,000
Evangelical Lutheran Church in America	4,542,868
National Baptist Convention of America, Inc.	3,500,000
Assemblies of God	2,914,669
Presbyterian Church (U.S.A.)	2,770,730
African Methodist Episcopal Church	2,500,000
National Missionary Baptist Convention of America	2,500,000
Lutheran Church—Missouri Synod (LCMS)	2,312,111
Episcopal Church	2,006,343
Churches of Christ	1,639,495
Greek Orthodox Archdiocese of America	1,500,000
Pentecostal Assemblies of the World, Inc.	1,500,000
African Methodist Episcopal Zion Church	1,400,000
American Baptist Churches in the U.S.A.	1,310,505
Jehovah's Witnesses	1,162,686
United Church of Christ	1,080,199
Church of God (Cleveland, TN)	1,076,254
Christian Churches and Churches of Christ	1,071,616
Seventh-Day Adventist Church	1,043,606
Progressive National Baptist Convention, Inc.	1,010,000

Note: Most recent data as of 2012.

SOURCE: Eileen Lindner (ed.) 2012. *Yearbook of American and Canadian Churches 2011*, Table 2, p. 12. Nashville, TN: Abingdon Press. Reprinted by permission from *Yearbook of American and Canadian Churches 2008.* Copyright © National Council of Churches of Christ in the USA.

denomination in the United States is Catholicism; yet at least 24 other Christian religious denominations have 1 million or more members (Lindner 2011).

At least four non-Christian religious groups in the United States have numbers that are comparable to any of these large denominations: Jews, Muslims, Buddhists, and Hindus. In the United States, each numbers more than 1 million members. Within each of these groups are branches or sects that distinguish themselves from each other. For example, the Judaic faith embraces several factions such as Orthodox, Conservative, Reconstructionist, and Reform that are similar in their roots but marked by sharp distinctions. Continuing the examples, in the United States and the rest of the world, some Muslims are Sunni and others Shia. Further divisions are present within these groups, just as among Protestants and, in turn, among Baptists.

The United States has long been described as a Judeo-Christian nation, but with interest in other faiths and continuing immigration, this description, if ever accurate, is not now. This is especially true with the growth of Muslim Americans.

Islam in the United States has a long history stretching from Muslim Africans who came as slaves to today's Muslim community, which includes immigrants and native-born Americans. President Obama, the son of a practicing Muslim and who lived for years in Indonesia, the country with the largest Muslim population, never sought to hide his roots. However, reflecting the prejudices of many toward non-Christians, his Christian upbringing was stressed throughout his presidential campaigns. Little wonder that a national survey showed that 55 percent believe the U.S. Constitution establishes the country as a "Christian nation" (Cose 2008; Thomas 2007).

Even if religious faiths have broad representation, they tend to be fairly homogeneous at the local church level. This is especially ironic, given that many faiths have played critical roles in resisting racism and in trying to bring together the nation in the name of racial and ethnic harmony.

Broadly defined, faiths represent a variety of ethnic and racial groups. In Figure 5.4, we consider the interaction of White, Black, and Hispanic races with religions. Muslims, Pentecostals, and Jehovah's Witnesses are much more diverse than Presbyterians or Lutherans. Religion plays an even more central role for Blacks and Latinos than Whites. A national survey indicated that 65 percent of African Americans and 51 percent of Latinos attend a religious service every week, compared to 44 percent of White non-Hispanics (Winseman 2004).

It would also be a mistake to focus only on older religious organizations when considering religion's role in society. Local churches that developed into national faiths in the 1990s, such as Calvary Chapel, Vineyard, and Hope Chapel, have a following among Pentecostal believers, who embrace a more charismatic form of worship devoid of many traditional ornaments, with pastors and congregations alike favoring informal attire. New faiths develop with increasing rapidity in what can only be called a very competitive market for individual religious faith. In addition, many people, with or without religious affiliation, become fascinated with spiritual concepts such as angels or become a part of

Figure 5.4 Racial and Ethnic Makeup of Selected Religions in the United States

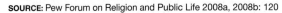

Note: "Other" includes self-identified mixed races. Evangelical includes Baptist, Lutheran (Missouri and Wisconsin Synods), and Pentecostal, among others. Mainline Protestant includes Methodist, Lutheran (ELCA), Presbyterian, Episcopal, and United Church of Christ, among others, but excludes historically Black churches. Based on a national survey of 35,556 adults conducted in August 2007.

SOURCE: Pew Forum on Religion and Public Life 2008a, 2008b: 120

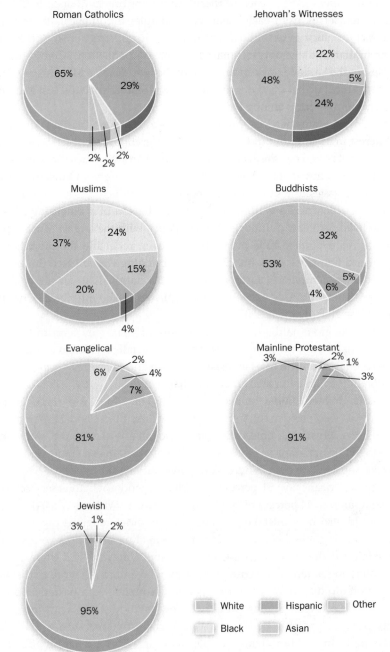

loose-knit fellowships. Religion in the United States is an ever-changing social phenomenon. Other nonmainstream faiths emerge in new arenas, as evidenced by the successful campaign of Mitt Romney, a Mormon, to win the Republican nomination for president in 2012 or the visible role of celebrities promoting the Church of Scientology (Schaefer and Zellner 2011).

Divisive conflicts along religious lines are muted in the United States compared with those in, say, the Middle East. Although not entirely absent, conflicts about religion in the United States seem to be overshadowed by civil religion. **Civil religion** is the religious dimension in the United States that merges public life with sacred beliefs. It also reflects that no single faith is privileged over all others. Indeed, it even encompasses the conversation of nonbelievers regarding the human condition.

Sociologist Robert Bellah (1967) borrowed the phrase *civil religion* from eighteenth-century French philosopher Jean-Jacques Rousseau to describe a significant phenomenon in the contemporary United States. Civil religion exists alongside established religious faiths, and it embodies a belief system that incorporates all religions but is not associated specifically with any one. It is the type of faith to which presidents refer in inaugural speeches and to which American Legion posts and Girl Scout troops swear allegiance. In 1954, Congress added the phrase *under God* to the Pledge of Allegiance as a legislative recognition of religion's significance. Elected officials in the United States, beginning with Ronald Reagan, often conclude even their most straightforward speeches with "God bless the United States of America," which in effect evokes the civil religion of the nation.

A rabbi blesses a young girl at her Bat Mitzvah in the temple. Jewish children often celebrate a coming-of-age ceremony. According to Jewish law, when Jewish children reach the age of maturity (12 years for girls, 13 years for boys), they become responsible for their actions. At this point a boy is said to become Bar Mitzvah; a girl is said to become Bat Mitzvah.

Functionalists see civil religion as reinforcing Central American values that may be more expressly patriotic than sacred in nature. The mass media, following major societal upheavals, from the 1995 Oklahoma City bombing to the 2001 terrorist attacks, often show church services with clergy praying and asking for national healing. Bellah (1967) sees no sign that the importance of civil religion has diminished in promoting collective identity, but he does acknowledge that it is more conservative than during the 1970s.

Beginning with the Clinton administration, the federal government has made explicit efforts to include religious organizations. The 1996 Welfare Reform Act President Clinton signed provided that religious groups could compete for grants. President George W. Bush created a White House Office of Faith-Based and Community Initiatives to provide for a significant expansion of charitable choice. President Barack Obama has continued the office, naming a Pentecostal minister to oversee it (Jacoby 2009).

In the following sections, we explore the diversity among the major Christian groups in the United States, such as Roman Catholics and Protestants, as well as how Islam has emerged as a significant religious force in the United States and can no longer be regarded as a marginal faith in terms of followers (Gorski 2010).

Diversity among Roman Catholics

Social scientists have persistently tended to ignore the diversity within the Roman Catholic Church in the United States. Recent research has not sustained the conclusions that Roman Catholics are melding into a single group, following the traditions of the American Irish Catholic model, or even that parishioners are attending English-language churches. Religious behavior has been different for each ethnic group within the Roman Catholic Church. The Irish and French Canadians left societies that were highly competitive both culturally and socially. Their religious involvement in the United States is more relaxed than it was in Ireland and Quebec. However, the influence of life in the United States has increased German and Polish involvement in the Roman Catholic Church, whereas Italians have remained largely inactive. Variations by ethnic background continue to emerge in studies of contemporary religious involvement in the Roman Catholic Church (Eckstrom 2001).

Since the mid-1970s, the Roman Catholic Church in America has received a significant number of new members from the Philippines, Southeast Asia, and particularly Latin America. Although these new members have been a stabilizing force offsetting the loss of White ethnics, they have also challenged a church that for generations was dominated by Irish, Italian, and Polish parishes. Perhaps the most prominent subgroup in the Roman Catholic Church is the Latinos, who now account for one-third of all Roman Catholic parishioners. Clearly immigrants are seen as a significant part of the Catholic Church's future. The Church nationwide mounts more than 150 immigration-oriented programs.

Often a program for a patron saint or national feast begins with two national anthems sung–that of the participant's native country and The Star-Spangled Banner. Some Los Angeles churches in or near Latino neighborhoods must schedule 14 masses each Sunday to accommodate the crowds of worshipers. In 2010, the Pope selected a Latino, Mexican-born archbishop, Jose H. Gomez, to lead the Los Angeles Archdiocese (Dolan 2013; Goodstein and Steinhauer 2010; Navarro-Rivera, Kosmin, and Keysar 2010).

The Roman Catholic Church, despite its ethnic diversity, has clearly been a powerful force in reducing the ethnic ties of its members, making it also a significant assimilating force. The irony in this role of Catholicism is that so many nineteenth-century Americans heaped abuse on Catholics in this country for allegedly being un-American and having a dual allegiance. The history of the Catholic Church in the United States may be portrayed as a struggle within the membership between the Americanizers and the anti-Americanizers, with the former ultimately winning. Unlike the various Protestant churches that accommodated immigrants of a single nationality, the Roman Catholic Church had to Americanize a variety of linguistic and ethnic groups. The Catholic Church may have been the most potent assimilating force after the public school system. Comparing the assimilationist goal of the Catholic Church and the current diversity in it leads us to the conclusion that ethnic diversity has continued in the Roman Catholic Church despite, not because of, this religious institution.

Diversity among Protestants

Protestantism, like Catholicism, often is portrayed as a monolithic entity. Little attention is given to the doctrinal and attitudinal differences that sharply divide the various denominations in both laity and clergy. However, several studies document the diversity. Unfortunately, many opinion polls and surveys are content to learn whether a respondent is a Catholic, a Protestant, or a Jew. Stark and Glock (1968) found sharp differences in religious attitudes within Protestant churches. For example, 99 percent of Southern Baptists had no doubt that Jesus was the divine Son of God as contrasted to only 40 percent of Congregationalists. We can identify four "generic theological camps":

1. **Liberals:** United Church of Christ (Congregationalists) and Episcopalians
2. **Moderates:** Disciples of Christ, Methodists, and Presbyterians
3. **Conservatives:** American Lutherans and American Baptists
4. **Fundamentalists:** Missouri Synod Lutherans, Southern Baptists, and Assembly of God

Roman Catholics generally hold religious beliefs similar to those of conservative Protestants, except on essentially Catholic issues such as papal infallibility (the authority of the spiritual role in all decisions regarding faith and morals).

Figure 5.5 Income and Denominations

Denominations attract different income groups. All groups have both affluent and poor members, yet some have a higher proportion of members with high incomes, whereas others are comparatively poor.

SOURCE: Based on interviews with a representative sample of 35,000 adults conducted May–August and reproduced in the Pew Forum on Religion and Public Life 2008a, 2008b: 78–79, 84–85.

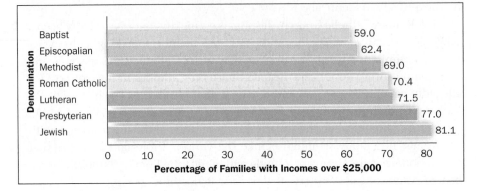

Whether or not there are four distinct camps is not important: The point is that the familiar practice of contrasting Roman Catholics and Protestants is clearly not productive. Some differences between Roman Catholics and Protestants are inconsequential compared with the differences between Protestant sects.

Secular criteria as well as doctrinal issues may distinguish religious faiths. Research has consistently shown that denominations can be arranged in a hierarchy based on social class. As Figure 5.5 reveals, members of certain faiths, such as Episcopalians, Jews, and Presbyterians, have a higher proportion of affluent members. Members of other faiths, including Baptists, tend to be poorer. Of course, all Protestant groups draw members from each social stratum. Nonetheless, the social significance of these class differences is that religion becomes a mechanism for signaling social mobility. A person who is moving up in wealth and power may seek out a faith associated with a higher social ranking. Similar contrasts are shown in formal schooling in Figure 5.6.

Protestant faiths have been diversifying, and many of their members have been leaving them for churches that follow strict codes of behavior or fundamental interpretations of biblical teachings. This trend is reflected in the gradual decline of the five mainline churches: Baptist, Episcopalian, Lutheran, Methodist, and Presbyterian. In 2006, these faiths accounted for about 58 percent of total Protestant membership, compared with 65 percent in the 1970s. With a broader acceptance of new faiths and continuing immigration, it is unlikely that these mainline churches will regain their dominance in the near future (Davis, Smith, and Marsden 2007: 171–172).

Although Protestants may seem to define the civil religion and the accepted dominant orientation, some Christian faiths feel they, too, experience

Figure 5.6 Education and Denominations

There are sharp differences in the proportion of those with some college education by denomination.

SOURCE: Based on interviews with a representative sample of 35,000 adults conducted May–August and reproduced in the Pew Forum on Religion and Public Life 2008a, 2008b: 78–79, 84–85.

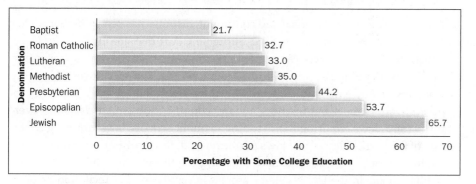

the discrimination usually associated with non-Christians such as Jews and Muslims. For example, representatives of the liberal and moderate faiths dominate the leadership of the military's chaplain corps. There are 16 Presbyterian soldiers for every Presbyterian chaplain, 121 Full Gospel worshippers for every Full Gospel chaplain, and 339 Muslim soldiers for every Muslim chaplain (Cooperman 2005).

As another example of denominational discrimination, in 1998, the Southern Baptist Convention amended its basic theological statements of beliefs to include a strong statement on family life. However, the statement included a declaration that a woman should "submit herself graciously" to her husband's leadership. There were widespread attacks on this position, which many Baptists felt was inappropriate because they were offering guidance for their denomination's members. In some respects, Baptists felt this was a form of respectable bigotry. It was acceptable to attack them for their views on social issues even though such criticism would be much more muted for many more liberal faiths that seem free to tolerate abortion (Bowman 1998; Niebuhr 1998).

Religion and the Courts

Religious pluralism owes its existence in the United States to the First Amendment declaration that "Congress shall make no law respecting an establishment of religion, or prohibiting the free exercise thereof." The U.S. Supreme Court has consistently interpreted this wording to mean not that government should ignore religion but that it should follow a policy of neutrality to maximize religious freedom. For example, the government may not help religion by financing a new church building, but it also may not obstruct religion by denying a church adequate police and fire protection. We examine four issues that continue to require clarification: school prayer, secessionist minorities and their rituals, creationism (including intelligent design), and the public display of religious (or sacred) symbols.

School Prayer

Among the most controversial and continuing disputes has been whether prayer has a role in the schools. The 1962 Supreme Court decision in *Engel v. Vitale*, which disallowed a purportedly nondenominational prayer drafted for use in the New York public schools, disturbed many people. The prayer was "Almighty God, we acknowledge our dependence upon Thee, and we beg Thy blessings upon us, our parents, our teachers, and our country." Subsequent decisions overturned state laws requiring Bible reading in public schools, laws requiring recitation of the Lord's Prayer, and laws permitting a daily one-minute period of silent meditation or prayer. Despite such judicial pronouncements, children in many public schools in the United States are led in regular prayer recitation or Bible reading. Contrary to what many people believe, religion has not been hounded out of public schools (Yemma 2013).

What about prayers at public gatherings? In 1992, the Supreme Court ruled 5–4 in *Lee v. Weisman* that prayer at a junior high school graduation in Providence, Rhode Island, violated the U.S. Constitution's mandate of separation of church and state. A rabbi had given thanks to God in his invocation. The district court suggested that the invocation would have been acceptable without that reference. The Supreme Court did not agree with the school board that a prayer at a graduation was not coercive. The Court did say in its opinion that it was acceptable for a student speaker voluntarily to say a prayer at such a program (Marshall 2001).

Public schools and even states have mandated a "moment of silence" at the start of the school day in what critics contend is a transparent attempt to get around *Lee v. Weisman*. While prayer or religious thoughts are clearly intended by legislators when they created these "moments," the courts have to date ruled such policies as constitutional and argued that the policy is secular, rather than sacred. Arkansas in 2013 became the latest state to mandate a minute of silence at the beginning of the school day (ABC Television 2013).

Secessionist Minorities

Several religious groups have been in legal and social conflict with the rest of society. Some can be called **secessionist minorities** in that they reject both assimilation and coexistence in some form of cultural pluralism. The Amish are one such group that comes into conflict with outside society because of its beliefs and way of life. The Old Order Amish shun most modern conveniences and maintain a lifestyle dramatically different from that of larger society.

Are there limits to the free exercise of religious rituals by secessionist minorities? Today, tens of thousands of members of Native American religions believe that ingesting the powerful drug peyote is a sacrament and that those who partake of peyote will enter into direct contact with God. In 1990, the Supreme Court ruled that prosecuting people who use illegal drugs as part of a religious ritual is not a violation of the First Amendment guarantee of religious freedom. The case arose because Native Americans were dismissed from their jobs for the religious use of peyote and were then refused unemployment benefits by the state of Oregon's employment division. In 1991, however, Oregon enacted a new law permitting the sacramental use of peyote by Native Americans (*New York Times* 1991).

In another ruling on religious rituals, in 1993, the Supreme Court unanimously overturned a local ordinance in Florida that banned ritual animal sacrifice. The High Court held that this law violated the free-exercise rights of adherents of the Santeria religion, in which the sacrifice of animals (including goats, chickens, and other birds) plays a central role. The same year, Congress passed the Religious Freedom Restoration Act, which said the government may not enforce laws that "substantially burden" the exercise of religion. Presumably, this action will give religious groups more flexibility in practicing their faiths. However, many local and state officials are concerned that the law has led to unintended consequences, such as forcing states to accommodate prisoners' requests for questionable religious activities or to permit a church to expand into a historic district in defiance of local laws (Greenhouse 1996).

The legal acceptance of different faiths has been illustrated in numerous decisions. For example, the courts have allowed Wiccan organizations to enjoy

After lobbying by Wiccans, the U.S. Department of Veterans Affairs eventually approved the pentacle symbol for use on the cemetery markers of fallen soldiers who self-identify as Witches.

non-profit status. In addition, the U.S. Department of Veterans Affairs approved of the pentacle symbol for use on national cemetery markers of those fallen soldiers who self-identify as Witches.

Creationism and Intelligent Design

The third area of contention has been whether the biblical account of creation should be or must be presented in school curricula and whether this account should receive the same emphasis as scientific theories. In the famous "monkey trial" of 1925, Tennessee schoolteacher John Scopes was found guilty of teaching the scientific theory of evolution in public schools. Since then, however, Darwin's evolutionary theories have been presented in public schools with little reference to the biblical account in Genesis. People who support the literal interpretation of the Bible, commonly known as **creationists**, have formed various organizations to crusade for creationist treatment in U.S. public schools and universities.

In a 1987 Louisiana case, *Edwards v. Aguillard,* the Supreme Court ruled that states may not require the teaching of creationism alongside evolution in public schools if the primary purpose of such legislation is to promote a religious viewpoint. The target to promote creationism is often to influence choice of textbooks by a local school district or, in states where statewide adoptions, by a state board of education. The teaching of evolution and creationism has remained a controversial issue in many communities across the United States (Applebome 1996; Rich 2013).

Beginning in the 1980s, those who believe in a divine hand in the creation of life have advanced **intelligent design** (ID), the idea that life is so complex it could only have been created by a higher intelligence. Although not explicitly drawn on the biblical account, creationists feel comfortable with ID and advocate that it is a more accurate account than Darwinism or, at the very least, that it be taught as an alternative alongside the theory of evolution. In 2005, a federal judge in *Kitzmiller v. Dove Area School District* ended a Pennsylvania school district intention to require the presentation of ID. In essence, the judge found ID to be "a religious belief" that was only a subtler way of finding God's fingerprints in nature than traditional creationism. Because the issue continues to be hotly debated, future court cases are certain to come (Clemmitt 2005; Goodstein 2005).

Public Displays

The fourth area of contention has been a battle over public displays that depict symbols of religion or appear to others to be sacred representations. Can manger scenes be erected on public property? Do people have a right to be protected from large displays such as a cross or a star atop a water tower overlooking an entire town? In a series of decisions in the 1980s through 1995, the Supreme Court ruled that tax-supported religious displays on public government property may be successfully challenged but may be permissible if made more secular. Displays that combine a crèche—the Christmas manger scene depicting the birth of Jesus—or the Hanukkah menorah and also include Frosty the Snowman or even Christmas trees have been ruled secular. These decisions have been dubbed "the plastic reindeer rules." In 1995, the Court clarified the issue by stating that privately sponsored religious displays may be allowed on public property if other forms of expression are permitted in the same location.

The final judicial word has not been heard, and all these rulings should be viewed as tentative because the Court cases have been decided by close votes. Changes in the Supreme Court's composition in the next few years also may alter the outcome of future cases (Bork 1995; Hirsley 1991; Mauro 1995).

Conclusion

5.8 Interpret how the courts have ruled on religion.

From his cramped basement apartment, Grigore Culian has been producing a biweekly Romanian-language paper called *New York Magazin* since 1997 that provides local news of interest to Romanians in the metro area and beyond. There are over 146,000 adults in the United States for whom Romanian is their primary language. While being a one-person operation is unusual, producing news for a small ethnic community is not. Language newspapers, radio stations, cable outlets, and more recently video streaming keep ethnic ties alive and go beyond symbolic ethnicity. Similar media outlets foster a sense of community for hundreds of religious denominations, Christian and non-Christian alike, to believers in the United States (Lazar 2013).

Considering ethnicity and religion reinforces our understanding of the Spectrum of Intergroup Relations first presented in Chapter 1. The Spectrum of Intergroup Relations figure shows the rich variety of relationships as defined by people's ethnic and religious identities. The profiles of German, Irish, Italian, and Polish Americans reflect the variety of White ethnic experiences.

Any study of life in the United States, especially one that focuses on dominant and subordinate groups, cannot ignore religion and ethnicity. The two are closely related, as certain religious faiths predominate in certain nationalities. Both religious activity and interest by White ethnics in their heritage continue to be prominent features of the contemporary scene. People have been and continue to be ridiculed or deprived of opportunities solely because of their ethnic or religious affiliation. To get a true picture of people's place in society, we need to consider both ethnicity and social class in association with their religious identification.

Religion is changing in the United States. As one commercial recognition of this fact, Hallmark created its first greeting card in 2003 for the Muslim holiday Eid-al-fitr, which marks the end of the monthlong fast of Ramadan. The

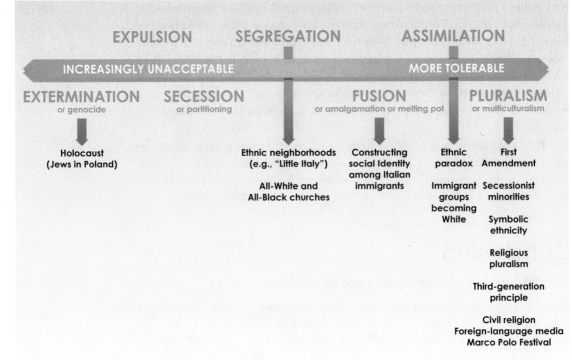

EXPULSION	SEGREGATION	ASSIMILATION

INCREASINGLY UNACCEPTABLE ————————————————— **MORE TOLERABLE**

| EXTERMINATION | SECESSION | | FUSION | | PLURALISM |
| or genocide | or partitioning | | or amalgamation or melting pot | | or multiculturalism |

Holocaust
(Jews in Poland)

Ethnic neighborhoods
(e.g., "Little Italy")

All-White and
All-Black churches

Constructing
social Identity
among Italian
immigrants

Ethnic
paradox

Immigrant
groups
becoming
White

First
Amendment

Secessionist
minorities

Symbolic
ethnicity

Religious
pluralism

Third-generation
principle

Civil religion
Foreign-language media
Marco Polo Festival

Blended identity

issue of the persistence of ethnicity is an intriguing one. Some people may only casually exhibit their ethnicity and practice what has been called symbolic ethnicity. However, can people immerse themselves in their ethnic culture without society punishing them for their will to be different? The tendency to put down White ethnics through respectable bigotry continues. Despite this intolerance, ethnicity remains a viable source of identity for many citizens today. There is also the ethnic paradox, which finds that practicing one's ethnic heritage often strengthens people and allows them to move successfully into the larger society.

The issue of religious expression in all its forms also raises a variety of intriguing questions. How can a country that is increasingly populated by diverse and often non-Christian faiths maintain religious tolerance? How might this change in the decades ahead? How will the courts and society resolve the issues of religious freedom? This is a particularly important issue in areas such as school prayer, secessionist minorities, creationism, intelligent design, and public religious displays. Some examination of religious ties is fundamental to completing an accurate picture of a person's social identity.

Ethnicity and religion are a basic part of today's social reality and of each individual's identity. The emotions, disputes, and debate over religion and ethnicity in the United States are powerful indeed.

Summary

1. While considering race and ethnicity in the United States, we often ignore how White people come to see themselves as a group and in relationship to others.

2. Feelings of ethnicity may be fading among the descendants of Europeans, but it may reemerge as reflected in either the third-generation principle or, in a more limited fashion, through symbolic ethnicity.

3. German Americans are the largest White ethnic group but have been largely incorporated into the core population with little visible distinctive cultural presence apart from food.

4. First regarded very much as "outsiders" and even not White, Irish immigrants have emerged as the fourth largest White ethnic group today.

5. Like the Irish, immigrants from Italy first encountered resistance in the United States but moved up from their lower and working-class place in the American social hierarchy.

6. The more recent immigration from Poland has created a more visible presence of Polonia in several American cities than that of Little Italy.

7. The ethnic diversity of the United States is matched by the many denominations among Christians as well as the sizable Jewish and Muslim presence.

8. In its interpretation of the First Amendment, the Supreme Court has tried to preserve religious freedom, but critics have argued that the Court has served to stifle religious expression.

Key Terms

blended identity, p. 150
civil religion, p. 175
creationists, p. 182
deficit model of ethnic
    identity, p. 150

denomination, p. 172
ethnic paradox, p. 152
intelligent design, p. 182
principle of third-generation
    interest, p. 151

religion, p. 171
secessionist minority, p. 180
symbolic ethnicity, p. 154
White privilege, p. 149

Review Questions

1. How is Whiteness socially constructed?

2. In what ways can White ethnicity be rediscovered?

3. Explain the impact that World War II had on German Americans both before and after the war.

4. Apply "Whiteness" to Irish Americans.

5. How does stereotyping relate to contemporary Italian Americans?

6. What role does Polonia play in the lives of contemporary Polish Americans?

7. To what extent has a non-Christian tradition been developing in the United States?

8. How have court rulings affected religious expression?

Critical Thinking

1. When do you see ethnicity becoming more apparent? When does it appear to occur only in response to other people's advancing their own ethnicity? From these situations, how can ethnic identity be both positive and perhaps counterproductive or even destructive?

2. How do White people you know seem to be aware or unaware of their ethnic roots? Of their Whiteness?

3. Why do you think we are so often reluctant to show our religion to others? Why might people of certain faiths be more hesitant than others?

4. How does religion reflect conservative and liberal positions on social issues? Consider services for the homeless, the need for childcare, the acceptance or rejection of gay men and lesbians, and a woman's right to terminate a pregnancy versus the fetus's right to survive.

Chapter 6
The Nation as a Kaleidoscope

Learning Objectives

THE GLASS HALF EMPTY

6-1 Characterize the amount or lack of progress that has been made by racial and ethnic minorities.

IS THERE A MODEL MINORITY?

6-2 Explain the model minority image.

ACTING WHITE, ACTING BLACK, OR NEITHER

6-3 What "acting White" means.

PERSISTENCE OF INEQUALITY

6-4 Discuss how inequality has persisted.

TALKING PAST ONE ANOTHER

6-5 Consider how intergroup communication occurs without truly communicating.

What metaphor do we use to describe a nation whose racial, ethnic, and religious minorities are now becoming numerical majorities in cities coast to coast, as already in the states of California, Hawaii, New Mexico, Texas, and a growing proportion of all counties within the United States? The outpouring of statistical data and personal experience documents the racial and ethnic diversity of the entire nation. The mosaic may be different in different regions and different communities; the tapestry of racial and ethnic groups is always close at hand wherever one is in the United States.

Significantly adding to the diversity of the United States is the growing Latino population. The Hispanic presence is everywhere. Here Dora the Explorer, an animated character on Nickelodeon, makes her appearance here in the annual Macy's Thanksgiving Day Parade.

Although *E Pluribus Unum* may be reassuring, it does not describe what a visitor sees along the length of Fifth Avenue in Manhattan or in Monterey Park outside Los Angeles. It is apparent in the increasing numbers of Latinos in the rural river town of Beardstown, Illinois, and the emerging Somali immigrant population in Lewiston, Maine.

For several generations, the melting pot has been used as a convenient description of our culturally diverse nation. The analogy of an alchemist's cauldron was clever, even if a bit jingoistic—in the Middle Ages, the alchemist attempted to change less costly metals into gold and silver.

The phrase *melting pot* originated as the title of a 1908 play by Israel Zangwill. In this play, a young Russian Jewish immigrant to the United States composes a symphony that portrays a nation that serves as a crucible (or pot) where all ethnic and racial groups dissolve into a new, superior stock.

The belief of the United States as a melting pot became widespread in the first part of the twentieth century, particularly because it suggested that the United States had an almost divinely inspired mission to destroy artificial divisions and create a single humankind. However, the dominant group had indicated its unwillingness to welcome Native Americans, African Americans, Hispanics, Jews, and Asians, among many others, into the melting pot.

Although the metaphor of the melting pot is still used today, observers recognize that it hides as much about a multiethnic United States as it discloses. Therefore, the metaphor of the salad bowl emerged in the 1970s to portray a country that is ethnically diverse. As we can distinguish the lettuce from the tomatoes from the peppers in a tossed salad, we can see the increasing availability of ethnic restaurants and the persistence of "foreign" language newspapers. The dressing over the ingredients is akin to the shared value system and culture covering, but not hiding, the different ingredients of the salad.

Yet even the notion of a salad bowl is wilting. Like its melting-pot predecessor, the picture of a salad is static—certainly not what we see in the United States. It also hardly calls to mind the myriad cultural pieces that make up the fabric or mosaic of our diverse nation.

The kaleidoscope offers another familiar, yet more useful, analogy. Patented in 1817 by Scottish scientist Sir David Brewster, the kaleidoscope is both a toy and increasingly a table artifact of upscale living rooms. Users of this optical device are aware that when they turn a set of mirrors, the colors and patterns reflected off pieces of glass, tinsel, or beads seem to be endless. The growing popularity of the phrase "people of color" seems made for the kaleidoscope that is the United States. The changing images correspond to the often-bewildering array of groups found in our country.

How easy is it to describe the image to someone else as we gaze into the eyepiece of a kaleidoscope? It is a challenge similar to that faced by educators who toil with what constitutes the ethnic history of the United States. We can forgive the faux pas by the *Washington Post* writer who described the lack of Hispanic-speaking (rather than Spanish-speaking) police as a factor contributing to hostilities in the capital. Little wonder, given the bewildering ethnic patterns, that Chicago politicians, who sought to maintain the "safe" Hispanic congressional district after the results of the 2010 Census, found themselves scrutinized by Blacks fearful of losing their "safe" districts and critiqued by Latinos for not creating a second or even third safe seat. We can forgive Marlon Brando for sending a Native American woman to refuse his Oscar, thus protesting Hollywood's portrayal of Native Americans. Was he unaware of Italian Americans' disbelief when his award-winning performance was in *The Godfather*? We can understand why the African Americans traumatized by Hurricane Katrina would turn their antagonism from the White power structure that they perceived as ignoring their needs to the Latinos who took advantage of reconstruction projects in New Orleans.

It is difficult to describe the image created by a kaleidoscope because it changes dramatically with little effort. As we can see in Figure 6.1, there is a rapid increase in the proportion of racial and ethnic minorities in schools and a decline in the proportion of White non-Hispanics. Similarly, in the kaleidoscope of the United States, we find it a challenge to describe the multiracial nature of this republic. Perhaps in viewing the multiethnic, multiracial United States as a kaleidoscope, we may take comfort that the Greek word *kalos* means "beautiful" (Schaefer 1992).

Figure 6.1 Changes in Minority School Population 1995 and 2021

As recently as 1995, all racial and ethnic minorities combined accounted for just a little more than one out of three of the nation's schoolchildren. By 2021, the "minorities" will be the numerical majority.

Note: Data for public elementary and secondary schools. Race categories exclude Hispanics.

SOURCE: National Center for Education Statistics 2013: Table 44.

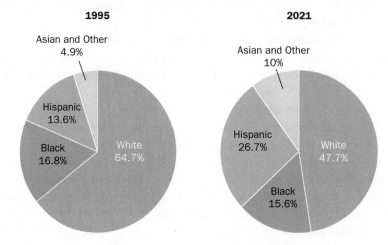

In order to develop a better understanding of the changing image through the kaleidoscope, we will first try to learn what progress has taken place and why miscommunication among our diverse peoples seems to be the rule rather than the exception.

The Glass Half Empty

6-1 **Characterize the amount or lack of progress that has been made by racial and ethnic minorities.**

A common expression makes reference to a glass half full or half empty of water. If one is thirsty, it is half empty and in need of being replenished. If one is attempting to clear dirty dishes, it is half full. For many people, especially Whites, the progress of subordinate groups or minorities makes it difficult to understand calls for more programs and new reforms and impossible to understand when minority neighborhoods erupt in violence.

In absolute terms, the glass of water has been filling up, but people in the early twenty-first century do not compare themselves with people in the 1960s. For example, Latinos and African Americans regard the appropriate reference group to be Whites today; compared with them, the glass is half empty at best.

In Figure 6.2, we have shown the current picture and recent changes by comparing African Americans and Hispanics with Whites as well as contemporary data for Native Americans (American Indians). We see that the nation's largest

Figure 6.2 Changes in Schooling, Income, and Life Expectancy

Note: Data for 1975 Hispanic education estimated by author from data for 1970 and 1980. White data are for non-Hispanic.

SOURCE: Bureau of the Census 1988:167; Bureau of the Census 2011a, 2013e; DeNavas-Walt et al. 2013: Tables A-1, B-1.

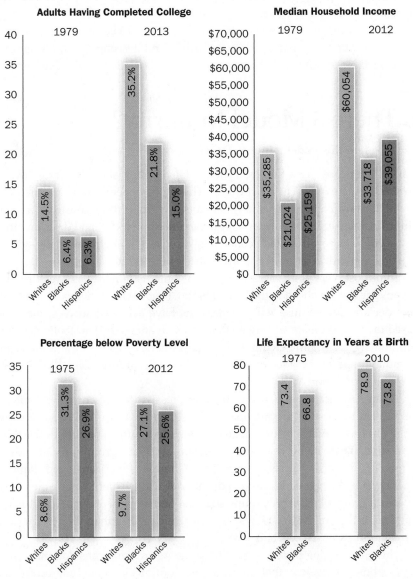

minority groups—African Americans and Hispanics—have higher household income, complete more schooling, and enjoy longer life expectancy today than in 1975. White Americans have made similar strides in all three areas. The greatest strides have been made in educational attainment. However, in other areas, the gap remains and, if one analyzes it closely, has actually increased in some instances. Black household median incomes in 2012 have yet to match the levels that Whites had in 1975, about four decades behind! Hispanics are not doing much better in this area. Latinos and African Americans still have triple the poverty rates of their White counterparts. Also, Black Americans today have barely matched the life expectancy that Whites had a generation earlier. Similarly, many minority Americans remain entrenched in poverty: nearly one out of four Hispanics and African Americans.

Little has changed since 1975. We have chosen 1975 because that was a year for which we have comparable data for Latinos, Whites, and African Americans. However, the patterns would be no different if we considered 1950, 1960, or 1970.

Is There a Model Minority?

6-2 **Explain the model minority image.**

"Asian Americans are a success! They achieve! They succeed! They have no protests, no demands. They just do it!" This is the general image people in the United States often hold of Asian Americans as a group. They constitute a **model minority** because, although they have experienced prejudice and discrimination, they seem to have succeeded economically, socially, and educationally without resorting to political or violent confrontations with Whites.

Some observers point to the existence of a model minority as a reaffirmation that anyone can get ahead in the United States. Proponents of the model-minority view declare that because Asian Americans have achieved success, they have ceased to be subordinate and are no longer disadvantaged. This labeling is only a variation of **blaming the victim**: With Asian Americans, it is praising the victim. Examining aspects of the socioeconomic status of Asian Americans allows a more thorough exploration of this view.

Asian Americans, as a group, have impressive school enrollment rates in comparison to the total population. In 2010, half of Asian Americans 25 years of age or older held bachelor's degrees, compared with 28 percent of the White population. These rates vary among Asian American groups: Asian Indians, Filipino Americans, Korean Americans, Chinese Americans, and Japanese Americans have higher levels of educational achievement than other Asian American groups. Yet other groups such as Vietnamese Americans and Pacific Islanders, including Native Hawaiians, fare much worse than White Americans (Bureau of the Census 2007b, 2011a).

This encouraging picture regarding some Asian Americans does have some qualifications, however, that question the optimistic model-minority view. According to a study of California's state university system, although Asian Americans often are viewed as successful overachievers, they have unrecognized and overlooked needs and experience discomfort and harassment on campus. As a group, they also lack Asian faculty and staff members to whom they can turn for support. They confront many identity issues and must do a "cultural balancing act" along with all the usual pressures faced by college students. The

report noted that an "alarming number" of Asian American students appear to be experiencing intense stress and alienation, problems that have often been "exacerbated by racial harassment" (Ohnuma 1991; Teranishi 2010).

Many point to the Asian American family as where the excellence begins. True, many immigrant Asian Americans and new arrivals often are dismayed by the more American behavior patterns of American youth. Change in family life is one of the most difficult cultural changes to accept. Children questioning parental authority, which Americans grudgingly accept, are a painful experience for the tradition-oriented Chinese. The 2011 bestseller *Battle Hymn of the Tiger Mother* by legal scholar Amy Chu touched off heated discussions in her indictment of parents indulging their children and holding up as a model strong parental guidance in children's activities and interests. In "Research Focus" we look more closely at this controversy.

Despite the widespread belief that they constitute a model minority, Asian Americans are victims of both prejudice and violence. After the terrorist attacks of September 11, 2001, anti-Asian violence increased dramatically for several months in the United States. The first fatality was an Asian Indian American who was shot and killed by a gunman in Mesa, Arizona, shouting, "I stand for America all the way" (National Asian Pacific American Legal Consortium 2002).

This anti–Asian American feeling is built on a long cultural tradition. The term *yellow peril* dates back to the view of Asian immigration, particularly from China, as unwelcome. **Yellow peril** came to refer to the generalized prejudice toward Asian people and their customs. The immigrants were characterized as heathen, morally inferior, drug addicted, savage, or lustful. Although the term was first used around the turn of the twentieth century, this anti-Asian sentiment is very much alive today. Many contemporary Asian Americans find this intolerance very unsettling given their conscientious efforts to extend their education, seek employment, and conform to the norms of society. Hate crimes

Research Focus

Tiger Mothers

It is not often a memoir sparks a national debate about parenting that extends around the world but such was the case with a Yale law professor. In 2011, Amy Chua authored *Battle Hymn of Tiger Mother*, which, in large part, is about how she raised her two American girls, now teenagers. Her parenting followed the childrearing she experienced from her Chinese parents who had immigrated from the Philippines and raised her in Illinois.

The quick takeaway readers, or even those who never opened the book, came away with was that "Tiger moms"—or Chinese American, maybe all Asian American, mothers—raise their children in a stern, but loving fashion that was highly competitive. **Tiger mother** has come to refer to a demanding mother who pushes her children to high levels of achievement following practices common in China and other parts of Asia.

Days are filled with music lessons and practice, and hand-making greeting cards with no sleepovers, no television, or video games and no accepting any grade but A. Married to a fellow law professor, Chua agreed to raise the children in his Jewish faith (Chua is Roman Catholic) but only if she could be a "Chinese mother." The book came to be seen as an indictment of the more permissive U.S. child-rearing practices. It was also seen by some as better too— the *Wall Street Journal* (2011) entitled its excerpt from the book " Why Chinese Mothers are Superior."

Chua does not claim to be a child development specialist and contends this was her story of one mother who came to be frustrated with when her second daughter became more rebellious at age 13 than her sister because she chose tennis over piano and violin. Since the ensuing firestorm about the book, Chua has admitted she has some regrets but would still basically raise her children strictly and

continues to defend her approach as taking the best from "Asian cultures."

Studies of Chinese parenting, much less parenting in all of Asia, stress that there is no one way that most parents rear their children. In addition Chua's relatively affluent lifestyle allowed her to hire many helpers and access experts while still being a full-time professional. All of this is well beyond the financial means of most parents. The book reinforces the model minority stereotype. There is more emphasis in Asia and among the immigrant households on stressing respect for authority and self-discipline. This approach has its roots in the ethnical and philosophical system developed from the teachings of the Chinese philosopher Confucius from the fifth century BC. Confucian parental goals do stress the importance of perseverance, working hard in school, being obedient, and being sensitive to parents' wishes.

Yet even if more common in Asia, this approach is not uniquely Chinese as Chua admits. The author said that NBC journalist Tom Brokaw told her that his working-class South Dakotan father was a "Chinese mom." There is also evidence that in China today, especially urban China, parents are becoming more relaxed with their children and growing critical of schools' emphasis on rote memorization.

Perhaps most telling about the notion of "tiger mother" and the ensuing debate is that it is set directly into viewing Asia and particularly China as a "threat" to America's superpower status. Chua makes explicit reference to how U.S. children are being outperformed in standardized tests by children in other countries and especially in China. So while *Tiger Mother* offers some insight into the caregiving culture in Asia, it also highlights how Americans see Asian and Asian Americans.

SOURCES: Chua 2011; Paul 2011; Pitt 2013; Russell, Crockett, and Chao 2010; Shah 2012; Wall Street Journal 2011.

against Asian Americans persist and have even risen in recent years (Hurh 1994; Lee et al. 2007).

The resentment against Asian Americans is not limited to overt expressions of violence. Like other subordinate groups, Asian Americans are subject to institutional discrimination. For example, some Asian American groups have large families and find themselves subject to zoning laws stipulating the number of people per room, which make it difficult for family members to live together. Kinfolk are unable to take in family members legally. Whereas we may regard these family members as distant relatives, many Asian cultures view cousins, uncles, and aunts as relatives to whom they have a great deal of familial responsibility.

The marginal status of Asian Pacific Islanders leaves them vulnerable to both selective and collective oppression. In 1999, news stories implicated Wen Ho Lee, a nuclear physicist at Los Alamos National Laboratory in New Mexico, as a spy for China. Subsequent investigation, during which Lee was imprisoned under very harsh conditions, concluded that the naturalized citizen scientist had indeed downloaded secret files to an unsecured computer, but there was no evidence that the information ever went further.

In the aftermath of the Wen Ho Lee incident, a new form of racial profiling emerged. We introduced **racial profiling** in Chapter 2 as any police-initiated action that relies on race, ethnicity, or national origin rather than a person's behavior. Despite Lee's being found not guilty, Asian Americans were viewed as security risks. A survey found that 32 percent of the people in the United States felt that Chinese Americans are more loyal to China than to the United States. In fact, the same survey showed that 46 percent were concerned about Chinese Americans passing secrets to China. Subsequent studies found that Asian Americans were avoiding top-secret science labs for employment because they became subject to racial profiling at higher security levels (Committee of 100 2001; Department of Energy 2000; Lee and Zia 2006; Wu 2002).

Another misleading sign of the apparent success of Asian Americans is their high incomes as a group. Like other elements of the image, however, this deserves closer inspection. Asian American family income approaches parity with that of Whites because of their greater achievement than Whites in formal schooling. If we look at specific educational levels, however, Whites earn more than their Asian counterparts of the same age. Asian Americans' average earnings increased by at least $2,300 for each additional year of schooling, whereas Whites gained almost $3,000. Asian Americans as a group have significantly more formal schooling but have lower household family income. We should note that to some degree, some Asian Americans' education is from overseas and, therefore, may be devalued by U.S. employers. Yet in the end, educational attainment does not pay off as much if one is of Asian descent as it does for White non-Hispanics (Kim and Sakamoto 2010; Zeng and Xie 2004).

So even with all the "tools" to succeed—supportive family, high achievement, and often attending prestigious schools—Asian Americans often hit what

Asian Americans are subject to stereotypes, one of which "straight-A," reflects the model minority image

has been termed a *bamboo ceiling*. The **bamboo ceiling** refers to the barrier that talented Asian Americans face because of resentment and intolerance directed toward Asian Americans. The bamboo ceiling is clearly a nod to the term *glass ceiling*, a term that has historically been used to address barriers that women and minority group men have faced in the workplace. The presence of the bamboo ceiling reflects the cultural values and social norms that impact Asian professionals' interactions with others and cause others to make negative judgments about them (Hyun 2006, 2009).

Asian Americans are just over 5 percent of the U.S. population, but they account for 15 to 25 percent of Ivy League college enrolment. At the same time, as of 2011, they represented fewer than 2 percent of Fortune 500 CEOs and corporate officers. A national survey showed that Asian Americans who are successful in the corporate world must manage themselves so they don't seem too ambitious or have too many ideas. Only 28 percent of Asian Americans feel very comfortable "being themselves" at the workplace, compared to 45 percent of African Americans, 41 percent of Latinos, and 42 percent of White workers (Center for Work-Life Policy 2011).

Even the positive stereotype of Asian American students as academic stars or whiz kids can be burdensome to the people so labeled. Asian Americans who do only modestly well in school may face criticism from their parents or teachers for their failure to conform to the whiz kid image. Some Asian American youths disengage from school when faced with these expectations or receive little support for their interest in vocational pursuits or athletics (Kibria 2002; Maddux et al. 2008; Ochoa 2013).

Striking contrasts are evident among Asian Americans. For every Asian American household in 2012 with an annual combined income of $200,000 or more, another earns fewer than $17,000 a year. Collectively, 11.7 percent of Asian Americans were below the poverty level in 2012 compared to 9.7 percent of White non-Hispanics. Almost every Asian American group has a higher poverty rate than non-Hispanic Whites. The lone exception is Filipinos, who tend to live in the relatively high-income states of Hawaii and California (DeNavas-Walt, Proctor, and Smith 2013: Tables HINC-02 and POV01; National CAPACD 2012).

At first, one might be puzzled to see criticism of a positive generalization such as "model minority." Why should the stereotype of adjusting without problems be a disservice to Asian Americans? The answer is that this incorrect view helps exclude Asian Americans from social programs and conceals unemployment and other social ills. When representatives of Asian groups seek assistance for those in need, people who have accepted the model-minority stereotype resent them. This is especially troubling given that problems of substance abuse and juvenile delinquency need to be addressed within the Asian American community.

If a minority group becomes viewed as successful, its members no longer will be included in any program designed to alleviate any problems they encounter as minorities. The positive stereotype reaffirms the U.S. system of mobility: New immigrants as well as established subordinate groups ought to achieve more merely by working within the system. At the same time, viewed from the conflict perspective outlined in Chapter 1, this is yet another instance of blaming the victim: If Asian Americans have succeeded, then Blacks and Latinos must be responsible for their own low status rather than recognizing society's responsibility (Bascara 2008; Chen 2012; Chou and Feagin 2008; Ryan 1976; Xu and Lee 2013).

For young Asian Americans, life in the United States often is a struggle for identity when their heritage is so devalued by those in positions of influence. Sometimes identity means finding a role in White America; other times, it involves finding a place among Asian Americans collectively and then locating oneself within one's own racial or ethnic community.

Acting White, Acting Black, or Neither

6-3   what "acting White" means.

A common view advanced by some educators is that African Americans, especially males, do not succeed in school because they do not want to be caught **acting White**. That is, they avoid at all costs taking school seriously and do not accept the authority of teachers and administrators. Whatever the accuracy of such a generalization, acting White clearly shifts the responsibility of low school attainment from the school to the individual and, therefore, can be seen as yet another example of blaming the victim. Acting White is also associated with speaking proper English or with cultural preferences like listening to rock music rather than hip-hop. This characterization is also sometimes referred to as *oppositional culture* (Fordham and Ogbu 1986; Lewis 2013; Ogbu 2004; Ogbu with Davis 2003).

In the context of high achievers, to what extent do Blacks *not* want to act White? Many scholars have noted that individuals' efforts to avoid looking like they want an education has a long history and is hardly exclusive to any one race. Students of all colors may hold back for fear of being accused of being "too hardworking."

Back in the 1950s, one heard disparaging references to "teacher's pet" and "brown nosing." Does popularity come to high school debaters and National Honor Society students or to cheerleaders and athletes? Academic-oriented classmates are often viewed as social misfits, nerds, and geeks and are seen as socially inept even if their skill building will later make them more economically independent and often more socially desirable. For minority children, including African Americans, to take school seriously means they must overcome their White classmates' same desire to be cool and not a nerd. In addition, Black youth must also come to embrace a curriculum and respect teachers who are much less likely to look or sound like them (Tyson, Darity, and Castellino 2005).

The acting-White thesis overemphasizes personal responsibility rather than structural features such as quality of schools, curriculum, and teachers. Therefore, it locates the source of Black miseducation—and by implication, the remedy—in the African American household. As scholar Michael Dyson (2005) observes, "When you think the problems are personal, you think the solutions are the same." Often one may hear the comment, If we could only get African American parents to encourage their children to work a little harder and act better

Is there a difference between Black and White schoolchildren in achievement orientation? Although some people feel that African American youth avoid acting White, research points to no difference in this respect. Members of high school science clubs, whether Black or White, are equally likely to overcome being regarded as "geeks" or "nerds."

(i.e., White), everything would be fine. As Dyson notes, "It's hard to argue against any of these things in the abstract; in principle such suggestions sound just fine."

Of course, not all Whites act White. To equate acting White with high academic achievement has little empirical or cultural support. Although more Whites between ages 18 and 19 are in school, the differences are relatively small—69 percent of Whites compared to 65 percent of Blacks. Studies comparing attitudes and performance show that Black students have the same attitudes—good and bad—about achievement as their White counterparts. Too often, we tend to view White slackers who give a hard time to the advanced placement kids as "normal," but when low-performing African Americans do the same thing, it becomes a systemic pathology undermining everything good about schools. The primary stumbling block is not acting White or acting Black but being presented with similar educational opportunities (Buck 2011; Bureau of the Census 2011a: Table 224; Downey 2008; Lewis 2013; Tyson 2011; Tyson, Darity, and Castellino 2005).

So if the notion of the difficulty that some Black students face in school is not due to their opposition to act White, why are so many people still advancing this as fact? It allows us to blame the student and "Black culture'" whatever one may wish that to mean, and not confront how our educational institutions are underperforming. This is another example of **color-blind racism**, first present in Chapter 2 when we use race-neutral principles to defend the racial unequal status quo. Majority-minority schools today persist with far fewer educational resources. Where African Americas attend more integrated schools, they are often relegated to less demanding curricular programs and face increased disciplinary actions compared to their fellow students (Lewis 2013).

Persistence of Inequality

6-4   **Discuss how inequality has persisted.**

Progress has occurred. Indignities and injustices have been eliminated, allowing us to focus on the remaining barriers to equity. But why do the gaps in income, living wages, education, and even life expectancy persist? Especially perplexing is whether the glass is half full or half empty, given the numerous civil rights laws, study commissions, favorable court decisions, and efforts by nonprofits, faith-based organizations, and private sectors.

Positive, forward steps need to be placed in the perspective of historical events. The most dramatic recent confrontation between Native Americans and the government happened in what came to be called the Battle of Wounded Knee II. In January 1973, AIM leader Russell Means led an unsuccessful drive to impeach Richard Wilson as tribal chairman of the Oglala Sioux tribe on the Pine Ridge Reservation. In the next month, Means, accompanied by some 300 supporters, started a 70-day occupation of Wounded Knee, South Dakota, site of the infamous cavalry assault in 1890 and now part of the Pine Ridge Reservation. The occupation received tremendous press coverage.

In "Speaking Out," journalist Tim Giago, born a member of the Oglala Sioux tribe on the Pine Ridge Reservation, draws attention to the harsh reality of the experience of the Plains Indians at the heads of the U.S. Army. Specifically he calls for a museum at Wounded Knee to recognize the millions of American Indians who lost their lives in the nineteenth century.

Speaking Out

Holocaust Museum of the Indigenous People Should Be Built at Wounded Knee

Tim Giago

Since 1492 the history of the Western Hemisphere has been marked by one of the greatest holocausts in the history of the world.

There are no true figures to quote about how many millions of indigenous people have perished in this land that was once their own. Those who wrote the history of the settlement of these lands often reduced the numbers of deaths because they were so high that it would make the invaders of this land appear in history as bloodthirsty barbarians. No culture wants to be remembered like this.

But somewhere in the books of man there is a compilation of the millions of indigenous people who died at the hands of the invaders whether by guns, knives, or diseases.

In Washington D.C. there is a museum to mark the Holocaust brought upon the Jewish people by Adolf Hitler. It is a place of tragedy and yet it reminds the world of what happened to the Jews in hopes that

this will never happen again. More than 6 million Jews died in the death camps operated by the Nazis and the Holocaust Museum stands as a stark reminder of these tragedies. Perhaps 5 to 10 times that number of indigenous people died beginning in 1492.

It would be prophetic if the Oglala Sioux Tribe would build a holocaust museum to educate and to remind the world of what happened to the indigenous people of the Western Hemisphere. From South America, Central America and North America, millions of indigenous people died protecting and defending what was theirs.

What happened to the Native people everywhere in the Western Hemisphere is one of the most shameful chapters in the history of mankind on this planet called earth.

Wounded Knee may have been the final chapter on this holocaust of indigenous people. It is only right that the Oglala Lakota build a Holocaust Museum of the Indigenous People right here on the grounds where the massacre of the Lakota took place on December 29, 1890.

The museum could house the history of the millions who died from the tip of South America to the top of North America. Every indigenous tribe has its stories of the death and destruction that was visited upon their people. A museum of this nature would draw visitors from around the world and it would inform and educate the masses as to the true history of the Natives of this hemisphere. But more than that, the museum would serve as a stark reminder that the hands of the invaders were not clean, but they were the hands of a people who tried in vain to destroy a culture and a people.

Whether that destruction came in the form of forced religions or in the quest for gold, indigenous people died in its wake. There are hundreds of stories to be told and hundreds of photos and artefacts to substantiate the holocaust of the Native people. It should be a priority venture for the Oglala Sioux Tribe and there should be many wealthy people and the United States government itself that would contribute money and the expertise to make the Holocaust Museum of the Indigenous People a reality.

It is time to stop talking about the genocide foisted upon us and to do something about it. This idea is one that is achievable. We now need the Lakota people of vision to cease upon it and make it happen. It is time to tell the true history of the invasion of the Americas and about the millions of deaths that ensued.

And the Lakota People should be the leaders in this endeavor because for all intent and purposes, the holocaust of the indigenous people ended on the Sacred Grounds at Wounded Knee.

SOURCE: Giago 2013.

In trying to comprehend the persistence of inequality among racial and ethnic groups, sociologists and other social scientists have found it useful to think in terms of the role played by social and cultural capital. Popularized by French sociologist Pierre Bourdieu, these concepts refer to assets that are not necessarily economic but do impact economic capital for one's family and future. Less cultural and social capital may be passed on from one generation to the next, especially when prejudice and discrimination make it difficult to overcome deficits. Racial and ethnic minorities reproduce disadvantage while Whites are more likely to reproduce privilege (Bourdieu 1983; Bourdieu and Passeron 1990).

Racial and ethnic minorities may not have the cultural and social capital of privileged Whites, but they treasure their rich heritage. The growing Black middle class owes part of its momentum to African American who have broken in to the upper ranks of corporate America. Don Thompson was named CEO of McDonald's in 2012, having begun his career with the corporation in 1990 as an electrical engineer with a degree from Purdue University. In 2012, just five other African Americans were heads of Fortune 500 corporations.

Cultural capital refers to noneconomic forces such as family background and past investments in education that are then reflected in knowledge about the arts and language. It is not necessarily book knowledge but the kind of education valued by the elites. African Americans and Native Americans have in the past faced significant restrictions in receiving a quality education. Immigrants have faced challenges due to English not being spoken at home. Muslim immigrants face an immediate challenge in functioning in a culture that advantages a different form of spirituality and lifestyle. The general historical pattern has been for immigrants, especially those who came in large numbers and settled in ethnic enclaves, to take two or three generations to reach educational parity. Knowledge of hip-hop and familiarity with Polish cuisine is culture, but it is not the culture that is valued and prestigious. Society privileges or values some lifestyles over others. This is not good, but it is social reality. Differentiating between *perogies* will not get you to the top of corporate America as fast as will differentiating among wines. This is, of course, not unique to the United States. Someone settling in Japan would have to deal with cultural capital that includes knowledge of Noh Theatre and tea ceremonies. In most countries, you are much better off following the run-up to the World Cup rather than the contenders for the next Super Bowl (DiMaggio 2005).

Social capital refers to the collective benefit of durable social networks and their patterns of reciprocal trust. Much has been written about the strength of family and friendship networks among all racial and ethnic minorities. Family reunions are major events. Family history and storytelling are rich and full. Kinfolk are not merely acquaintances but truly living assets upon which one depends or, at the very least, feels comfortable to call upon repeatedly. Networks outside the family are critical to coping in a society that often seems to be determined to keep anyone who looks like you down. But given past as well as current discrimination and prejudice, these social networks may help you become a construction worker, but they are less likely to get you into a boardroom. Residential and school segregation make developing social capital more difficult. Immigrant professionals find that their skills or advanced degrees are devalued, and they are shut out of networks of the educated and influential. Working-class Latino and Black workers have begun to develop informal social ties with their White coworkers and neighbors. Professional immigrants, in time, become accepted as equals, but racial and ethnic minority communities continue to resist institutional marginalization (Coleman 1988; Cranford 2005).

As the ranks of the powerful and important have been reached by all racial and ethnic groups, social capital is more widely shared, but this process has proven to be slower than advocates of social equality would wish. Perhaps accelerating it will be the tendency for successful minority members to be more likely to network with up-and-coming members of their own community, while Whites are more likely to be more comfortable, even complacent, with the next generation making it on their own. We are increasingly appreciative of the importance of aspirations and motivations that are often much more present among people with poor or immigrant backgrounds than those born of affluence. We know that bilingualism is an asset, not a detriment. Children who have translated for their parents develop "real-world" skills at a much earlier age than their monolingual English counterparts (Bauder 2003; Monkman, Ronald, and Théraméne 2005; Portes 1998; Yosso 2005).

Considering cultural and social capital does leave room for measured optimism. Racial and ethnic groups have shared their cultural capital, whether it is the music we dance to or the food we eat. As the barriers to privilege weaken and eventually fall, people of all colors will be able to advance. The particular strength that African Americans, tribal people, Latinos, Asian Americans, and arriving immigrants bring to the table is that they also have the ability to resist and to refuse to accept second-class status. The role that cultural and social capital plays also points to the need to embrace strategies of intervention that will increasingly acknowledge the skills and talents found in a pluralistic society.

Talking Past One Another

6-5   Consider how intergroup communication occurs without truly communicating.

African Americans, Italian Americans, Korean Americans, Puerto Ricans, Native Americans, Mexican Americans, and many others live in the United States and interact daily, sometimes face-to-face and constantly through the media. But communication does not mean we listen to, much less understand, one another. Sometimes we assume that, as we become an educated nation, we will set aside our prejudices. Yet, in recent years, our college campuses have been the scenes of tension, insults, and even violence. Fletcher Blanchard, Teri Lilly, and Leigh Ann Vaughn (1991) conducted an experiment at Smith College and found that even overheard statements can influence expressions of opinion on the issue of racism.

The researchers asked a student who said she was conducting an opinion poll for a class to approach seventy-two White students as each was walking across the campus. Each time she did so, she also stopped a second White student—actually a confederate working with the researchers—and asked her to participate in the survey as well. Both students were asked how Smith College should respond to anonymous racist notes actually sent to four African American students in 1989. However, the confederate was always instructed to answer first. In some cases, she condemned the notes; in others, she justified them. Blanchard and his colleagues (1991) concluded that "hearing at least one other person express strongly antiracist opinions produced dramatically more strongly antiracist public reactions to racism than hearing others express equivocal opinions or opinions more accepting of racism" (pp. 102–103). However, a second experiment demonstrated that when the confederate expressed sentiments justifying racism, the subjects were much less likely to express antiracist opinions than were those who heard no one else offer opinions. In this

People of different races, religions, and ethnic backgrounds talk to each other, but do we talk past one another?

experiment, social control (through the process of conformity) influenced people's attitudes and the expression of those attitudes.

Why is there so much disagreement and tension? There is a growing realization that people do not mean the same thing when they are addressing problems of race, ethnicity, gender, or religion. A husband regularly does the dishes and feels he is an equal partner in doing the housework, not recognizing that the care of his infant daughter is left totally to his wife. A manager is delighted that he has been able to hire a Puerto Rican salesperson but makes no effort to see that the new employee will adjust to an all-White, non-Hispanic staff.

We talk, but do we talk past one another? Surveys regularly show that different ethnic and racial groups have different perceptions, whether on immigration policies or racial profiling, or on whether discrimination occurs in the labor force. Sociologist Robert Blauner (1969, 1972) contends that Blacks and Whites see racism differently. Minorities see racism as central to society, as ever present, whereas Whites regard it as a peripheral concern and a national concern only when accompanied by violence or involving a celebrity. African Americans and other minorities consider racist acts in a broader context: "It is racist if my college fails to have Blacks significantly present as advisers, teachers, and administrators." Whites would generally accept a racism charge if there had been an explicit denial of a job to an appropriately qualified minority member. Furthermore, Whites would apply the label "racist" only to the person or the few people who were actually responsible for the act. Members of minority groups would be more willing to call most of the college's members racist for allowing racist practices to persist. For many Whites, the word *racism* is a red flag, and they are reluctant to give it the wide use typically employed by minorities, that is, those who have been oppressed by racism (Lichtenberg 1992).

Community studies and fieldwork show the slights that African Americans feel in everyday interactions with Whites such as at restaurants and retail outlets. Now not all these perceived slights may be real nor are they always do to racial prejudice or discrimination. Nonetheless African Americans and other racial minorities are much more likely to assess them as results of intolerance and typically dismiss them as "here we go again" rather than drawing attention to bigotry. Whites, however, would be more likely to be even annoyed that such slights could be interpreted as racial in nature and generally perceive the same interactions quite differently or due to the obnoxious nature of the offending White person (Anderson 2011; Duneier 2013).

People today evoke a color-blind racism and see little evidence of intolerance except when confronted by a horrendous hate crime. Others contend that racism is often couched in a "backstage" manner through discussions of immigration, affirmative action, anti-poverty programs, and profiling for national security.

Is one view correct—the broader minority perspective of what is racism or the more limited White outlook of what constitutes a racist action? No, but both are a part of the social reality in which we all live. We need to recognize both interpretations.

As we saw when we considered Whiteness in Chapter 5, the need to confront racism, however perceived, is not to make Whites guilty and absolve Blacks, Asians, Hispanics, and Native Americans of any responsibility for their present plight. Rather, to understand racism, past and present, is to understand how its impact has shaped both a single person's behavior and that of the entire society (Bonilla-Silva and Baiocchi 2001; Duke 1992).

Conclusion

As the United States promotes racial, ethnic, and religious diversity, it strives also to impose universal criteria on employers, educators, and realtors so that subordinate racial and ethnic groups can participate fully in the larger society. In some instances, to bring about equality of results—not just equality of opportunity—programs have been developed to give competitive advantages to women and minority men. Only more recently have similar strides been made on behalf of people with disabilities. These latest answers to social inequality have provoked much controversy over how to achieve the admirable goal of a multiracial, multiethnic society, undifferentiated in opportunity and rewards.

Relations between racial, ethnic, or religious groups take two broad forms, as situations characterized by either consensus or conflict. Consensus prevails where assimilation or fusion of groups has been completed. Consensus also prevails in a pluralistic society in the sense that members have agreed to respect differences between groups. By eliminating the contending group, extermination and expulsion also lead to a consensus society. In the study of intergroup

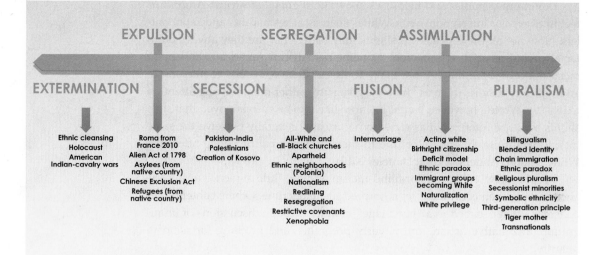

relations, it is often easy to ignore conflict where there is a high degree of consensus because it is assumed that an orderly society has no problems. In some instances, however, this assumption is misleading. Through long periods of history, misery inflicted on a racial, ethnic, or religious group was judged to be appropriate, if not actually divinely inspired.

In recent history, harmonious relations between all racial, ethnic, and religious groups have been widely accepted as a worthy goal. The struggle against oppression and inequality is not new. It dates back at least to the revolutions in England, France, and the American colonies in the seventeenth and eighteenth centuries. The twentieth century was unique in the extension of equality to the less-privileged classes, many of whose members are racial and ethnic minorities. Conflict along racial and ethnic lines is especially bitter now because it evokes memories of slavery, colonial oppression, and overt discrimination. Today's African Americans are much more aware of slavery than contemporary poor people are of seventeenth-century debtors' prison.

Unquestionably, the struggle for justice among racial and ethnic groups has not completely met its goals. Many people are still committed to repression, although they may see it only as the benign neglect of those less privileged. Such repression leads to the dehumanization of both the subordinated individual and the oppressor. Growth in equal rights movements and self-determination for Third World countries largely populated by non-White people have moved the world onto a course that seems irreversible. The old ethnic battle lines now renewed in Iran, Kenya, Sudan, and the Ukraine have only added to the tensions.

Self-determination, whether for groups or individuals, often is impossible in societies as they are currently structured. Bringing about social equality, therefore, will entail significant changes in existing institutions. Because such changes are not likely to come about with everyone's willing cooperation, the social costs will be high. However, if there is a trend in racial and ethnic relations in the world today, it is the growing belief that the social costs, however high, must be paid to achieve self-determination.

It is naive to foresee a world of societies in which one person equals one vote and all are accepted without regard to race, ethnicity, religion, gender, age, disability status, or sexual identity. It is equally unlikely to expect to see a society, let alone a world, that is without a privileged class or prestigious jobholders. Contact between different peoples, as we have seen numerous times, precedes conflict. Contact also may initiate mutual understanding and appreciation.

Assimilation, even when strictly followed, does not necessarily bring with it acceptance as an equal, nor does it even mean that one will be tolerated. Segregation persists. Efforts toward pluralism can be identified, but we can also easily see the counterefforts, whether they are the legal efforts to make English the official language or acts of intimidation by activists patrolling the nation's borders. However, the sheer changing population of the United States guarantees that we will learn, work, and play in a more diverse society.

The task of making this kaleidoscopic image of diverse cultures, languages, colors, and religions into a picture of harmony is overwhelming. But the images of failure in this task, some of which we have witnessed in our news media, are even more frightening. We can applaud success and even take time to congratulate ourselves, but we must also review the unfinished agenda.

Summary

1. There is an agreement that racial and ethnic minority groups have made great strides during the last two generations in the United States, but typically the gap between them and White men and women has remained the same.

2. Often Asian Americans are labeled as a model minority, which overlooks the many problems they face and serves to minimize the challenges of succeeding despite prejudice and discrimination.

3. African Americans have made gains in all levels of formal schooling but still fall behind the gains made by others. Debate continues over the appropriateness of the notion that Black youths avoid appearances of acting White.

4. Inequality persists despite visible improvement because most racial and ethnic groups are unable to accumulate social and cultural capital.

5. While interaction across racial and ethnic lines occurs with increasing significance, it is less clear whether we are all listening to what each other has to say. White people generally apply the charge of racism when it is operating explicitly, whereas members of racial and ethnic groups are more likely to apply it more generally where disadvantages persist.

Key Terms

acting White, p. 197
bamboo ceiling, p. 196
blaming the victim, p. 192
color-blind racism, p. 199

cultural capital, p. 202
model minority, p. 192
racial profiling, p. 195

social capital, p. 202
tiger mother, p. 194
yellow peril, p. 193

Review Questions

1. Pose views of some issue facing contemporary society that takes the position of "half full" and then "half empty."
2. Why is it harmful to be viewed as a model minority?
3. What are the accurate and inaccurate aspects of identifying people as "acting White" or "acting Black"?
4. Selecting three measures, how has inequality declined or persisted over the last generation between racial and ethnic groups.
5. Increased intergroup contact is usually encouraged, but how may the communication that naturally follows be misunderstood?

Critical Thinking

1. What contributes to the changing image of diversity in the United States?
2. Considering the stereotypes that persist, how does it affect both the people who are stereotyped as well as those who express them?
3. Consider conversations you have with people very different than yourself. Why do you feel those people are very different? To what degree did you talk to them or past them? To what degree do they talk to you or past you?
4. How have places where you have worked, even part time, been different from those of your parents or grandparents in terms of diversity of the workforce? What explains these changes?

Glossary

Parenthetical numbers refer to the pages on which the term is introduced.

absolute deprivation   The minimum level of subsistence below which families or individuals should not be expected to exist. (79)

acting White   Taking school seriously and accepting the authority of teachers and administrators. (197)

affirmative action   Positive efforts to recruit subordinate group members, including women, for jobs, promotions, and educational opportunities. (96)

Afrocentric perspective   An emphasis on the customs of African cultures and how they have pervaded the history, culture, and behavior of Blacks in the United States and around the world. (38)

amalgamation   The process by which a dominant group and a subordinate group combine through intermarriage to form a new group. (33)

anti-Semitism   Anti-Jewish prejudice or discrimination. (50)

apartheid   The policy of the South African government intended to maintain separation of Blacks, Coloureds, and Asians from the dominant Whites. (32)

assimilation   The process by which a subordinate individual or group takes on the characteristics of the dominant group. (34)

asylees   Foreigners who have already entered the United States and now seek protection because of persecution or a well-founded fear of persecution. (140)

authoritarian personality   A psychological construct of a personality type likely to be prejudiced and to use others as scapegoats. (51)

bamboo ceiling   The barrier that talented Asian Americans face because of resentment and intolerance directed toward Asian Americans. (196)

bilingual education   A program designed to allow students to learn academic concepts in their native language while they learn a second language. (126)

bilingualism   The use of two or more languages in places of work or education and the treatment of each language as legitimate. (126)

biological race   The mistaken notion of a genetically isolated human group. (11)

blaming the victim   Portraying the problems of racial and ethnic minorities as their fault rather than recognizing society's responsibilities. (22, 192)

blended identity   Self-image and worldview that is a combination of religious faith, cultural background based on nationality, and current residency. (150)

Bogardus scale   Technique to measure social distance toward different racial and ethnic groups. (67)

brain drain   Immigration to the United States of skilled workers, professionals, and technicians who are desperately needed in their home countries. (122)

chain immigration   Immigrants sponsor several other immigrants who, on their arrival, may sponsor still more. (110)

civil religion   The religious dimension in American life that merges the state with sacred beliefs. (175)

class   As defined by Max Weber, people who share similar levels of wealth. (19)

colonialism   A foreign power's maintenance of political, social, economic, and cultural dominance over people for an extended period. (26)

color-blind racism   Use of race-neutral principles to defend the racially unequal status quo. (57, 199)

conflict perspective   A sociological approach that assumes that the social structure is best understood in terms of conflict or tension between competing groups. (21)

contact hypothesis   An interactionist perspective stating that intergroup contact between people of equal status in noncompetitive circumstances will reduce prejudice. (68)

creationists   People who support a literal interpretation of the biblical book of Genesis on the origins of the universe and argue that evolution should not be presented as established scientific thought. (182)

cultural capital   Noneconomic forces such as family background and past investments in education that are then reflected in knowledge about the arts and language. (201)

deficit model of ethnic identity   One's ethnicity is viewed by others as a factor of subtracting away the characteristics corresponding to some ideal ethnic type. (150)

denomination A large, organized religion not officially linked with the state or government. (172)

discrimination The denial of opportunities and equal rights to individuals and groups because of prejudice or for other arbitrary reasons. (46, 78)

dysfunction An element of society that may disrupt a social system or decrease its stability. (21)

emigration Leaving a country to settle in another. (24)

environmental justice Efforts to ensure that hazardous substances are controlled so that all communities receive protection regardless of race or socioeconomic circumstances. (95)

environmental refugees People forced to leave their communities because of natural disasters, or the effects of climate change and global warming. (139)

ethnic cleansing Forced deportation of people accompanied by systematic violence. (28)

ethnic group A group set apart from others because of its national origin or distinctive cultural patterns. (9)

ethnic paradox The maintenance of one's ethnic ties in a way that can assist with assimilation in larger society. (152)

ethnocentrism The tendency to assume that one's culture and way of life are superior to all others. (44)

ethnophaulisms Ethnic or racial slurs, including derisive nicknames. (45)

exploitation theory A Marxist theory that views racial subordination in the United States as a manifestation of the class system inherent in capitalism. (51)

functionalist perspective A sociological approach emphasizing how parts of a society are structured to maintain its stability. (20)

fusion A minority and a majority group combining to form a new group. (33)

genocide The deliberate, systematic killing of an entire people or nation. (28)

glass ceiling The barrier that blocks the promotion of a qualified worker because of gender or minority membership. (102)

glass escalator The male advantage experienced in occupations dominated by women. (104)

glass wall A barrier to moving laterally in a business to positions that are more likely to lead to upward mobility. (104)

globalization Worldwide integration of government policies, cultures, social movements, and financial markets through trade, movements of people, and the exchange of ideas. (25, 137)

hate crime Criminal offense committed because of the offender's bias against a race, religion, ethnic or national origin group, or sexual orientation group. (79)

Holocaust The state-sponsored systematic persecution and annihilation of European Jewry by Nazi Germany and its collaborators. (28)

immigration Coming into a new country as a permanent resident. (24)

income Salaries, wages, and other money received. (86)

institutional discrimination A denial of opportunities and equal rights to individuals or groups resulting from the normal operations of a society. (84)

intelligence quotient (IQ) The ratio of a person's mental age (as computed by an IQ test) to his or her chronological age, multiplied by 100. (12)

intelligent design View that life is so complex that it must have been created by a higher intelligence. (182)

labeling theory A sociological approach introduced by Howard Becker that attempts to explain why certain people are viewed as deviants and others engaging in the same behavior are not. (22)

marginality The status of being between two cultures at the same time, such as the status of Jewish immigrants in the United States. (18)

melting pot Diverse racial or ethnic groups or both, forming a new creation, a new cultural entity. (33)

migration A general term that describes any transfer of population. (24)

minority group A subordinate group whose members have significantly less control or power over their own lives than do the members of a dominant or majority group. (5)

mixed status Families in which one or more members are citizens and one or more are noncitizens. (124)

model minority A group that, despite past prejudice and discrimination, succeeds economically, socially, and educationally without resorting to political or violent confrontations with Whites. (192)

nativism Beliefs and policies favoring native-born citizens over immigrants. (114)

naturalization Conferring of citizenship on a person after birth. (134)

normative approach The view that prejudice is influenced by societal norms and situations that encourage or discourage the tolerance of minorities. (52)

occupational segregation The tendency for a racial, ethnic, or gender group to be employed in different occupations from each other. (128)

panethnicity The development of solidarity between ethnic subgroups as reflected in the terms Hispanic and Asian American. (18)

pluralism Mutual respect for one another's culture, a respect that allows minorities to express their own culture without suffering prejudice or discrimination. (36)

prejudice A negative attitude toward an entire category of people such as a racial or ethnic minority. (45)

principle of third-generation interest Marcus Hansen's contention that ethnic interest and awareness increase in the third generation, among the grandchildren of immigrants. (151)

racial formation A sociohistorical process by which racial categories are created, inhibited, transformed, and destroyed. (15)

racial group A group that is socially set apart because of obvious physical differences. (8)

racial profiling Any arbitrary police-initiated action based on race, ethnicity, or national origin rather than a person's behavior. (55)

racism A doctrine that one race is superior. (14)

redlining The pattern of discrimination against people trying to buy homes in minority and racially changing neighborhoods. (90)

refugees People living outside their country of citizenship for fear of political or religious persecution. (139)

relative deprivation The conscious experience of a negative discrepancy between legitimate expectations and present actualities. (79)

religion A unified system of sacred beliefs and practices that encompass elements beyond everyday life that inspire awe, respect, and even fear. (171)

remittances The monies that immigrants return to their countries of origin. (130)

resegregation The physical separation of racial and ethnic groups reappearing after a period of relative integration. (32)

reverse discrimination Actions that cause better-qualified White men to be passed over for women and minority men. (100)

scapegoating theory A person or group blamed irrationally for another person's or group's problems or difficulties. (50)

secessionist minority Groups that reject assimilation and promote coexistence and pluralism. (180)

segmented assimilation The outcome of immigrants and their descendants moving in to different classes of the host society. (35)

segregation The physical separation of two groups, often imposed on a subordinate group by the dominant group. (30)

self-fulfilling prophecy The tendency to respond to and act on the basis of stereotypes, a predisposition that can lead one to validate false definitions. (23)

sexism The ideology that one sex is superior to the other. (54)

social capital Collective benefits of durable social networks and their patterns of reciprocal trust. (202)

social distance Tendency to approach or withdraw from a racial group. (67)

sociology The systematic study of social behavior and human groups. (19)

stereotypes Unreliable, exaggerated generalizations about all members of a group that do not take individual differences into account. (53)

stratification A structured ranking of entire groups of people that perpetuates unequal rewards and power in a society. (19)

symbolic ethnicity Herbert Gans's term that describes emphasis on ethnic food and ethnically associated political issues rather than deeper ties to one's heritage. (154)

Tiger mother A demanding mother who pushes her children to high levels of achievement following practices common in China and other parts of Asia. (194)

transnationals Immigrants who sustain multiple social relationships that link their societies of origin and settlement. (138)

wealth An inclusive term encompassing all of a person's material assets, including land and other types of property. (86)

White privilege Rights or immunities granted as a particular benefit or favor for being White. (48, 149)

world systems theory A view of the global economic system as divided between nations that control wealth and those that provide natural resources and labor. (27)

xenophobia The fear or hatred of strangers or foreigners. (114)

yellow peril A term denoting a generalized prejudice toward Asian people and their customs. (193)

References

Abbott, Andrew, and Ranier Egloff. 2008. The Polish Peasant in Oberlin and Chicago. The Intellectual Trajectory of W. I. Thomas. *American Sociologist* 39: 217–258.

ABC Television. 2013. *Arkansas Schools to Start Moment of Silence When Classes Begin* (August 2). Accessed September 8, 2013, at http://www.4029tv.com.

Abdo, Geneive. 2004a. A Muslim Rap Finds Voice. *Chicago Tribune* (June 30): 1, 19.

Adorno, T. W., Else Frenkel-Brunswik, Daniel J. Levinson, and R. Nevitt Sanford. 1950. *The Authoritarian Personality*. New York: Wiley.

Alliance for Board Diversity. 2009. *Women and Minorities on Fortune 100 Boards*. New York: Catalyst, the Executive Leadership Council, and the Hispanic Association on Corporate Responsibility.

Allport, Gordon W. 1979. *The Nature of Prejudice*, 25th anniversary ed. Reading, MA: Addison-Wesley.

American Community Survey. 2009. *American Community Survey 2008*. Data released August 2009. Accessible at http://www.census.gov.

American Community Survey. 2011b. *American Community Survey 2010*. Data released August 2011. Accessible at http://www.census.gov.

American Community Survey. 2013a. *American Community Survey 2012*. Data released August 2013. Accessible at http://www.census.gov.

American Financial Resources. 2012. *Craigslist Has New Policy for Discriminatory Ads* (June 17). Accessed August 7, 2013, at http://www.afr-mortgage.com.

Anderson, Elijah. 2011. *The Cosmopolitan Canopy: Race and Civility in Everyday Life*. New York: W. W. Norton and Company.

Ansell, Amy E. 2008. Color Blindness. Pp. 320–322 in vol. 1, *Encyclopedia of Race, Ethnicity, and Society*, Richard T. Schaefer, ed. Thousand Oaks, CA: Sage.

Applebome, Peter. 1996. 70 Years After Scopes Trial, Creation Debate Lives. *New York Times* (March 10): 1, 22.

Archibold, Randal C. 2007. A City's Violence Feeds on Black-Hispanic Rivalry. *New York Times* (January 17): A1, A15.

Asante, Molefi Kete. 2007. *An Afrocentric Manifesto: Toward an African Renaissance*. Cambridge, UK: Polity.

Asante, Molefi Kete. 2008. Afrocentricity. Pp. 41–42 in vol. 1, *Encyclopedia of Race, Ethnicity, and Society*, Richard T. Schaefer, ed. Thousand Oaks, CA: Sage.

Asi, Maryam, and Daniel Beaulieu. 2013. *Arab Households in the United States 2006–2010*. ACSBR/10-20. Accessible at http://www.census.gov.

Badgett, M. V. Lee, and Heidi I. Hartmann. 1995. The Effectiveness of Equal Employment Opportunity Policies. Pp. 55–83 in *Economic Perspectives in Affirmative Action*, Margaret C. Simms, ed. Washington, DC: Joint Center for Political and Economic Studies.

Baker, Bryan C. 2009. *Trends in Naturalization Rates: 2008 Update*. Washington, DC: Department of Homeland Security.

Baltzell, E. Digby. 1964. *The Protestant Establishment: Aristocracy and Caste in America*. New York: Vintage Books.

Bamshad, Michael J., and Steve E. Olson. 2003. Does Race Exist? *Scientific American* (December): 78–85.

Banton, Michael. 2008. The Sociology of Ethnic Relations. *Ethnic and Racial Studies* (May): 1–19.

Barringer, Felicity. 2004. Bitter Division for Sierra Club on Immigration. *New York Times* (March 14): A1, A16.

Bascara, Victor. 2008. Model Minority. Pp. 910–912 in vol. 2, *Encyclopedia of Race, Ethnicity, and Society*, Richard T. Schaefer, ed. Thousand Oaks, CA: Sage.

Bash, Harry M. 2001. *If I'm So White, Why Ain't I Right? Some Methodological Misgivings on Taking Identity Ascriptions at Face Value*. Paper presented at the annual meeting of the Midwest Sociological Society, St. Louis.

Bauder, Harald. 2003. Brain Abuse, or the Devaluation of Immigrant Labour in Canada. *Antipode* 35 (September): 699–717.

Bayoumi, Moustafa. 2009. *How Does it Feel to be a Problem? Being Young and Arab in America.* New York: Penguin Books.

Bayoumi, Moustafa. 2010. My Arab Problem. *Chronicle of Higher Education* (October 29): B13–B14.

Bean, Frank D., and G. Stevens. 2003. *America's Newcomers and the Dynamics of Diversity.* New York: Russell Sage Foundation.

Beisel, Nicola, and Tamara Kay. 2004. Abortion: Race and Gender in Nineteenth Century America. *American Sociological Review* 69 (August): 498–518.

Bell, Derrick. 1994. The Freedom of Employment Act. *The Nation* 258 (May 23): 708, 710–714.

Bell, Wendell. 1991. Colonialism and Internal Colonialism. Pp. 52–53 in *The Encyclopedic Dictionary of Sociology*, 4th ed., Richard Lachmann, ed. Guilford, CT: Dushkin Publishing Group.

Bellah, Robert. 1967. Civil Religion in America. *Daedalus* 96 (Winter): 1–21.

Belton, Danielle C. 2009. Blacks in Space. *American Prospect* (June): 47–49.

Bernard, Tara Siegel. 2012. Blacks Face Bias in Bankruptcy, Study Suggests. *New York Times* (January 21): A1.

Best, Joel. 2001. Social Progress and Social Problems: Toward a Sociology of Gloom. *Sociological Quarterly* 42 (1): 1–12.

Bjerk, David. 2008. Glass Ceilings or Sticky Floors? Statistical Discrimination in a Dynamic Model of Hiring and Promotion. *The Economic Journal* 118 (530): 961–982.

Blanchard, Fletcher A., Lilly, Teri, and Vaughn, Leigh Ann. 1991. Reducing the Expression of Racial Prejudice. *Psychological Science* (March 2): 101–105.

Blauner, Robert. 1969. Internal Colonialism and Ghetto Revolt. *Social Problems* 16 (Spring): 393–408.

Blauner, Robert. 1972. *Racial Oppression in America.* New York: Harper & Row.

Blazak, Randy. 2011. Isn't Every Crime a Hate Crime? The Case for Hate Crime Laws. *Sociology Compass* 5 (4): 244–255.

Bloom, Leonard. 1971. *The Social Psychology of Race Relations.* Cambridge, MA: Schenkman Publishing.

Bobo, Lawrence. 2013. The Antinomes of Racial Change. *DuBois Review* 10 (1): 1–5.

Bogardus, Emory. 1968. Comparing Racial Distance in Ethiopia, South Africa, and the United States. *Sociology and Social Research* 52 (January): 149–156.

Bohmer, Susanne, and Kayleen V. Oka. 2007. Teaching Affirmative Action: An Opportunity to Apply, Segregate, and Reinforce Sociological Concepts. *Teaching Sociology* 35 (October): 334–349.

Bonilla-Silva, Eduardo. 1996. Rethinking Racism: Toward a Structural Interpretation. *American Sociological Review* 62 (June): 465–480.

Bonilla-Silva, Eduardo. 2002. The Linguistics of Color Blind Racism: How to Talk Nasty about Blacks without Sounding Racist. *Critical Sociology* 28 (1–2): 41–64.

Bonilla-Silva, Eduardo. 2006. *Racism without Racists*, 2nd ed. Lanham, MD: Rowman & Littlefield.

Bonilla-Silva, Eduardo. 2012. The Invisible Weight of Whiteness: The Racial Grammar of Everyday Life in Contemporary America. *Ethnic and Racial Studies* 35 (February): 173–194.

Bonilla-Silva, Eduardo, and Gianpaolo Baiocchi. 2001. Anything but Racism: How Sociologists Limit the Significance of Racism. *Race and Society* 4: 117–131.

Bonilla-Silva, Eduardo, and David Dietrich. 2011. The Sweet Enchantment of Color-Blind Racism in Obamerica. *The ANNALS of the American Academy of Political and Social Science* 634 (March): 190–206.

Bonilla-Silva, Eduardo, and David G. Embrick. 2007. "Every Place Has a Ghetto…" The Significance of Whites' Social and Residential Segregation. *Symbolic Interaction* 30 (3): 323–345.

Bonilla-Silva, Eduardo, and David G. Embrick, with Louise Seamster. 2011. The Sweet Enchantment of Color Blindness in Black Face: Explaining the "Miracle," Debating the Politics, and Suggesting a Way for Hope to be "For Real" in America. *Political Power and Social Theory* 22: 139–175.

Borjas, George J., Jeffery Grogger, and Gordon H. Hanson. 2006. *Immigration and African-American Employment Opportunities: The Response of Wages, Employment, and Incarceration to Labor Supply Shocks.* Working Paper 12518. Cambridge, MA: National Bureau of Economic Research.

Bork, Robert H. 1995. What to Do About the First Amendment. *Commentary* 99 (February): 23–29.

Bourdieu, Pierre. 1983. The Forms of Capital. Pp. 241–258 in *Handbook of Theory and Research for the Sociology of Education*, J. G. Richardson, ed., Westport, CT: Greenwood.

Bourdieu, Pierre, and Jean-Claude Passerson. 1990. *Reproduction in Education, Society and Culture*, 2nd ed. London. Sage. Originally published as *La reproduction*.

Bowles, Scott. 2000. Bans on Racial Profiling Gain Steam. *USA Today* 2 (June): 3A.

Bowman, Tom. 1998. Evangelicals Allege Bias in U.S. Navy, Marine Chaplain Corps. *Baltimore Sun* 23 (August): A12.

Bowser, Benjamin, and Raymond G. Hunt, eds. 1996. *Impacts of Racism on White Americans*. Beverly Hills, CA: Sage Publications.

Braxton, Gregory. 2009. "Reality Television" in More Ways Than One. *Los Angeles Times* (February 17): A1, A15.

Breines, Winifred. 2007. Struggling to Connect: White and Black Feminism in the Movement Years. *Contexts* 6 (1): 18–24.

Brennan Center. 2006. *Citizens without Proof*. November. New York: Brennan Center for Justice at NYU School of Law.

Brennan Center. 2013. *Election 2012 Laws Roundup*. Accessed January 13, 2013, at http://www.brennancenter.org.

Brooks-Gunn, Jeanne, Pamela K. Klebanov, and Greg J. Duncan. 1996. Ethnic Differences in Children's Intelligence Test Scores: Role of Economic Deprivation, Home Environment, and Maternal Characteristics. *Child Development* 67 (April): 396–408.

Browne, Irene, ed. 2001. *Latinas and African American Women at Work: Race, Gender, and Economic Inequality*. New York: Russell Sage Foundation.

Brulliard, Karin. 2006. A Proper Goodbye: Funeral Homes Learn Immigrants' Traditions. *Washington Post National Weekly Edition* (May 7): 31.

Buchanan, Angela B., Nora G. Albert, and Daniel Beaulieu. 2010. *The Population with Haitian Ancestry in the United States: 2009*. ACSR/09-18. Accessible at http://www.census.gov.

Buck, Stuart. 2011. *Acting White: The Ironic Legacy of Desegregation*. New Haven: Yale University Press.

Budig, Michelle J. 2002. Male Advantage and the Gender Composition of Jobs: Who Rides the Glass Escalator? *Social Problems* 49 (2): 258–277.

Bukowczyk, John J. 2007. *A History of Polish Americans*. New Brunswick, NJ: Transaction Books.

Bureau of the Census. 2007b. *The American Community—Pacific Islanders: 2004*. ACS-06. Washington, DC: U.S. Government Printing Office.

Bureau of the Census. 2009b. *Irish-American Heritage Month (March) and St. Patrick's Day (March 17): 2009*. Washington, DC: U.S. Census Bureau.

Bureau of the Census. 2010a. *Statistical Abstract of the United States, 2011*. Washington, DC: U.S. Government Printing Office.

Bureau of the Census. 2010b. *U.S. Population Projections*. Accessible at http://www.census.gov/population/www/projections/2009projections.html.

Bureau of the Census. 2011a. *Statistical Abstract of the United States: 2012*. Accessible at http://www.census.gov.

Bureau of the Census. 2011b. *Irish-American Heritage Month (March) and St. Patrick's Day (March 17): 2011*. Census Brief CB11-FF, 03, January 13.

Bureau of the Census. 2012d. *Most Children Younger Than Age 1 are Minorities, Census Bureau Reports* (May 17). Accessible at http://www.census.gov/newsroom/releases/archives/population/cb12-90.html.

Bureau of the Census. 2013b. *2012 National Projections*. Updated May 2013. Accessible at http://www.census.gov/newsroom/releases/archives/population/cb13-211.html.

Burgess, Melinda, Karen E. Dill, S. Paul Stermer, Stephen R. Burgess, and Brian P. Brown. 2011. Playing with Prejudice: The Prevalence and Consequences of Racial Stereotypes in Video Games. *Media Psychology* 14: 289–311.

Cafaro, Philip, and Winthrop Staples III. 2009. *The Environmental Argument for Reducing Immigration to the United States*. Washington, DC: Center for Immigration Studies.

Calavita, Kitty. 2007. Immigration Law, Race, and Identity. *Annual Reviews of Law and Social Sciences* 3: 1–20.

Camarota, Steven A. 2007a. *Immigrants in the United States, 2007: A Profile of America's Foreign-Born Population*. Washington, DC: Center for Immigrant Statistics.

Camarota, Steven A., and Karen Jensenius. 2009. *A Shifting Tide: Recent Trends in the Illegal*

Immigrant Population. Washington DC: Center for Immigration Studies.

Campion, Siah. 2013. *Interview* (September). Montello WI.

Canfield, Clarke. 2012. Maine Major: Somalis Should Leave Culture at Door. *Twin City Times* (Lewiston Auburn ME) (October 4). Accessed November 12, 2012, at http://www.twincitytimes.com/columns/enough-is-enough-extremist-liberals-widen-the-divide-with-somalis.

Capps, Randy, Ku Leighton, and Michael Fix. 2002. *How Are Immigrants Faring after Welfare Reform? Preliminary Evidence from Los Angeles and New York City.* Washington, DC: Urban Institute.

Carlson, Allan C. 2003. The Peculiar Legacy of German-Americans. *Society* 40 (January/February): 77–88.

Carr, James H., and Nandinee K. Kutty, eds. 2008. *Segregation: The Rising Costs for America.* New York: Routledge.

Carroll, Joseph. 2006. Public National Anthem Should Be Sung in English. *The Gallup Poll* (May): 3.

Catalyst. 2001. *Women Satisfied with Current Job in Financial Industry but Barriers Still Exist.* Press release July 25, 2001. Accessed January 31, 2002, at http://www.catalystwomen.org.

Cave, Damien. 2011. Crossing Over, and Over. *New York Times* (October 3): A1, A6.

Center for Constitutional Rights. 2011. *Stop-and-Frisks of New Yorkers in 2010 Hit All-Time High at 600, 601; 87 percent of Those Stopped Black and Latino.* Accessed March 2, 2011, at http://ccrjustice.org.

Center for Work-Life Policy. 2011. *Asian-Americans Still Feel Like Outsiders in Corporate America, New Study from the Center for Work-Life Policy Finds.* July 20. New York: Center for Work-Life Policy.

Chazan, Guy, and Ainsley Thomson. 2011. Tough Irish Economy Turns Migration Influx to Exodus. *Wall Street Journal* (January 21): A8.

Chen, Carolyn. 2012. Asians: Too Smart for Their Own Good? *New York Times* (December 20): A35.

Chirot, Daniel, and Jennifer Edwards. 2003. Making Sense of the Senseless: Understanding Genocide. *Contexts* 2 (Spring): 12–19.

Chou, Roslaind S., and Joe R. Feagin. 2008. *The Myth of the Model Minority: Asian Americans Facing Racism.* Boulder: Paradigm Publishers.

Chu, Judy. 2011. *Chinese Exclusion Act.* Congressional Record 157 (No. 77, June 1): H3809–H3810.

Chua, Amy. 2011. *Battle Hymn of the Tiger Mother.* New York: Penguin Press.

Citrin, Jack, Amy Lerman, Michael Murakami, and Kathryn Pearson. 2007. Testing Huntington: Is Hispanic Immigration a Threat to American Identity? *Perspectives on Politics* 5 (March): 31–48.

Clark, Kenneth B., and Mamie P. Clark. 1947. Racial Identification and Preferences in Negro Children. Pp. 169–178 in *Readings in Social Psychology*, Theodore M. Newcomb and Eugene L. Hartley, eds. New York: Holt, Rinehart & Winston.

Clemmitt, Marcia. 2005. Intelligent Design. *CQ Researcher* 95 (July 29): 637–660.

Cognard-Black, Andrew J. 2004. Will They Stay, or Will They Go? Sex—Atypical among Token Men Who Teach. *Sociological Quarterly* 45 (1): 113–139.

Cohen, Patricia. 2010a. Discussing That Word That Prompts Either a Fist Pump or a Scowl. *New York Times* (January 23): C1, C5.

Coker, Tumaini et al. 2009. Perceived Racial/Ethnic Discrimination Among Fifth-Grade Students and Its Association with Mental Health. *American Journal of Public Health* 99 (5): 878–884.

Coleman, James S. 1988. Social Capital in the Creation of Human Capital. *American Journal of Sociology* 94 (Suppl.): S95–S120.

Collins, Patricia Hill. 2000. *Black Feminist Thought: Knowledge, Consciousness, and the Politics of Empowerment,* 2nd ed. New York: Routledge.

Collins, Patricia Hill. 2013. *On Intellectual Activism.* Philadelphia: Temple University Press.

Commission on Civil Rights. 1976. *Fulfilling the Letter and Spirit of the Law: Desegregation of the Nation's Public Schools.* Washington, DC: U.S. Government Printing Office.

Commission on Civil Rights. 1981. *Affirmative Action in the 1980s: Dismantling the Process of Discrimination.* Washington, DC: U.S. Government Printing Office.

Committee of 100. 2001. *American Attitudes Towards Chinese Americans and Asian Immigrants.* New York: Committee of 100.

Conyers, James L., Jr. 2004. The Evolution of Africology: An Afrocentric Appraisal. *Journal of Black Studies* 34 (May): 640–652.

Coontz, Stephanie. 2010. *A Strange Stirring: "The Feminine Mystique" and American Women at the Dawn of the 1960s.* New York: Basic Books.

Cooperman, Alan. 2005. One Way to Pray? *Washington Post National Weekly Edition* 22 (September 5): 10–11.

Cornacchia, Eugene J., and Dale C. Nelson. 1992. Historical Differences in the Political Experiences of American Blacks and White Ethnics: Revisiting an Unresolved Controversy. *Ethnic and Racial Studies* (January 15): 102–124.

Correll, Joshua, Bernadette Park, Charles M. Judd, Bernd Wittenbrink, Melody S. Sadler, and Tracie Keesee. 2007a. Across the Thin Blue Line: Police Officers and Racial Bias in the Decision to Shoot. *Journal of Personality and Social Psychology* 92 (6): 1006–1023.

Correll, Joshua, Bernadette Park, Charles M. Judd, Bernd Wittenbrink, Melody S. Sadler, and Tracie Keesee. 2007b. The Influence of Stereotypes and Decisions to Shoot. *European Journal of Social Psychology* 37: 1102–1117.

Cose, Ellis. 1993. *The Rage of a Privileged Class.* New York: HarperCollins.

Cose, Ellis. 2008. So What if He Were Muslim? *Newsweek* (September 1): 37.

Cox, Oliver C. 1942. The Modern Caste School of Social Relations. *Social Forces* 21 (December): 218–226.

Cranford, Cynthia J. 2005. Networks of Exploitation: Immigrant Labor and the Restructuring of the Los Angeles Janitorial Industry. *Social Problems* 52 (3): 379–397.

Cullen, Andrew. 2011. Struggle and Progress: 10 Years of Somalis in Lewiston. *Lewiston-Auburn Sun Journal* (December 18). Accessed April 16, 2012, at http://www.sunjournal.com/news/city/2011/12/18/struggle-and-progress-10-years-somalis-lewiston/1127846.

DaCosta, Kimberly McClain. 2007. *Making Multiracials: State, Family, and Market in the Redrawing of the Color Line.* Stanford, CA: Stanford University Press.

Dade, Corey. 2012a. *Census Bureau Rethinks The Best Way to Measure Race.* Accessed December 29, 2012, at http://www.wbur.org.

Dade, Corey. 2012b. *The Fight Over Voter ID Laws Goes to the United Nations* (March 9). Accessible at http://www.npr.org.

Dally, Chad. 2011. Hmong Heritage Month Refocuses on Health. *Wausau Daily Herald* (April 3): A3.

David, Gary C. 2003. Rethinking Who's an Arab American: Arab-American Studies in the New Millennium. *Al-Jadid* (Fall): 9.

David, Gary C. 2007. The Creation of "Arab American": Political Activism and Ethnic (Dis) Unity. *Critical Sociology* 32: 833–862.

Davis, James A., Tom W. Smith, and Peter V. Marsden. 2007. *General Social Surveys, 1972–2006: Cumulative Codebook.* Chicago: NORC.

Davis, Michelle R. 2008. Checking Sources: Evaluating Web Sites Requires Careful Eye. Released by *Education Week* (March 6). Accessed June 20, 2008, at http://www.edweek.org.

De Anda, Roberto M. 2004. *Chicanas and Chicanos in Contemporary Society,* 2nd ed. Lanham, MD: Rowman & Littlefield & Bacon.

de la Garza, Rodolfo O., Louis DeSipio, F. Chris Garcia, John Garcia, and Angelo Falcon. 1992. *Latino Voices: Mexican, Puerto Rican, and Cuban Perspectives on American Politics.* Boulder, CO: Westview Press.

DellaPergola, Sergio. 2007. World Jewish Population, 2007. Pp. 551–600 in *American Jewish Yearbook 2007,* David Singer and Lawrence Grossman, eds. New York: American Jewish Committee.

DellaPergola, Sergio. 2012. *Jewish Population of the World.* Accessible at http://www.jewishvirtual-library.org

Del Olmo, Frank. 2003. Slow Motion Carnage at the Border. *Los Angeles Times* (May 18): M5.

DeNavas-Walt, Carman, Bernadette D. Proctor, and Jessica C. Smith. 2013. *Income, Poverty, and Health Insurance Coverage in the United States: 2012.* Washington, DC: U.S. Government Printing Office.

Department of Agriculture. 2010. *2007 Census Publications: Wisconsin.* Accessed August 13, at http://www.agcensus.usda.gov/Publications/2007/Full_Report/Census_by_State/Wisconsin.

Department of Energy. 2000. *Final Report: Task Force against Racial Profiling.* Washington, DC: U.S. Government Printing Office.

Department of Homeland Security. 2013. *Naturalization Self Test.* Accessed August 7, 2013, at http://www.uscis.gov.

Department of Justice. 2001. *Report to the Congress of the United States: A Review of Restrictions on*

Persons of Italian Ancestry During World War II. Accessed February 1, 2002, at http://www.house.gov/judiciary/Italians.pdf.

Department of Justice. 2011. *Hate Crime Statistics, 2010.* Accessible at http://www.fbi.gov.

Department of State. 2013. *US State Department Services Dual Nationality.* Accessed August 7, 2013, at http://travel.state.gov/travel/cis_pa_tw/cis/cis_1753.html.

DeSante, Christopher D. 2012. Working Twice as Hard to Get Half as Far: Race, Work Ethnic, and America's Deserving Poor. *American Journal of Political Science* 57 (April): 342–356.

Desmond, Scott A., and Charise E. Kubrin. 2009. The Power of Place: Immigrant Communities and Adolescent Violence. *Sociological Quarterly* 50 (2009): 581–607.

Deutscher, Irwin, Fred P. Pestello, and H. Frances Pestello. 1993. *Sentiments and Acts.* New York: Aldine de Gruyter.

Diamond, Jared. 2003. Globalization, Then. *Los Angeles Times* (September 14): M1, M3.

Dickson, Lisa M. 2006. Book Review: Italians Then, Mexicans Now. *Industrial and Labor Relations Review* 60 (2): 293–295.

DiMaggio, Paul. 2005. Cultural Capital. Pp. 167–170 in *Encyclopedia of Social Theory*, George Ritzer, ed. Thousand Oaks, CA: Sage Publications.

DiTomaso, Nancy, Corinne Post, and Rochelle Parks-Yancy. 2007. Workforce Diversity and Inequality: Power, Status, and Numbers. *Annual Review of Sociology* 33: 473–501.

Dobbin, Frank, and Alexandra Kalev. 2013. The Origins and Effects of Corporate Diversity Programs. Pp. 253–281 in *Oxford Handbook of Diversity and Work*, Quintetta M. Roberson, ed. New York: Oxford University Press.

Dobbin, Frank, Alexandra Kalev, and Erin Kelly. 2007. Diversity Management in Corporate America. *Contexts* 6 (4): 21–27.

Dobbin, Frank, Soohan Kim, and Alexandra Kalev. 2011. You Can't Always Get What You Need: Organizational Determinants of Diversity Programs. *American Sociological Review* 76 (3): 386.

Dolan, Sean, and Sandra Stotsky. 1997. *The Polish Americans.* New York: Chelsea House.

Dolan, Timothy. 2013. Immigration and the Welcome Church. *Wall Street Journal* (October 18): A11.

Dorschner, Cheryl. 2013. *The New Face of Vermont Dairy Farming.* Accessed August 13, 2013, at http://www.uvm.edu/~cals/?Page=news&storyID=15296&category=calshome.

Downey, Douglas B. 2008. Black/White Differences in School Performance: The Oppositional Culture Explanation. *Annual Review of Sociology* 34: 107–126.

Du Bois, W. E. B. 1903. *The Souls of Black Folks: Essays and Sketches* (reprint). New York: Facade Publications, 1961.

Du Bois, W. E. B. 1969a. *An ABC of Color* [1900]. New York: International Publications.

Duke, Lynne. 1992. You See Color-Blindness, I See Discrimination. *Washington Post National Weekly Edition* 9 (June 15): 33.

Duneier, Mitchell. 2013. Elijah Anderson on Race Relations and Public Space: Beyond the Primacy of the Street. *Contemporary Sociology* 42 (6): 809–814.

Durkheim, Émile. 2001. *The Elementary Forms of Religious Life* [1912]. New translation by Carol Cosman. New York: Oxford University Press.

Duszak, Thomas. 1997. Lattimer Massacre Centennial Commemoration. *Polish American Journal* (August). Accessed June 4, 2008, at http://www.polamjournal.com/Library/APHistory/Lattimer/lattimer.html.

Dyson, Michael Eric. 2005. *Is Bill Cosby Right?* New York: Basic Civitas, Perseus Books.

Eckstrom, Kevin. 2001. New, Diverse Take Spot on Catholic Altars. *Chicago Tribune* (August 31): 8.

Economist. 2013a. *Secure Enough* (June 22): 31–32.

El-Haj, Nadia Abu. 2007. The Genetic Reinscription of Race. *Annual Review of Anthropology* 16: 283–300.

Ennis, Sharon R., Merarys Rios-Vargas, and Nora G. Albert. 2011. *The Hispanic Population: 2010.* C2010BR-404. Accessible at http://www.census.gov/prod/cen2010/briefs/c2010br-04.pdf.

Epstein, Cynthia Fuchs. 1999. The Major Myth of the Women's Movement. *Dissent* (Fall): 83–111.

Erdmans, Mary Patrice. 1998. *Opposite Poles: Immigrants and Ethnics in Polish Chicago, 1976–1990.* University Park: Pennsylvania State University.

Erdmans, Mary Patrice. 2006. New Chicago Polonia: Urban and Suburban. Pp. 115–127 in *The New*

Chicago, John Koval et al., eds. Philadelphia: Temple University Press.

Espiritu, Yen Le. 1992. *Asian American Panethnicity: Bridging Institutions and Identities.* Philadelphia: Temple University Press.

Fallows, Marjorie R. 1979. *Irish Americans: Identity and Assimilation.* Englewood Cliffs, NJ: Prentice Hall.

Farkas, Steve. 2003. *What Immigrants Say About Life in the United States.* Washington, DC: Migration Policy Institute.

Feagin, Joe R., and José A. Cobas. 2008. Latinos/as and White Racial Frame: The Procrustean Bed of Assimilation. *Sociological Inquiry* 78 (February): 39–53.

Feagin, Joe R., José A. Cobas, and Sean Elias. 2012. Rethinking Racial Formation Theory: A Systematic Racism Critique. *Ethnic and Racial Studies* (April): 1–30.

Feagin, Joe R., and Karyn D. McKinney. 2003. *The Many Costs of Racism.* Lanham, MD: Rowan and Littlefield.

Feagin, Joe R., and Eileen O'Brien. 2003. *White Men on Race, Power, Privilege, and the Shaping of Cultural Consciousness.* Boston: Beacon Press.

Feagin, Joe R., Hernán Vera, and Pinar Batur. 2000. *White Racism,* 2nd ed. New York: Routledge.

Federal Bureau of Investigation. 2013. *Hate Crime Statistics, 2012.* Accessible at http://www.fbi.gov.

Feldman, Marcus W. 2010. The Biology of Race. Pp. 136–159 in *Doing Race,* Hazel Rose Markus and Paula M. L. Moya, eds. New York: W. W. Norton.

Ferber, Abby L. 2008. Privilege. Pp. 1073–1074 in vol. 3, *Encyclopedia of Race, Ethnicity, and Society,* Richard T. Schaefer, ed. Thousand Oaks, CA: Sage.

Fernandez, Manny, and Kareem Fahim. 2006. Five on Plane Are Detained at Newark but Later Freed. *New York Times* (May 5): 29.

Fine, Gary. 2008. Robber's Cave. Pp. 1163–1164 in vol. 3, *Encyclopedia of Race, Ethnicity, and Society,* Richard T. Schaefer, ed. Thousand Oaks, CA: Sage.

Foerstrer, Amy. 2004. Race, Identity, and Belonging: "Blackness" and the Struggle for Solidarity in a Multiethnic Labor Union. *Social Problems* 51 (3): 386–409.

Foner, Eric., and Joanna Dreby. 2011. Relations Between the Generations In Immigrant Families. *Annual Reviews of Sociology* 37: 545–564.

Fordham, Signithia, and John U. Ogbu. 1986. Black Students' School Success: Coping with the Burden of "Acting White." *Urban Review* 18 (3): 176–206.

Fox, Stephen. 1990. *The Unknown Internment.* Boston: Twayne.

Frank, Reanne, Ilana Redstone A Krech, and Bob Lu. 2010. Latino Immigrants and the U.S. Racial Order: How and Where Do They Fit In? *American Sociological Review* 75 (3): 378–401.

Frey, William H. 2011. *Census Data: Blacks and Hispanics Take Different Segregation Paths* (February 24). Accessible at http://www.brookings.edu.

Fryer, Roland G., Lisa Kahn, Steven D. Levitt, and Jörg L. Spenkuch. 2012. The Plight of Mixed Race Adolescents. *Review of Economics and Statistics* 94 (August): 6231–6234.

Fuller, Chevon. 1998. Service Redlining. *Civil Rights Journal* 3 (Fall): 33–36.

Gans, Herbert J. 1979. Symbolic Ethnicity: The Future of Ethnic Groups and Cultures in America. *Ethnic and Racial Studies* 2 (January): 1–20.

Gerth, H. H., and C. Wright Mills. 1958. *From Max Weber: Essays in Sociology.* New York: Galaxy Books.

Giago, Tim. 2013. Holocaust Museum of the Indigenous People Should Be Built at Wounded Knee. *Huffington Post* (April 29). Accessible at http://www.huffingtonpost.com.

Gibson, Campbell, and Kay Jung. 2006. *Historical Census Statistics on the Foreign-Born Population of the United States: 1850–2000.* Working Paper No. 81. Washington, DC: Bureau of the Census.

Girardelli, Davide. 2004. Commodified Identities: The Myth of Italian Food in the United States. *Journal of Communication Inquiry* 28 (October): 307–324.

Giroux, Henry A. 1997. Rewriting the Discourse of Racial Identity: Towards a Pedagogy and Politics of Whiteness. *Harvard Educational Review* 67 (Summer): 285–320.

Gleason, Philip. 1980. American Identity and Americanization. Pp. 31–58 in *Harvard Encyclopedia of American Ethnic Groups,* Stephen Therstromm, ed. Cambridge, MA: Belknap Press of Harvard University Press.

Goering, John M. 1971. The Emergence of Ethnic Interests: A Case of Serendipity. *Social Forces* 48 (March): 379–384.

Goldstein, Joseph. 2013. Judge Rejects New York Stop-And-Frisk Policy. *New York Times* (August 12): A1, A16.

Gomez, Alan. 2010. Rise Seen in Births to Illegal Dwellers. *USA Today* (August 12): A1.

Gonzales, Roberto G. 2011. Learning to Be Illegal: Undocumented Youth And Shifting Legal Contexts in the Transition to Adulthood. *American Sociological Review* 76 (45): 602–619.

Gonzalez, David. 2009. A Family Divided by 2 Worlds, Legal and Illegal. *New York Times* (April 26): 1, 20–21.

Goodstein, Laurie. 2005. Issuing Rebuke: Judge Rejects Teaching of Intelligent Design. *New York Times* (December 21): A1, A21.

Goodstein, Laurie, and Jennifer Steinhauer. 2010. Pope Picks Latino to Lead Los Angeles Archdiocese. *New York Times* (April 7): A17.

Gordon, Milton M. 1964. *Assimilation in American Life: The Role of Race, Religion, and National Origins.* New York: Oxford University Press.

Gorski, Phillip S. 2010. *Civil Religion Today* (ARDA Guiding Paper Series). State College: Association of Religion Data Archives at the Pennsylvania State University. Accessible at http://www. thearda.com/rrh/papers/guidingpapers.asp.

Gose, Ben. 2013. Diversity Offices Aren't What They Used to Be. *Chronicle of Higher Education* (June 14): A14–A15, A17.

Gray-Little, Bernadette, and Hafdahl, Adam R. 2000. Factors Influencing Racial Comparisons of Self-Esteem: A Qualitative Review. *Psychological Bulletin* 126 (1): 26–54.

Greeley, Andrew M. 1981. *The Irish Americans: The Rise to Money and Power.* New York: Harper & Row.

Greenhouse, Linda. 1996. Court Accepts Case Tied to Separation Powers. *New York Times* (October 16). Accessed November 20, 2013, at http://www.nytimes.com/1996/10/16/us/court-accepts-case-tied-to-separation-ofpowers.html?pagewanted=all&src=pm.

Greenhouse, Steven. 2012. Equal Opportunity Panel Updates Hiring Policy. *New York Times* (April 26): B3.

Grieco, Elizabeth M., Yesenia D. Acosta, G. Patricia de la Cruz, Christine Gambino, Thomas Gryn, Luke J. Larsen, Edward N. Trevelyan, and Nathan P. Watters. 2012. *The Foreign-Born Population in the United States: 2010.* May 2012 ACS-19. Accessible at http://www.census.gov.

Grieco, Elizabeth M., and Rachel C. Cassidy. 2001. Overview of Race and Hispanic Origin. *Current Population Reports.* Ser. CENBR/01-1. Washington, DC: U.S. Government Printing Office.

Grossman, Cathy Lynn. 2010. Day of Prayer Divides Some. *USA Today* (May 5): 6D.

Guest, Kenneth J. 2003. *God in Chinatown: Religion and Survival in New York's Evolving Immigrant Community.* New York: University Press.

Guglielmo, Jennifer, and Salvatore Salerno, eds. 2003. *Are Italians White?* New York: Routledge.

Gupta, Sanjay. 2012. Interview of Dr. Alfredo Quinones-Hinojosa. *CNN Interview* (May 18).

Hakimzadeh, Shirin, and D'Vera Cohn. 2007. *English Usage among Hispanics in the United States.* Washington, DC: Pew Hispanic Center.

Haller, William, Alejandro Portes, and Scott M. Lynch. 2011. Dreams Fulfilled, Dreams Shattered: Determinants of Segmented Assimilation in the Second Generation. *Social Forces* 89 (3): 733–762.

Hammond, Laura. 2010. Obliged to Give: Remittances and the Maintenance of Transitional Networks Between Somalis at Home and Abroad. *Bildhaan: An International Journal of Somali Studies* 10 (Article 11). Accessible at http://digitalcommons.macalester.edu/bildhaan/.

Handlin, Oscar. 1951. *The Uprooted: The Epic Story of the Great Migrations That Made the American People.* New York: Grossett and Dunlap.

Hansen, Marcus Lee. 1952. The Third Generation in America. *Commentary* (November 14): 493–500.

Harlow, Caroline Wolf. 2005. Hate Crime Reported by Victims and Police. *Bureau of Justice Statistics Special Report* (November). Accessed May 8, 2008, at http://www.ojp.usdoj.gov/bjs/pub/pdf/hcrvp.pdf.

Harrison, Jill Lindsay, and Sarah E. Lloyd. 2012. Illegality at Work: Deportability and the Productive New Era of Immigration Enforcements. *Antipode* 44 (2): 365–385.

Harrison, Jill Lindsay, Sarah E. Lloyd, and Trish O'Kane. 2009. *Overview of Immigrant Workers on Wisconsin Dairy Farmers.* Briefing No. 1. Madison WI: Program on Agricultural Technology Studies.

Harzig, Christine. 2008. German Americans. Pp. 540–544 in vol. 1, *Encyclopedia of Race, Ethnicity, and Society*, Richard T. Schaefer, ed. Thousand Oaks, CA: Sage.

Hassrick, Elizabeth McGhee. 2007. *The Transnational Production of White Ethnic Symbolic Identities*. Paper presented at the Annual Meeting of the American Sociological Association.

Helmore, Edward. 2013. Desert "Death Map" Aims to Save Lives of Mexican Migrants. *The Guardian* (May 7): 30–31.

Herbert, Bob. 2010. Jim Crow Policy. *New York Times* (February 2): A27.

Herrnstein, Richard J., and Charles Murray. 1994. *The Bell Curve: Intelligence and Class Structure in American Life*. New York: Free Press.

Hirsley, Michael. 1991. Religious Display Needs Firm Count. *Chicago Tribune* (December 20), section 2: 10.

Hisnanick, John J., and Katherine G. Giefer. 2011. *Dynamics of Economic Well-Being: Fluctuations in the U.S. Income Distribution 2004–2007*. Washington, DC: U.S. Government Printing Office.

Hixson, Lindsay; Bradford B. Hepler, and Myoung Ouk Kim. 2012. *Islander Population: 2010*. May 2012. C2010BR-12. Washington DC: U.S. Government Printing Office.

Hoeffel, Elizabeth M., Sonya Rastogi, Myoung Ouk Kim, and Hasan Shahid. 2012. *The Asian Population: 2010*. C2010BR-11. Accessible at http://www.census.gov.

Holzer, Harry J. 2008. The Effects of Immigration on the Employment Outcomes of Black Americans. Testimony before the U.S. Commission on Civil Rights.

Hondagneu-Sotelo, Pierette, ed. 2003. *Gender and U.S. Immigration: Contemporary Trends*. Berkeley: University of California Press.

Hooks, Bell. 2000. *Feminist Theory: From Margin to Center*, 2nd ed. Boston: South End Press.

Hoover, Eric. 2013. Colleges Contemplate a "Race Neutral" Future. *Chronicle of Higher Education* (October 18): 30, 32–33.

Hughley, Matthew W., and Jessie Daniels. 2013. Racist Comments at Online News Sites: A Methodological Dilemma for Discourse Analysis. *Media, Culture & Society* 35 (3): 332–347.

Huisman, Kimberly A., Mazie Hough, Kristin M. Langellier, and Carol Nordstrom Toner. 2011. *Somalis in Maine: Crossing Cultural Currents*. Berkeley: North Atlantic Books.

Humes, Karen R., Nicholas A. Jones, and Roberto R. Ramirez. 2011. Overview of Race and Hispanic Organization. *2010 Census Briefs*. C2010 BR-02. Washington DC: U.S. Government Printing Office.

Hundley, Tom. 2009. Return Trip. *Chicago Tribune Magazine* (January 18): 8–14.

Huntington, Samuel P. 1993. "The Clash of Civilizations?" *Foreign Affairs* 73 (No. 3, Summer): 22–49.

Huntington, Samuel P. 1996. *The Clash of Civilizations and the Remaking of World Order*. New York: Simon & Schuster.

Hurh, Won Moo. 1994. Majority Americans' Perception of Koreans in the United States: Implications of Ethnic Images and Stereotypes. Pp. 3–21 in *Korean Americans: Conflict and Harmony*, H. Kwon, ed. Chicago: Center for Korean Studies.

Hyun, Jane. 2006. *Breaking the Bamboo Ceiling: Career Strategies for Asians*. New York: Harper Business.

Hyun, Jane. 2009. Better Luck Tomorrow: Breaking the Bamboo Ceiling. *Interview with Peter Nguyen* (October 14). Accessed July 30, 2012, at http://diversitymbamagazine.com.

IAAMS. 2009. *Italian-Americans Against Media Stereotypes*. Accessed January 4, 2011, at http://iaams.blogspot.com.

Iceland, John, Gregory Sharp, and Jeffrey M. Timberlake. 2013. Sun Belt Rising: Regional Population Change and the Decline in Residential Segregation, 1970–2009. *Demography* 50 (1): 97–123.

Ignatiev, Noel. 1994. Treason to Whiteness Is Loyalty to Humanity. Interview with Noel Ignatiev. *Utne Reader* (November–December): 83–86.

Ignatiev, Noel. 1995. *How the Irish Became White*. New York: Routledge.

Institute for Jewish and Community Research. 2008. *How Many Jews Are in World Today*. Accessed September 7, 2008, at http://bechollashon.org/population/today.php.

Institute on Taxation and Economic Policy. 2013. *Undocumented Immigrants' Share and Local Tax Contributions* (July). Washington DC: ITEP.

International Organization for Migration. 2009. *Migration, Climate Change and the Environment.* Geneva, Switzerland: IOM.

Jacoby, Susan. 2009. Keeping the Faith, Ignoring the History. *New York Times* (March 1): 11.

Jaroszyn'ska-Kirchmann. 2004. *The Exile Mission: The Polish Political Diaspora and Polish Americans, 1939–1956.* Athens: Ohio University Press.

Jefferies, Sierra M. 2007. Environmental Justice and the Skull Valley Goshute Indians' Proposal to Store Nuclear Waste. *Journal of Land, Resources, and Environmental Law* 27 (2): 409–429.

Jiménez, Tomás R. 2007. The Next Americans. *Los Angeles Times* (May 27): M1, M7.

Johnson, Kevin. 2004. *Immigration and Civil Rights.* Philadelphia: Temple University Press.

Johnston, Tim. 2008. Australia to Apologize to Aborigines for Past Mistreatment. *New York Times* (January 31).

Jones, Adele. 2008. A Silent but Mighty River: The Costs of Women's Economic Migration. *Signs: Journal of Women in Culture and Society* 33 (4): 761–769.

Jones, Jeff and Lydia Saad. 2013. *Gallup Poll Social Series: Minority Rights and Relations* (July 5). Accessible at www.gallup.com.

Jones, Nicholas, and Amy Symens Smith. 2001. *The Two or More Races Population: 2000.* Series C2KBR/01-6. Washington, DC: U.S. Government Printing Office.

Jones-Puthoff, Alexa. 2013. *Is the U.S. Population Getting Older and More Diverse?* (June 14). Accessible at http://www.census.gov/newsroom/cspan/pop_diverse/.

Jordan, Miriam. 2009. Got Workers? Dairy Farmers Run Low on Labor. *Wall Street Journal* (July 30). Accessible at http://online.wsj.com.

Kagan, Jerome. 1971. The Magical Aura of the IQ. *Saturday Review of Literature* 4 (December 4): 92–93.

Kahlenberg, Richard D. 2010. 10 Myths About Legacy Preference in College Admissions. *Chronicle of Higher Education* (October 1): A23–A25.

Kalev, Alexandria, Frank Dobbin, and Erin Kelly. 2006. Best Practices or Best Guesses? Diversity Management and the Remediation of Inequality. *American Sociological Review* 71: 589–617.

Kang, Jerry, and Kristen Lane. 2010. Seeing Through Colorblindness: Implicit Bias and the Law. *UCLA Law Review* 58 (2): 465–520.

Katz, Jeffrey. 2012. Google's Monopoly and Internet Freedom. *Wall Street Journal* (June 8): A15.

Katz, Michael B., Mark J. Stern, and Jamie J. Fader. 2007. The Mexican Immigration Debate. *Social Science History* 3 (Summer): 157–189.

Kazal, Russell A. 2004. The Interwar Origins of the White Ethnic: Race, Residence, and German Philadelphia, 1917–1939. *Journal of American Ethnic History* (Summer): 78–131.

Keen, Judy. 2011. Transmitting the Immigrant Life. *USA Today* (June 16): 3A.

Kenji America. 2013. *Cheerios Parody "Just Checking" Response to Haters.* Accessed August 5, 2013, at http://www.youtube.com/user/kenjiamerica.

Kibria, Nazli. 2002. *Becoming Asian American: Second-Generation Chinese and Korean American Identities.* Baltimore: Johns Hopkins Press.

Kim, ChangHwan, and Arthur Sakamoto. 2010. Have Asian American Men Achieved Labor Market Parity with White Men? *American Sociological Review* 73 (6): 934–957.

Kinloch, Graham C. 1974. *The Dynamics of Race Relations: A Sociological Analysis.* New York: McGraw-Hill.

Kivisto, Peter. 2008. Third Generation Principle. Pp. 1302–1304 in vol. 3, *Encyclopedia of Race, Ethnicity, and Society,* Richard T. Schaefer, ed. Thousand Oaks, CA: Sage.

Koch, Wendy. 2006. Push for "Official" English Heats Up. *USA Today* (October 9): 1A.

Kochhar, Rakesh. 2006. *Growth in the Foreign-Born Workforce and Employment of the Native Born.* Washington, DC: Pew Hispanic Center.

Kochhar, Rakesh, Richard Fry, and Paul Taylor. 2011. *Twenty-to-One: Wealth Gaps Rise to Record Highs Between Whites, Blacks and Hispanics.* Washington DC: Pew Social and Demographic Trends.

Kolpack, Dave. 2012. *ND Voters Dump Fighting Sioux Nickname.* Minnesota Public Radio (June 11). Accessible at http://minnesotat.publicradio.org.

Kopacz, Maria A., and Bessie Lee Lawton. 2013. Talking About the YouTube Indians: Images of Native Americans and Viewer Comments on a Viral Video Site. *Howard Journal of Communications* 24: 17–37.

Kotkin, Joel. 2010. Ready Set Grow. *Smithsonian* (July/August): 61–73.

Krammer, Arnold. 1997. *Undue Process: The Untold Story of America's German Alien Internees.* Lanham, MD: Rowman & Littlefield.

Krase, Jerome. 2006. Seeing Ethnic Succession in Little Italy: Change Despite Resistance. *Modern Italy* 11 (February): 79–95.

Kristof, Nicholas D. 2010. America's History of Fear. *New York Times* (September 5): A10.

Kroeger, Brooke. 2004. When a Dissertation Makes a Difference. *New York Times* (March 20). Accessed January 15, 2005, at http://www.racematters.org/devahpager.htm.

Krysan, Maria, Reynolds Farley, and Mick P. Couper. 2008. In the Eye of the Beholder. *DuBois Review* 5 (1): 5–26.

Kuebler, Meghan. 2013. Closing the Wealth Gap: A Review of Racial and Ethnic Inequalities in Homeownership. *Sociology Compass* 7 (8): 670–685.

Lal, Barbara Ballis. 1995. Symbolic Interaction Theories. *American Behavioral Scientist* 38 (January): 421–441.

LaPiere, Richard T. 1934. Attitudes vs. Actions. *Social Forces* (October 13): 230–237.

LaPiere, Richard T. 1969. Comment of Irwin Deutscher's Looking Backward. *American Sociologist* 4 (February): 41–42.

Lazar, Louie. 2013. Delivering News from the Homeland. *Wall Street Journal* (September 6): A16, A17.

Leavitt, Paul. 2002. Bush Calls Agent Kicked Off Flight "Honorable Fellow." *USA Today* (January 8).

Lee, J. J., and Marion R. Casey. 2006. *Making the Irish American.* New York: New York University Press.

Lee, Jennifer., and Frank D. Bean. 2007. Redrawing the Color Line. *City and Community* 6 (March): 49–62.

Lee, Wen Ho, with Helen Zia. 2006. *My Country Versus Me: The First-Hand Account by the Los Alamos Scientist Who Was Falsely Accused of Being a Spy.* New York: Hyperion.

Lee, Yueh-Ting, Sandy Vue, Richard Seklecki, and Yue Ma. 2007. How Did Asian Americans Respond to Negative Stereotypes and Hate Crimes? *American Behavioral Scientist* 51 (October): 271–293.

Leehotz, Robert. 1995. Is Concept of Race a Relic? *Los Angeles Times* (April 15): A1, A14.

Leung, Angela Ka-yee, William W. Maddux, Adam D. Galinsky, and Chi-yue Chiu. 2008. Multicultural Experience Enhances Creativity. *American Psychologist* 63 (April): 169–181.

Levin, Jack, and Jim Nolan. 2011. *The Violence of Hate: Confronting Racism, Anti-Semitism, and Other Forms of Bigotry,* 3rd ed. Upper Saddle River, NJ: Pearson.

Levitt, Peggy, and B. Nadya Jaworsky. 2007. Transnational Migration Studies: Past Developments and Future Trends. *Annual Review of Sociology* 33: 129–156.

Lewin, Tamar. 2006. Campaign to End Race Preferences Splits Michigan. *New York Times* (October 31): A1, A19.

Lewis, Amanda E. 2004. "What Group?" Studying Whites and Whiteness in the Era of "Color-Blindness." *Sociological Theory* 22 (December): 623–646.

Lewis, Amanda E. 2013. The "Nine Lives" of Oppositional Culture? *DuBois Review* 10 (1): 279–289.

Lichtenberg, Judith. 1992. Racism in the Head, Racism in the World. *Report from the Institute for Philosophy and Public Policy* 12 (Spring–Summer): 3–5

Lindner, Eileen. 2011. *Yearbook of American and Canadian Churches.* Nashville, TN: Abingdon Press.

Lindner, Eileen, ed. 2012. *Yearbook of American and Canadian Churches 2011,* Table 2, p. 12. Nashville, TN: Abingdon Press. Reprinted by permission from *Yearbook of American and Canadian Churches 2008.* Copyright © National Council of Churches of Christ in the USA.

Lipman, Francine J. 2008. *The Undocumented Immigrant Tax: Enriching Americans from Sea to Shining Sea.* Chapman University Law Research Paper No. 2008. Accessible at http://ssrn.com/abstract=1292960.

Livingston, Gretchen, and D'Vera Cohn. 2012. *U.S. Birth Rate Falls to a Record Low; Decline Is Greatest Among Immigrants.* Washington DC: Pew Research Center.

Llosa, Alvaro Vargas. 2013. *Global Crossings: Immigration, Civilization, and America.* Oakland CA: The Independent Institute.

Lofquist, Daphne, Terry Lugaila, Martin O'Connell, and Sarah Feliz. 2012. *Households and Families: 2010.* C2012BR-14. Accessible at http://www.census.gov/newsroom/releases/archives/2012_census/cb12-68.html.

Logan, John R., and Brian J. Stults. 2011. *The Persistence of Segregation in the Metropolis: New Findings from the 2010 Census.* Providence RI: US 2010 Project.

Lopata, Helena Znaniecki. 1994. *Polish Americans,* 2nd ed. New Brunswick, NJ: Transaction Books.

Lopez, David, and Yen Espiritu. 1990. Panethnicity in the United States: A Theoretical Framework. *Ethnic and Racial Studies* (April 13): 198–224.

Lopez, Julie Amparano. 1992. Women Face Glass Walls as Well as Ceilings. *Wall Street Journal* (March 3).

Lopez, Mark Hugo, and Ana Gonzalez-Barrera. 2013. If They Could, How Many Unauthorized Immigrants Would Become U.S. Citizens? (June 27). Accessible at http://www.pewresearch.org.

Luconi, Stefano. 2001. *From Peasant to White Ethnics: The Italian Experience in Philadelphia.* Albany: State University Press of New York.

Mack, Raymond W. 1996. Whose Affirmative Action? *Society* 33 (March–April): 41–43.

Maddux, William W., Adam D. Galinsky, Amy J. C. Cuddy, and Mark Polifroni. 2008. When Being a Model Minority Is Good…and Bad: Realistic Threat Explains Negativity Toward Asian Americans. *Personality and Social Psychology Bulletin* 34 (January): 74–89.

Madigan, Nick. 2013. In the Shadow of 'Old Smokey," A Toxic Legacy. *New York Times* (September 23): A10, A13.

Malhotra, Nei, and Yotam Margalit. 2009. State of the Nation: Anti-Semitism and the Economic Crisis. *Boston Review* (May/June). Accessible at http://bostonreview.net/BR34.3/malhotra_margalit.php.

Manning, Robert D. 1995. Multiculturalism in the United States: Clashing Concepts, Changing Demographics, and Competing Cultures. *International Journal of Group Tensions* (Summer): 117–168.

Martin, Timothy W., Josh Dawsey, and Betsy McKay. 2012. The Gender Barrier Falls at Augusta. *Wall Street Journal* (August 21): B1.

Marshall, Patrick. 2001. Religion in Schools. *CQ Research* 11 (July 12): 1–24.

Martin, Daniel C., and James E. Yankay. 2013. *Refugees and Asylees: 2012.* Washington DC: Office of Immigration Statistics.

Marx, Karl, and Frederick Engels. 1955. *Selected Works in Two Volumes.* Moscow: Foreign Languages Publishing House.

Marubbio, M. Elise. 2006. *Killing the Indian Maiden: Images of Native American Women in Film.* Lexington: University Press of Kentucky.

Massey, Douglas S. 2011. The Past and Future of American Civil Rights. *Daedalus* 140 (Spring): 37–54.

Massey, Douglas S. 2012. Reflections on the Dimensions of Segregation. *Social Forces* 91 (1): 39–43.

Massey, Douglas S., and Karen A. Pren. 2012. Unintended Consequences of US Immigration Policy: Explaining the Post-1965 Surge from Latin America. *Population and Development Review* 38 (1): 1–29.

Massey, Douglas S., and Margarita Mooney. 2007. The Effects of America's Three Affirmative Action Programs on Academic Performance. *Social Problems* 54 (1): 99–117.

Massey, Douglas S., and Nancy A. Denton. 1993. *American Apartheid: Segregation and the Making of the Underclass.* Cambridge, MA: Harvard University Press.

Mastony, Colleen. 2013. Poland Calling Them Home. *Chicago Tribune* (January 13): 1, 12.

Mauro, Tony. 1995. Ruling Helps Communities Set Guidelines. *USA Today* (December 21): A1, A2.

Mazzocco, Philip J., Timothy C. Brock, Gregory J. Brock, Kristen R. Olson, and Mahzarin R. Banaji. 2006. The Cost of Being Black: White Americans' Perceptions and the Question of Reparations. *DuBois Review* 3 (2): 261–297.

McCabe, Kristen. 2012. *Foreign-Born Health Care Workers in the United States* (June). Accessible at http://www.migrationinformation.org/USfocus/display.cfm?id=898.

McGurn, William. 2009. New Jersey's 'Italian' Problem. *Wall Street Journal* (July 28): A15.

McIntosh, Peggy. 1988. *White Privilege: Unpacking the Invisible Knapsack.* Wellesley, MA: Wellesley College Center for Research on Women.

McKernan, Signe-Mary, Caroline Radcliffe, Eugene Steuerle, and Sisi Zhang. 2013. *Less than Equal: Racial Disparities in Wealth Accumulation* (April 2013). Accessible at http://www.urban.org.

McKinney, Karyn D. 2003. I Feel "Whiteness" When I Hear People Blaming Whites: Whiteness as Cultural Victimization. *Race and Society* 6: 39–55.

McKinney, Karyn D. 2008. Confronting Young People's Perceptions of Whiteness: Privilege or Liability? *Social Compass* 2. Accessible at http://www.blackwell-compass.com/subject/sociology.

Meagher, Timothy J. 2005. *The Columbia Guide to Irish American History.* New York: Columbia University Press.

Media Matters for America. 2013. *Diversity in Evening Cable News in 13 Charts* (May 13). Accessible at mediamatters.org.

Merton, Robert K. 1949. Discrimination and the American Creed. Pp. 99–126 in *Discrimination and National Welfare,* Robert M. MacIver, ed. New York: Harper & Row.

Merton, Robert K. 1976. *Sociological Ambivalence and Other Essays.* New York: Free Press.

Meyers, Dowell. 2007. *Immigrants and Boomers: Forging a New Social Contract for the Future of America.* New York: Russell Sage.

Meyers, Norma. 2005. *Environment Refugees: An Emergent Security Issue.* Paper presented at the 13th Economic Forum (May), Prague.

Migration News. 2012b. *DHS: Border, Interior, USCIS.* April 19 (2). Accessible at http://migration.ucdavis.edu/mn/comments.php?id-3745_0_2_0.

Miller, David L. 2014. *Introduction to Collective Behavior and Collective Action,* 3rd ed. Long Grove IL: Waveland Press.

Miller, Norman. 2002. Personalization and the Promise of Contact Theory. *Journal of Social Issues* 58 (Summer): 387–410.

Mocha, Frank, ed. 1998. *American "Polonia" and Poland.* New York: Columbia University Press.

Monkman, Karen, Margaret Ronald, and Florence Délimon Théraméne. 2005. Social and Cultural Capital in an Urban Latino School Community. *Urban Education* 40 (January): 4–33.

Montagu, Ashley. 1972. *Statement on Race.* New York: Oxford University Press.

Mosisa, Abraham T. 2013. *Foreign-born workers in the U.S. Labor Force. Spotlight on Statistics* (July). Accessible at http://www.bls.gov.

Mostofi, Nilou. 2003. Who We Are: The Perplexity of Iranian-American Identity. *Sociological Quarterly* 44 (Fall): 681–703.

Moulder, Frances V. 1996. *Teaching about Race and Ethnicity: A Message of Despair or a Message of Hope?* Paper presented at annual meeting of the American Sociological Association, New York.

Muste, Christopher P. 2013. The Polls—Trends. The Dynamics of Immigration Opinion in the United States: 1992–2012. *Public Opinion Quarterly* 77 (Spring): 398–416.

Myers, Dowell, John Pitkin, and Julie Park. 2004. *California's Immigrants Turn the Corner. Urban Initiative Policy Relief.* Los Angeles: University of Southern California.

Myrdal, Gunnar. 1944. *An American Dilemma: The Negro Problem and Modern Democracy.* New York: Harper & Row.

NAACP. 2008. *Out of Focus—Out of Sync Take 4.* Baltimore MD: NAACP.

Nahm, H. Y. 2012. 23 *Big Milestones in Asian American History.* Accessed November 9, 2013, at http://goldsea.com/AAD/Milestones/milestones.html.

Naimark, Norman M. 2004. Ethnic Cleaning, History of. Pp. 4799–4802 in *International Encyclopedia of Social and Behavioral Sciences,* N. J. Smelser and P. B. Baltes, eds. New York: Elsevier.

Nash, Manning. 1962. Race and the Ideology of Race. *Current Anthropology* 3 (June): 285–288.

National Asian Pacific American Legal Consortium. 2002. *Backlash: When America Turned on its Own.* Washington, DC: NAPALC.

National CAPACD. 2012. *Data Points: Asian American and Pacific Islander Poverty* (May 1). Accessible at http://www.nationalcapacd.org/.

National Center for Education Statistics. 2013. *Digest of Education Statistics.* Accessible at http://nces.ed.gov/programs/digest/2012menu_tables.asp.

National Italian American Foundation. 2006. Stop Ethnic Bashing. *New York Times* (January). Accessed June 4, 2008, at http://www.niaf.org/news/index.asp?id=422.

National Park Service. 2009. *Chinatown and Little Italy Historic District.* Accessible at http://www.nps.gov.

National Park Service. 2012. *The War Relocation Camps of World War II: When Fear Was Stronger than Justice—Supplementary Resources.* Accessed July 16, 2012, at http://www.nps.gov/history/nr/twhp/wwwlps/lessons/89nanzanar/89lrnmore.htm.

National Public Radio. 2013. *Impossible Choice Faces America's First "Climate Refugees"* (May 18). Accessible at http//wwww.wbur.org/npr/185068648/impossible-choice-faces-americas-first-climate-refugees.

Navarro-Rivera, Juhem, Marry A. Kosmin, and Ariela Keysar. 2010. *U.S. Latino Religious Identification 1990–2008 Growth, Diversity & Transformation.* Hartford, CT: American Religious Identification Project, Trinity College. Accessible at http://www.americanreligionsurvey-aris.org/latinos2008.pdf.

Nawa, Fariba. 2011. Struggling to Stay Bilingual. *Christian Science Monitor* (October 17): 38–39.

Nelsen, Frank C. 1973. The German-American Immigrants Struggle. *International Review of History and Political Science* 10 (2): 37–49.

New America Media. 2007. *Deep Divisions, Shared Destiny.* San Francisco: New America Media.

Newman, William M. 1973. *American Pluralism: A Study of Minority Groups and Social Theory.* New York: Harper & Row.

Newport, Frank. 2011. *Very Religious Have Higher Wellbeing Across All Faiths* (January 6). Accessible at http://www.gallup.com.

New York Times. 1991. For Two, an Answer to Years of Doubt on Use of Peyote in Religious Rite (July 9): A14.

New York Times. 2005. Warnings Raised About Exodus of Philippine Doctors and Nurses (November 27): 13.

Niebuhr, Gustav. 1998. Southern Baptists Declare Wife Should "Submit" to Her Husband. *New York Times.*

Norris, Tina, Paula L. Vines, and Elizabeth M. Hoeffel. 2012. *The American Indian and Alaska Native Population: 2010.* C2010BR-10. Accessible at http://www.census.gov.

Norton, Michael I., and Samuel R. Sommers. 2011. Whites See Racism as a Zero-Sum Game That They are Now Losing. *Perspectives on Psychological Science* 6 (3): 215.

Nudd, Tim. 2013. It's 2013, and People are Still Getting Worked Up about Interracial Couples in Ads. *Adweek* (May 30). Accessible at http://www.adweek.com.

Ochoa, Gilda L. 2013. *Academic Profiling: Latinos, Asian Americans, and the Achievement Gap.* Minneapolis: University of Minnesota Press.

Office of Immigration Statistics. 2009. *Yearbook of Immigration Statistics: 2008.* Accessible at www.dhs.gov.

Office of Immigration Statistics. 2012. *Yearbook of Immigration Statistics: 2011.* Accessible at http://www.dhs.gov/files/statistics/publications/LPR10.shtm.

Office of Immigration Statistics. 2013. *2012 Yearbook of Immigration Statistics.* Accessible at http://www.dhs.gov/yearbook-immigration-statistics.

Ogbu, John U. 2004. Collective Identity and the Burden of "Acting White" in Black History, Community, and Education. *Urban Review* 36 (March): 1–35.

Ogbu, John U., with Astrid Davis. 2003. *Black American Students in an Affluent Suburb: A Study of Academic Disengagement.* Mahwah, NJ: Lawrence Erlbaum Associates.

Ohnuma, Keiko. 1991. Study Finds Asians Unhappy at CSU. *AsianWeek* 12 (August 8): 5.

Oliveri, Rigel C. 2009. Discriminatory Housing Advertisements On-Line: Lessons from Craigslist. *Indiana Law Review* 43: 1126–1183.

Omi, Michael, and Howard Winant. 1994. *Racial Formation in the United States,* 2nd ed. New York: Routledge.

Omniglot. 2013. *Links: Online Radio Stations.* Accessed November 3, at http://www.omniglot.com/links/radio.htm.

O'Neill, Maggie. 2008. Authoritarian Personality. Pp. 119–121 in vol. 1, *Encyclopedia of Race, Ethnicity, and Society,* Richard T. Schaefer, ed. Thousand Oaks, CA: Sage.

Orfield, Gary. 2007. The Supreme Court and the Resegregation of America's Schools. *Focus* (September–October): 1, 15–16.

Orfield, Gary, and Chungmei Lee. 2005. *Why Segregation Matters: Poverty and Educational Inequality.* Cambridge, MA: Civil Rights Project.

Orfield, Gary, John Kucsera, and Genevieve Siegel-Hawley. 2012. *E Pluribus...Separation: Deepening Double Segregation for More Students.* Los Angeles: The Civil Rights Project. Accessible at http://civilrightsproject.ucla.edu/research/k-12-education/integration-and-diversity/mlk-national/e-pluribus...separation-deepening-double-segregation-for-more-students.

Page, Scott E. 2007. *The Difference: How the Power of Diversity Creates Better Groups, Firms, Schools, and Societies.* Princeton, NJ: Princeton University Press.

Pager, Devah. 2003. The Mark of a Criminal. *American Journal of Sociology* 108: 937–975.

Pager, Devah, and Bruce Western. 2012. Identifying Discrimination at Work: The Use of Field Experiments. *Journal of Social Issues* 68 (2): 221–237.

Pager, Devah, Bruce Western, and Bart Bonikowski. 2009. Discrimination in a Low-Wage Labor Market: A Field Experiment. *American Sociological Review* 74 (October): 777–799.

Paluck, Elizabeth Levy, and Donald P. Green. 2009. Prejudice Reduction: What Works? A Review and Assessment of Research and Practice. *Annual Review of Psychology* 60: 339–367.

Pariser, Eli. 2011a. The Filter Bubble: What the Internet Is Hiding from You. *New York: Penguin Press.*

Pariser, Eli. 2011b. In Our Own Little Internet Bubbles. *The Guardian Weekly* (June 24): 32–33.

Park, Robert E. 1928. Human Migration and the Marginal Man. *American Journal of Sociology* 33 (May): 881–893.

Park, Robert E. 1950. Race and Culture: Essays in the Sociology of Contemporary Man. New York: Free Press.

Park, Robert E., and Ernest W. Burgess. 1921. *Introduction to the Science of Sociology.* Chicago: University of Chicago Press.

Parrillo, Vincent. 2008. Italian Americans. Pp. 766–771 in vol. 2, *Encyclopedia of Race, Ethnicity, and Society,* Richard T. Schaefer, ed. Thousand Oaks, CA: Sage.

Passel, Jeffrey S., and D'Vera Cohn. 2009. *A Portrait of Unauthorized Immigrants in the United States.* Washington, DC: Pew Hispanic Center.

Passel, Jeffrey S., D'Vera Cohn, and Ana Gonzalez-Barrera. 2013. *Population Decline of Unoauthorized Immigrants Stalls, May Have Reverse* (September 23). Accessible at http://www.pewresearch.org/hispanic.

Passel, Jeffrey S., Wendy Wang, and Paul S. Taylor. 2010. *Marrying Out: One-in-Seven New U.S. Marriages is Interracial or Interethnic.* Washington, DC: Pew Research Center. Accessible at http://www.pewsocialtrends.org/files/2010/10/755-marrying-out.pdf.

Pastor, Jr., Manuel, Rachel Morello-Frosch, and James L. Saad. 2005. The Air Is Always Cleaner on the Other Side: Race, Space, and Ambient Air Toxics Exposure in California. *Journal of Urban Affairs* 27 (2): 127–148.

Paul, Annie Murphy. 2011. The Roar of the Tiger Mother. *Time* (January 31): 34–40.

Pearson, Bryan. 2006. Brain Drain Human Resource Crisis. *The Africa Report* (October): 95–98.

Pellow, David Naguib, and Hollie Nyseth Brehm. 2013. An Environmental Sociology for the Twenty-First Century. *Annual Review of Sociology* 39: 229–250.

Pellow, David Naguib, and Robert J. Brulle. 2007. Poisoning the Planet: The Struggle for Environmental Justice. *Contexts* 6 (Winter): 37–41.

Perlmann, Joel. 2005. *Italians Then, Mexicans Now: Immigrant Origins and Second-Generation Progress, 1890–2000.* New York: Russell Sage Foundation.

Perry, Barbara, ed. 2003. *Hate and Bias Crime: A Reader.* New York: Routledge.

Pew Forum on Religion and Public Life. 2008a. *U.S. Religious Landscape Survey.* Washington, DC: Pew Forum. Accessible at http://religions.pewforum.org/pdf/report2-religious-landscape-study-full.pdf.

Pew Forum on Religion and Public Life. 2008b. *U.S. Religious Landscape Survey: Religious Beliefs and Practices: Diverse and Political Relevant.* Washington DC: Pew Forum on Religion and Public Life.

Pew Forum on Religion and Public Life. 2010. *Growing Number of Americans Say Obama Is a Muslim.* Washington, DC: Pew Forum.

Pew Hispanic Center. 2011a. *Mapping the Latino Electorate.* Accessible at http://pewhispanic.org/docs/?DocID=26.

Pew Hispanic Center. 2011b. *Unauthorized Immigrants: Length of Residency, Patterns of*

Parenthood (December 1). Washington, DC: Pew Hispanic Center.

Pew Research Center. 2010. *Blacks Upbeat about Black Progress, Prospects.* Accessible at http://pewsocialtrends.org/2010/01/12/blacks-upbeat-about-black-progress-prospects.

Pew Social and Demographic Trends. 2012. *The Rise of Asian Americans.* Washington DC: Pew Social and Demographic Trends.

Pincus, Fred L. 2003. *Reverse Discrimination: Dismantling the Myth.* Boulder, CO: Lynne Rienner.

Pincus, Fred L. 2008. *Reverse Discrimination.* Pp. 1159–1161 in vol. 3, *Encyclopedia of Race, Ethnicity, and Society,* Richard T. Schaefer, ed. Thousand Oaks, CA: Sage.

Pitt, Nicola Ann. 2013. *The Cultural and Political Significance of Tiger Mothering.* Doctorate. Monash University.

Polzin, Theresita. 1973. *The Polish Americans: Whence and Whither.* Pulaski, WI: Franciscan Publishers.

Porter, Eduardo. 2005. Illegal Immigrants Are Bolstering Social Security with Billions. *New York Times* (April 5): A1, C6.

Portes, Alejandro. 1998. Social Capital: Its Origins and Applications in Modern Society. *Annual Review of Sociology* 24 (1): 1–24.

Portes, Alejandro. 2006. Paths of Assimilation in the Second Generation. *Sociological Forum* 21 (September): 499–503.

Portes, Alejandro, and Rubén G. Rumbaut. 2006. *Immigrant America,* 3rd ed. Berkeley: University of California Press.

Powell-Hopson, Darlene, and Derek Hopson. 1988. Implications of Doll Color Preferences Among Black Preschool Children and White Preschool Children. *Journal of Black Psychology* 14 (February): 57–63.

Preston, Julia. 2007. Polls Surveys Ethnic Views among Chief Minorities. *New York Times* (December 13).

Preston, Julia. 2010. On Gangs, Asylum Law Offers Little. *New York Times* (June 30): A15, A19.

Preston, Julia. 2013a. Huge Amounts Spent on Immigration, Study Finds. *New York Times* (January 8): A11.

Preston, Julia. 2013b. Legal Immigrants Seek Reward for Years of Following the Rules. *New York Times* (July 16): A1, A13.

Pryor, John H., Kevin Egan, Laura Palucki Blake, Sylvia Hurtado, Jennifer Berdan, Matthew H. Case, and Linda DeAngelo. 2012. *The American Freshman: National Norms for Fall 2012.* Los Angeles: Higher Education Research Institute, UCLA.

Purdy, Matthew. 2001. Ignoring and Then Embracing the Truth about Racial Profiling. *New York Times* (March 11).

Quillian, Lincoln. 2006. New Approaches to Understanding Racial Prejudice and Discrimination. Pp. 299–328 in *Annual Reviews of Sociology 2006,* Karen S. Cook, ed. Palo Alto, CA: Annual Reviews Inc.

Quiñoes-Hinojosa, Alfredo, with Mim Eichler Rivas. 2011. *Becoming Dr. Q: My Journey from Migrant Farm Worker to Brain Surgeon.* Berkeley: University of California Press.

Ramos, Jorge. 2010. *A Country for All.* New York: Vintage Books.

Ratledge, Ingela. 2012. Is the Bachelor Racist? *TV Guide* (May 6): 6.

Reskin, Barbara F. 2012. The Race Discrimination System. *Annual Review of Sociology*: 38.

Rich, Meghan Ashlin. 2008. Resegregation. Pp. 1152–1153 in vol. 3, *Encyclopedia of Race, Ethnicity, and Society*, Richard T. Schaefer, ed. Thousand Oaks, CA: Sage.

Rich, Motoko. 2013. Creationists on Texas Panel for Biology Textbooks. *New York Times* (September 29): 16, 20.

Richmond, Anthony H. 2002. Globalization: Implications for Immigrants and Refugees. *Ethnic and Racial Studies* 25 (September): 707–727.

Roberts, Sam. 2011. Little Italy, Littler by the Year. *New York Times* (February 22): A19.

Robnett, Belinda, and Cynthia Feliciano. 2011. Patterns of Racial-Ethnic Exclusion by Internet Daters. *Social Forces* 80 (No. 3, March): 807, 828.

Roediger, David R. 1994. *Towards the Abolition of Whiteness: Essays on Race, Politics, and Working Class History (Haymarket).* New York: Verso Books.

Roediger, David R. 2006. Whiteness and Its Complications. *Chronicle of Higher Education* 52 (July 14): B6–B8.

Roediger, David R. 2009. To Be Continued? The "Problem of the Color-Line" in the Twenty-First

Century. Pp. 281–286 in *Twenty-First Century Color Lines*, Andrew Grant-Thomas and Gary Orfield, eds. Philadelphia: Temple University Press.

Roof, Wade Clark. 2007. Introduction. *The Annals* 612 (July): 6–12.

Rose, Arnold. 1951. *The Roots of Prejudice*. Paris: UNESCO.

Rusk, David. 2001. *The "Segregation Tax": The Cost of Racial Segregation to Black Homeowners*. Washington, DC: Brookings Institution.

Russell, Stephen T., Lisa J. Crockett, and Ruth K. Chao. 2010. Asian American Parenting and Parent-Adolescent Relationships. *Journal of Youth and Adolescence* 40: 245–247.

Ryan, Camile. 2013. Language Use in the United States: 2011. *American Community Survey Report* (August 2013). Accessible at http://www.census.gov.

Ryan, William. 1976. *Blaming the Victim*, rev. ed. New York: Random House.

Ryo, Emily. 2013. Deciding to Cross: Norms and Economics of Unauthorized Migration. *American Sociological Review* 78 (4): 574–603.

Saad, Lydia. 2006. Anti-Muslim Sentiments Fairly Commonplace. *The Gallup Poll* (August 10).

Saperstein, Aliya, and Andrew M. Penner. 2012. Racial Fluidity and Inequality in the United States. *American Journal of Sociology* 118 (3): 676–727.

Sassler, Sharon L. 2006. School Participation among Immigrant Youths: The Case of Segmented Assimilation in the Early 20th Century. *Sociology of Education* 79 (January): 1–24.

Saulny, Susan. 2011. Black? White? Asian? More Young Americans Choose All of the Above. *New York Times* (January 29): A1, A17–A18.

Schaefer, Richard T. 1976. *The Extent and Content of Racial Prejudice in Great Britain*. San Francisco: R&E Research Associates.

Schaefer, Richard T. 1986. Racial Prejudice in a Capitalist State: What Has Happened to the American Creed? *Phylon* 47 (September): 192–198.

Schaefer, Richard T. 1992. People of Color: The "Kaleidoscope" May Be a Better Way to Describe America than "the Melting Pot." *Peoria Journal Star* (January 19): A7.

Schaefer, Richard T. 1996. Education and Prejudice: Unraveling the Relationship. *Sociological Quarterly* 37 (January): 1–16.

Schaefer, Richard T. 2008b. Nativism. Pp. 611–612 in vol. 1, *Encyclopedia of Social Problems*, Vincent N. Parrillo, ed. Thousand Oaks, CA: Sage.

Schaefer, Richard T., and William Zellner. 2011. *Extraordinary Groups*, 9th ed. New York: Worth.

Schwartz, Alex. 2001. *The State of Minority Access to Home Mortgage Lending: A Profile of the New York Metropolitan Area*. Washington, DC: Brooking Institution Center on Urban and Metropolitan Policy.

Scott, Janny. 2003. Debating Which Private Clubs Are Acceptable and Private. *New York Times* (December 8), section 7: 5.

Scully, Marc. 2012. Whose Day Is It Anyway? St. Patrick's Day as a Contested Performance of National And Diasporic Irishness. *Studies in Ethnicity and Nationalism* 12 (1): 118–135.

Semple, Kirk. 2012. Many U.S. Immigrants' Children Seek American Dream Abroad. *New York Times* (April 16). Accessed April 21, 2013, at http://www.nytimes.com/2012/04/16/us/more-us-children-of-immigrants-are-leaving-us.html?ref=kirksemple.

Shah, Priyank G. 2012. *Asian Americans' Achievement Advantage: When and Why Does it Emerge*. Dissertation. The Ohio State University.

Shanklin, Eugenia. 1994. *Anthropology and Race*. Belmont, CA: Wadsworth.

Shapiro, Thomas M., Tatjana Meschede, and Laura Sullivan. 2010. *The Racial Wealth Gap Increases Fourfold*. Research and Policy Brief (May), Institute on Assets and Social Policy: University of Michigan.

Sherwood, Jessica Holden. 2010. *Wealth, Whiteness, and the Matrix of Privilege: The View from the Country Clubs*. Lanham, MD: Rowman and Littlefield.

Shin, Hyon B., and Robert A. Kominski. 2010. Language Use in the United States 2007. *Census Brief ACS-12*. Washington, DC: U.S. Government Printing Office.

Siegal, Erin. 2013. Amnesty: Back to the Future. *Christian Science Monitor* (April 8): 26–31.

Sigelman, Lee, and Steven A. Tuch. 1997. Metastereotypes: Blacks' Perception of Whites'

Stereotypes of Blacks. *Public Opinion Quarterly* 61 (Spring): 87–101.

Simon Wiesenthal Center. 2008. *iReport: Online Terror + Hate: The First Decade.* Los Angeles: Simon Wiesenthal Center.

Simpson, Jacqueline C. 1995. Pluralism: The Evolution of a Nebulous Concept. *American Behavioral Scientist* 38 (January): 459–477.

Skrentny, John D. 2008. Culture and Race/Ethnicity: Bolder, Deeper, and Broader. *Annals* 619 (September): 59–77.

Slavin, Robert E., and Alan Cheung. 2003. *Effective Reading Programs for English Language Learners.* Baltimore: Johns Hopkins University, Center for Research on the Education of Students Placed at Risk.

Smith, Tom W. 2006. *Taking America's Pulse III. Intergroup Relations in Contemporary America.* Chicago: National Opinion Research Center, University of Chicago.

Society for Human Resource Management. 2010. *Workplace Diversity Practices: How Has Diversity and Inclusion Changed Over Time?* Alexandra VA: SHRM.

Society for Human Resource Management. 2011. *SHRM Survey Findings: An Examination of Organizational Commitment to Diversity and Inclusion.* Alexandra VA: SHRM.

Soltero, Sonia White. 2008. *Bilingual Education.* Pp. 142–146 in vol. 1, *Encyclopedia of Race, Ethnicity, and Society,* Richard T. Schaefer, ed. Thousand Oaks, CA: Sage.

Song, Tae-Hyon. 1991. *Social Contact and Ethnic Distance between Koreans and the U.S. Whites in the United States.* M.A. Thesis, Western Illinois University, Macomb.

Southern Poverty Law Center. 2010. *Ten Ways to Fight Hate: A Community Response Guide.* Montgomery, AL: SPLC.

Stark, Rodney, and Charles Glock. 1968. *American Piety: The Nature of Religious Commitment.* Berkeley: University of California Press.

Steinberg, Stephen. 2005. Immigration, African Americans, and Race Discourse. *New Politics* (Winter): 10.

Steinberg, Stephen. 2007. *Race Relations: A Critique.* Stanford, CT: Stanford University Press.

Steinhauer, Jennifer. 2006. An Unwelcome Light on Club Where Legends Teed Off. *New York Times* (September 23): A8.

Stern, Nucolas. 2007. *Review on the Economics of Climate Change.* London: HM Treasury.

Stone, Emily. 2006. Hearing the Call—In Polish. *Chicago Tribune* (October 13): 15.

Stonequist, Everett V. 1937. *The Marginal Man: A Study in Personality and Culture Conflict.* New York: Scribner's.

Stretesky, Paul, and Michael Lynch. 2002. Environmental Hazards and School Segregation in Hillsborough County, Florida, 1987–1999. *Sociological Quarterly* 43: 553–573.

Takaki, Ronald. 1998. *Strangers from a Different Shore: A History of Asian Americans.* Updated and revised. Boston, MA: Little, Brown, Back Bay edition.

Taylor, Stuart, Jr. 1987. High Court Backs Basing Promotion on a Racial Quota. *New York Times* (February 26): 1, 14.

Taylor, Stuart, Jr. 1988. Justices Back New York Law Ending Sex Bias by Big Clubs. *New York Times* (June 21): A1, A18.

Teranishi, Robert T. 2010. *Asians in the Ivory Tower: Dilemmas of Racial Inequity in American Higher Education.* New York: Teachers College Press.

Thomas, Oliver. 2007. So What Does the Constitution Say about Religion? *USA Today* (October 15): 15A.

Thomas, William I. 1923. *The Unadjusted Girl.* Boston: Little, Brown.

Thomas, William Isaac, and Florian Znaniecki. 1996. *The Polish Peasant in Europe and America* (5 vols.), Eli Zaretsky, ed. Urbana: University of Illinois Press.

Tice, Lindsay. 2007. Another Side of Brent Matthews. *Lewiston-Auburn Sun Journal* (April 29). Accessed April 16, 2012, at http://www.sunjournal.com/node/239728.

Tomaskovic-Devey, Donald, and Patricia Warren. 2009. Explaining and Eliminating Racial Profiling. *Contexts* 8 (Spring): 34–39.

Tonelli, Bill. 2004. *Arrivederci, Little Italy* (September 27). Accessed August 28, 2013, at http://nymag.com/nymetro/urban/features/9904/.

Torkelson, Jason and Douglas Hartmann. 2010. White Ethnicity in Twenty-First-Century

America: Findings from a New National Survey. *Ethnic and Racial Studies* 33 (8): 1310–1331.

Townsend, Sarah S. M., Hazel R. Markos, and Hilary Bergsieker. 2009. My Choice, Your Categories: The Denial of Multiracial Identities. *Journal of Social Issues* 65 (1): 185–204.

Ture, Kwame, and Charles Hamilton. 1992. *Black Power: The Politics of Liberation.* New York: Vintage Books.

Turner, Margery Austin, Fred Freiburg, Erin Godfrey, Clark Herbig, Diane K. Levy, and Robin R. Smith. 2002. *All Other Things Being Equal: A Paired Testing Study of Mortgage Lending Institutions.* Washington, DC: Urban Institute.

Turner, Margery Austin, Fred Freiburg, Erin Godfrey, Clark Herbig, Diane K. Levy, and Robin R. Smith et al. 2013. *Housing Discrimination Against Racial and Ethnic Minorities 2012.* Washington DC: The Urban Institute.

Two Bridges. 2013. *Celebrate the 5th Anniversary of New York City's Marco Polo Festival!* Accessed August 20, 2013, at http://www.twobridges.org.

Tyson, Karolyn. 2011. *Integration Interrupted: Tracking, Black Students, & Acting White After Brown.* New York: Oxford University Press.

Tyson, Karolyn, William Darity, Jr., and Domini R. Castellino. 2005. It's Not "a Black Thing": Understanding the Burden of Acting White and Other Dilemmas of High Achievement. *American Sociological Review* 70 (August): 582–605.

United Nations High Commission on Refugees. 2008. *2007 Global Trends: Refugees, Asylum-seekers, Returnees, Internally Displaced and Stateless Persons.* Geneva: UNHCR.

U.S. English. 2013. *Official English.* Accessed August 9, 2013, at http://us-english.org.

Wagley, Charles, and Marvin Harris. 1958. *Minorities in the New World: Six Case Studies.* New York: Columbia University Press.

Wall Street Journal. 2011. Tiger Mom's Long-Distance Cub. (December 24).

Wallerstein, Immanuel. 1974. *The Modern World System.* New York: Academic Press.

Wark, Colin, and John F. Galliher. 2007. Emory Bogardus and the Origins of the Social Distance Scale. *American Sociologist* 38: 383–395.

Warner, W. Lloyd, and Leo Srole. 1945. *The Social Systems of American Ethnic Groups.* New Haven: Yale University.

Waters, Mary. 1990. *Ethnic Options. Choosing Identities in America.* Berkeley: University of California Press.

Weber, Max. 1947. *The Theory of Social and Economic Organization* [1913–1922], trans. by Henderson and T. Parsons. New York: Free Press.

Weinberg, Daniel H. 2004. Evidence from Census 2000 About Earnings by Detailed Occupation for Men and Women. *CENSR-15.* Washington, DC: U.S. Government Printing Office.

Welch, William M. 2011. More Hawaii Resident Identify as Mixed Race. *USA Today* (February 28).

Wessel, David. 2001. Hidden Costs of Brain Drain. *Wall Street Journal* (March 1): 1.

West, Darrel M. 2010. *Brain Grain: Rethinking U.S. Immigration Policy.* Washington, DC: Brookings Institution Press.

White House. 2012. *Remarks by the President on the Nomination of Dr. Jim Kim for World Bank President* (March 23). Accessible at http://www.whitehouse.gov/photos-and-video/video/2012/03/23/president-obama-nominated-jim-yong-kim-world-bank-president#transcript.

Wickham, De Wayne. 1993. Subtle Racism Thrives. *USA Today* (October 25): 2A, 15, A1, A26.

Williams, Kim M. 2005. Multiculturalism and the Civil Rights Future. *Daedalus* 134 (1): 53–60.

Willoughby, Brian. 2004. *10 Ways to Fight Hate on Campus.* Montgomery, AL: Southern Poverty Law Center.

Winant, Howard. 1994. *Racial Conditions: Politics, Theory, Comparisons.* Minneapolis, MN: University of Minnesota Press.

Winant, Howard. 2004. *The New Politics of Race: Globalism, Difference, Justice.* Minneapolis: University of Minnesota Press.

Winant, Howard. 2006. Race and Racism: Towards a Global Future. *Ethnic and Racial Studies* 29 (September): 986–1003.

Winerip, Michael. 2011. New Influx of Haitians, But Not Who Was Expected. *New York Times* (January 16): 15, 22.

Winseman, Albert L. 2004. *U.S. Churches Looking for a Few White Men.* Accessed July 27, 2004, at http://www.gallup.com.

Winter, S. Alan. 2008. *Symbolic Ethnicity.* Pp. 1288–1290 in vol. 3, *Encyclopedia of Race, Ethnicity, and Society*, Richard T. Schaefer, ed. Thousand Oaks, CA: Sage.

Withrow, Brian L. 2006. *Racial Profiling: From Rhetoric to Reason.* Upper Saddle River, NJ: Prentice Hall.

Witt, Bernard. 2007. What Is a Hate Crime? *Chicago Tribune* (June 10): 1, 18.

Working, Russell. 2007. Illegal Abroad, Hate Web Sites Thrive Here. *Chicago Tribune* (November 13): A1, A15.

World Bank. 2013a. *Work Bank Launches Initiative on Migration, Releases New Projections on Remittances Flows* (April 19). Accessible at http://www.worldbank.org.

World Bank. 2013b. *World Databank.* Accessed August 7, 2013, at http://databankl.wpr;dbanl.org/data/views/reports/tableview.aspx.

Writers Guild of America West. 2013. *Diversity on TV Writing Staffs: Writers Guild Releases Latest Research Findings* (March 26). Accessible at http://www.wga.org.

Wrong, Dennis H. 1972. How Important Is Social Class? *Dissent* 19 (Winter): 278–285.

Wu, Frank M. 2002. *Yellow: Race in America beyond Black and White.* New York: Basic Books.

Wyatt, Edward. 2009. No Smooth Ride on TV Networks' Road to Diversity. *New York Times* (March 18): 1, 5.

Wyman, Mark. 1993. *Round-Trip to America. The Immigrants Return to Europe, 1830–1930.* Ithaca, NY: Cornell University Press.

Xu, Jun, and Jennifer C. Lee. 2013. The Marginalized "Model" Minority: An Empirical Examination of the Racial Triangulation of Asian Americans. *Social Forces* 91 (4): 1363–1397.

Yancey, George. 2003. *Who Is White? Latinos, Asians, and the New Black–Nonblack Divide.* Boulder, CO: Lynne Rienner.

Yemma, John. 2013. Teaching the Freedom to Believe. 2013. *Christian Science Monitor* (June 17): 5.

Yinger, John. 1995. *Closed Doors, Opportunities Lost: The Continuing Costs of Housing Discrimination.* New York: Russell Sage Foundation.

Yosso, Tara J. 2005. Whose Culture Has Capital? A Critical Race Theory Discussion of Community Cultural Wealth. *Race Ethnicity and Education* 8 (March): 69–91.

Young, Jeffrey R. 2003. Researchers Change Racial Bias on the SAT. *Chronicle of Higher Education* (October 10): A34–A35.

Zeng, Zhen, and Yu Xie. 2004. Asian-Americans' Earnings Disadvantage Reexamined: The Role of Place of Education. *American Journal of Sociology* 109 (March): 1075–1108.

Zia, Helen. 2000. *Asian American Dreams: The Emergence of an American People.* New York: Farrar, Straus & Giroux.

Zimmerman, Seth. 2008. *Immigration and Economic Mobility.* Washington, DC: Economic Mobility Project.

Zittrain, Jonathan. 2008. *The Future of the Internet and How to Stop It. With a New Forward by Lawrence Lessig and New Preface by the Author.* New Haven: Yale University Press.

Zogby, James. 2001. *National Survey: American Teen-Agers and Stereotyping.* Submitted to the National Italian American Foundation by Zogby International. Accessed June 3, 2008, at http://www.niaf.org/research/report_zogby.asp?print=1&.

Zogby, James. 2010. *51% Expect Major Terror Attack This Year and 25% Plan to Fly Less* (February 4). Accessed March 2, 2011, at http://www.zogby.com.

Photo Credits

Name Index

Subject Index